# Psychotherapy, Mindfulness and Buddhist Meditation

Tullio Giraldi

# Psychotherapy, Mindfulness and Buddhist Meditation

palgrave
macmillan

Tullio Giraldi
University of Trieste
Trieste, Italy

ISBN 978-3-030-29002-3 ISBN 978-3-030-29003-0 (eBook)
https://doi.org/10.1007/978-3-030-29003-0



Cover illustration: Leks_Laputin/gettyimages

This Palgrave Macmillan imprint is published by the registered company Springer Nature Switzerland AG
The registered company address is: Gewerbestrasse 11, 6330 Cham, Switzerland

*To my family, with a huge thankfulness for the support and patience during the writing of this book, which must have been a challenge greater than that they have to face during my previous writings.*
*I have an even greater debt of gratitude to my wife Vlady for her unfailing love, accompanied during my writings by generous supplies of coffee and macaroon biscuits.*

# Acknowledgements

This work should not have been possible without the personal and professional growth which I had thanks to the encounter with numerous outstanding personalities and institutions which I had the privilege to meet and to work with. I shall not attempt to name all of them to avoid omissions which would be inexcusable, and I shall necessarily make impersonal references.

My Alma mater is the University of Trieste, Italy, where I completed my studies and later spent large part of my academic career as a professor of pharmacology and related topics. There I had the occasion to develop a critical mind towards the understanding of the world in an objective ("scientific") perspective, aware of the fallacies of the beliefs affecting human attempts to understand the inner and outer world.

My initial interests on pharmacology were on chemotherapy, and later moved towards the brain and the drugs modifying its functions. In this connection, I could participate to the dramatic changes in psychiatric care which happened in Trieste beginning in the 60s, thanks to the realization of the revolutionary approaches of Franco Basaglia in the local Department of Mental Health of the community care services of the National Health System. These initiatives led to marked changes of the legislation in Italy, and are still at the focus of the attention by the international psychiatric community and WHO. My psychiatric interests were also enriched by becoming a clinical psychologist with a training in psychotherapy as a transactional analyst which I received in Bologna, Italy.

A distinct enrichment was provided to me by outstanding British institutions. As a young visiting scientist I had a remarkable experience at the old Chester Beatty Research Institute, London, in mid-70s. This had to be followed much later by my current visiting professorship at the Global Health and Social Medicine Department of the King's College, London. This is a place of excellence, where the founder and past director, together with a growing academic staff, provided original critical views of the continuously debated critical issues of mental health: it is while in this department that I had the occasion to develop some of the ideas which led to writing this book.

A crucial event in my life was the encounter with Buddhism, which led me to the practice of Rinzai Zen which I began in the late 70s at the Zenshin-ji monastery in Orvieto, Italy. I followed there the teachings of master Engaku Taino along the lineage of Yamada Mumon Roshi, and it is with this master at this temple that in 1971 I was ordained a lay Buddhist monk.

These are the experiences along which my experiences developed, and I mentioned them to let the reader of this book to understand the background of my efforts to provide a critical perspective for the recent explosive growth of mindfulness, with its isolation from Buddhist meditation which occurred with its transplantation into current Western culture.

These are also hints which will allow to understand why I cannot cite name by name all the numerous and beautiful persons and minds, teachers and students, researchers and discoverers, and companions along the Way of life, from which I learnt so much and to whom I have an incommensurable debt of gratitude that I recognize and acknowledge here with the greatest gratefulness.

I wish finally to thank Tristan Grove for his careful work of copy editing.

# Introductory Note

Since this work is intended also for a general readership, the terms of Pali and Sanskrit origins are transliterated without the diacritical marks that would have been appropriate in a work of a more scholarly nature.

Similarly, the Japanese words will be used retaining the system of Romanization used in the original documents cited.

Mindfulness is the word which had been used as a translation of the Pali term *sati* since the early English translations of Buddhist scriptures. With the diffusion of the mindfulness movement and applications in the West, and particularly with its diffusion into the world of medicine and psychology, the term of mindfulness began to be used also in an undifferentiated way as a synonym of *meditation*. The terms of *mindfulness* and *meditation* will be therefore retained without further specification as used in the original documents cited.

# Contents

# Abbreviations

| | |
|---|---|
| ACT | Acceptance Behaviour Therapy, Acceptance and Commitment Therapy |
| AIPT | Adult Improving Access to Psychological Therapies |
| APA | American Psychiatric Association |
| BA | Behavioural Activation |
| BDI | Beck Depression Inventory |
| BNF | British National Formulary |
| CAM | Complimentary Alternative Medicine |
| CBT | Cognitive Behavioural Therapy |
| CCBT | Computerized Cognitive Behavioural Therapy |
| CEDAR | Clinical Education Development and Research |
| CT | Cognitive Therapy |
| DALY | Disability Adjusted Life Years |
| DBT | Dialectical Behaviour Therapy |
| DMH | Department of Mental Health |
| DSM | Diagnostic and Statistical Manual (of Mental Disorders) |
| EBT | Evidence Based Treatment |
| EEG | Electroencephalogram |
| EPDS | Edinburgh Postnatal Depression Scale |
| FDA | US Food and Drug Administration |
| f-MRI | Functional Magnetic Resonance |

| | |
|---|---|
| FOIA | US Freedom of Information Act |
| GP | General Practitioner |
| GSR | Galvanic Skin Response |
| GWAS | Genome-Wide Association Studies |
| HAM-D | Hamilton Rating Scale for Depression |
| HDRS | Hamilton Depression Rating Scale |
| IAPT | Improving Access to Psychotherapy |
| IBS | Irritable Bowel Syndrome |
| IMS | Insight Meditation Society |
| IPT | Interpersonal Psychotherapy |
| ITT | Intention to Treat |
| LSE | London School of Economics |
| MAPPG | Mindfulness All-Party Parliamentary Group |
| MARC | Meditation Awareness Research Center |
| MBCT | Mindfulness-Based Cognitive Therapy |
| MBCT-AS | MBCT Adherence Scale |
| MBCT-TS | MBCT—Taper or Discontinue Antidepressant Treatment |
| MBI | Mindfulness Based Interventions |
| MBRP | Mindfulness Based Relapse Prevention |
| MBSR | Mindfulness-Based Stress Reduction |
| MDD | Major Depressive Disorder |
| MIT | Massachusetts Institute of Technology |
| MMFT | Mindfulness-Based Mind Fitness Training |
| MRI | Magnetic Resonance Imaging |
| NHS | National Health Service |
| NICE | National Institute for Health and Care Excellence |
| NIH | US National Institutes of Health |
| NMIH | US National Mental Health Institute |
| PBCT | Personalized-Based Cognitive Therapy |
| PET | Positron Emission Tomography |
| PHQ | Patients Health Questionnaire Scale |
| PNIRS | Psychoneuroimmunology Research Society |
| PTSD | Post Traumatic Stress Disorder |
| PUVA | Photochemotherapy |
| PWP | Psychological Well-being Practitioner |
| RCT | Randomized Controlled Trial |
| RDoC | Research Domain Criteria |
| REBT | Rational Emotive Behavior Therapy |
| SPECT | Single-Photon Emission Computed Tomography |

| | |
|---|---|
| SSRI | Selective Serotonin Reuptake Inhibitor |
| STAR*D | Sequenced Treatment Alternatives to Relieve Depression |
| TASU | Treatment As Usual |
| TAU | Treatment As Usual |
| TCBT | Therapist Led CBT |
| TM | Transcendental Meditation |
| UCLA | University of California—Los Angeles |
| USPSTF | US Preventive Services Task Force |
| UV | Ultraviolet |
| UVB | Phototherapy |
| WHO | World Health Organization |
| YLD | Years Lived with Disability |

# 1
# Prologue

Every seat in the amphitheatre lecture hall was taken. Late comers squeezed along the walls and the back of the auditorium. The event? A lecture called: "*From theory to practice: The psychological and neuropsychological foundations of mindfulness meditation and their applications for children.*" It was part of the weekly series organised by the university's Ph.D. School of Neuroscience and Cognitive Sciences. The room was so full not only because a considerable number of undergraduate students had been pressed to attend by their lecturers, but also because many others were simply interested in the subject.

The person who had been invited to host the lecture was a young researcher working at a nearby university. His credentials were first-rate: according to his CV, after getting a degree in Psychology he also gained a Ph.D. in Neuroscience from an internationally renowned institution. Not only that: he was also now training as a psychotherapist, and had gained the title: 'Instructor of Mindfulness-Based Approaches' in stress reduction and cognitive psychotherapy. He was doing experimental research in various fields of applied psychology, and many of his results had already been published in scientific journals and presented at national and international scientific meetings. Most of the research he


T. Giraldi, *Psychotherapy, Mindfulness and Buddhist Meditation*,
https://doi.org/10.1007/978-3-030-29003-0_1

was presenting at that time was on the very popular subject of mindfulness. And as well as his research, he was also holding courses on introducing mindfulness into schools, hospitals, centres for psychological support and psychotherapy, and professional training organisations.

He gave the talk with the professional tone of voice of a young, active researcher. It was a captivating and convincing style, which quite often resembled that of a missionary keen to proselytise new followers.

He examined many of the main issues to do with mindfulness, beginning with how you define it, and moving on to show its astonishing diffusion in the thirty years since it was introduced into psychology and psychotherapy. In the course of the lecture, he also referred to a recent paper (Van Dam et al., 2017) which delved into the difficulties with the definition of mindfulness, as well as the concerns about its explosive diffusion, uses and effectiveness. As well as this, he also briefly mentioned the relationship of mindfulness to meditation and its roots in Buddhism.

One key part of the presentation was an examination of the results when mindfulness-based approaches were applied in clinical psychology and medicine. He also showed the results when more advanced cognitive science and brain imaging techniques were used to study the effects of mindfulness on the mind and brain. He devoted a significant part of the presentation to his own experimental research too. And most of his results showed the variation in the scoring on psychometric scales before and after mindfulness-based interventions. These were in a range of clinical settings, including primary schools attended by young children.

The part of the talk on clinical intervention also included the positive results obtained when mindfulness techniques were used with patients suffering from mental disorders—as diagnosed using the criteria and the Diagnostic and Statistical Manual of Mental Disorders (DSM) of the American Psychiatric Association. There was no discussion at the end of the talk: instead the speaker proposed a series of guided meditation sessions with the audience.

The presentation I have just described is recent and real, and it is a perfect example of how the proponents of mindfulness enthusiastically expound its virtues both to specialists and the general public.

During the course of this presentation, I began to feel progressively uneasy: I knew that what was being offered to the audience was a distinctly biased perspective. It gave the students attending the lecture a limited and distorted view of the substantial body of evidence on the subject. And the results the speaker was claiming were based on methods that were, to be frank, inadequate to sustain them. In short, the lecture was based on a poor standard of scientific inquiry. It was nevertheless catchy and captivating, which may well account for the hype and ever-growing popularity of mindfulness.

The approach to mindfulness presented by the lecturer, however, is essentially the same as the approach taken in neuroscience and the cognitive sciences. The question, then, is can we really be satisfied with this approach—or is it, at base, biased and one-sided?

It is also important to clearly examine the phenomenon of mindfulness because of the enormous number of books, studies and articles published on the subject—not only in scientific journals, but also in non-specialist publications and media. "Sales of Mind, Body, Spirit Books Boom in UK Amid 'Mindfulness Mega-Trend'" is the title of an article which appeared in *The Guardian* on 31 July 2017. It describes the unrelenting proliferation of books on mindfulness after Jon Kabat-Zinn first proposed a Mindfulness-Based Stress Reduction (MBSR) programme at the University of Massachusetts Medical School in the late 70s (Flood, 2019). This same astonishing popularisation of mindfulness even led Jon Kabat-Zinn to worry in a recent interview with *The Guardian* that "People are losing their minds. That is what we need to wake up to" (Booth, 2019).

A search of "mindfulness" in the PubMed database of the US National Library of Medicine National Institutes of Health shows there were almost no scientific journal articles on the subject before the year 2000. Then the number quickly began to increase, reaching 100 in 2008, 500 in 2013 and 900 in 2017. Meanwhile, more than 30,000 articles appeared in the general press in 2015 alone. The number of books on mindfulness is similarly astonishing. When, for example, Ruby Wax was publicising her last book—*A Mindfulness Guide for the Frazzled*—in *The Guardian*, she asked herself and her readers: "Do we really need more guides to mindfulness?" (Burkeman, 2019)

Mindfulness has now become so pervasive that in 2016, mindfulness-related health practices and other applications created a market of approximately $1.2 billion in the US. That figure is still growing—alongside a large market of apps for smartphones and wearable devices (Wieczner, 2016).

Critical articles and books on mindfulness have also begun to appear, there are now critical reviews of the plentiful literature on mindfulness emerging, and it is now also finally possible to perform meta-analysis on the subject. New studies are being conducted following more appropriate research protocols. And as a result, in many cases the positive results initially reported have been shown to be markedly less pronounced—or even completely insignificant. A noteworthy example is the recent, provocatively-titled book *Mindlessness*, by Thomas Joiner—on the deviations of mindfulness from its original conception (Joiner, 2017).

This book will consider these issues in detail, taking into account the best evidence available in the literature on mindfulness and its relationship to meditation. It sets out to develop as objective, comprehensive and balanced view as possible on the subject of mindfulness.

It is important to note how closely the applications and developments of meditation that Jon Kabat-Zinn termed "mindfulness"—and which have since become so popular—are still interwoven with meditation and the heightened awareness and attention attained through various Buddhist practices. This point will be examined as appropriate in the relevant chapters of this book. For the sake of simplicity, however, the term "mindfulness" will still be used throughout this book because of its general meaning and common usage.

The best place to start here is the origin of mindfulness: meditation. This practice, which has been at the core of Buddhism since its beginnings 2500 years ago in India, only really became accessible to the Western cultural world approximately one century ago.

In this limited time, Buddhism—and therefore meditation—also spread out of Asia as a religion, brought by a small number of immigrants, as well as intellectual elites who saw it as a cultural curiosity. Its reach also extended through a growing number of people who were dissatisfied with the restraints of a Western society increasingly based on materialist and consumerist values.

In the last thirty years, meditation was transformed in the West into "mindfulness". Since then its popularity extended remarkably until it attained the astonishing pervasiveness we see today. The first chapter of this book, *What Is Mindfulness?*, will examine the definition of mindfulness and its relationship to meditation, its historical and operative development, as well as its current applications.

The next chapter is called "Buddhism Spreads from East to West". It charts the rise of Buddhism in India 2500 years ago, and traces its spread to China and to other countries in South Asia. Buddhist teachings first became accessible to Western cultures in the late nineteenth and early twentieth Centuries—largely thanks to translations into English by devoted pioneers. The first Western devotees were trained in Eastern monasteries, where they had direct experience of Buddhist teachings—and from there brought them back to America and Europe.

Monks from Asian countries established themselves in the West to deliver religious services to communities of migrants who came from Buddhist countries—which also helped to give Western devotees easy access to Buddhist teachings. The phenomenon was particularly prominent in the 1960s, when Zen Buddhism—one of the most widespread forms in Japanese culture—received great attention from the Beat Generation as well as noted US intellectuals. And it was from these tradition that "mindfulness" emerged.

The practice of Buddhism, in the various forms it has taken throughout history, has always involved the adherence to a precise set of moral and existential precepts, which in the monasteries are accompanied by specific meditative practices. The main message of Buddhism is that awakening and enlightenment can be achieved by practising the Middle Way during one's life—essentially by attaining specific states of consciousness and liberating oneself from the existential sufferings of life. It is therefore not surprising that when Buddhism gained a hold in the West after the Second World War, people interested in the relationship between Eastern spirituality and mental health—including mental health professionals—turned to Buddhism.

What is peculiar, however, is that their attention was specifically focused on meditation, leaving aside all the complexities of Buddhist teachings and practices. In Japan, there were seminal physiological and psychiatric investigations into the matter, which soon sparked the interest of psychiatrists, psychologists and psychotherapists in the USA. Numerous different approaches were involved, such as psychoanalysis, Gestalt, as well as existential and humanist psychotherapies.

It was then in the 70s when the phenomenon of "mindfulness" really began, based on the seminal proposal to practice Buddhist meditation without Buddhism. Then the explosive popularisation of "mindfulness" began. In general, people then also began conflating the term "mindfulness"—the "sati" of the Noble Eightfold Path—with the "mindfulness" increasingly practised in the West, which had moved some distance from Buddhist traditions. The next chapter, called 'Psychologists and Psychiatrists Became Interested in Buddhism', will examine how exactly this happened.

Much of the force behind the popularisation of "mindfulness" in the West came from Jon Kabat-Zinn's original stress reduction programme. His mindfulness intervention was based on regular periods of guided meditation throughout an eight-week programme. Large efforts were made to prove the effectiveness of this for evidence-based medicine. And many studies have since been published that aim to show that mindfulness interventions are effective for promoting wellbeing, overcoming emotional difficulties, helping to adapt to life events—and for treating mental disorders.

Mindfulness has been adopted in the fields of biological psychiatry and neuroscience. Particular attention has been given to the treatment of conditions such as depression, which is currently being diagnosed so widely as to effectively constitute a mental health epidemic. When psychotropic drugs were introduced for the treatment of mental diseases in the 1950s, psychiatry shifted from a psychodynamic to a more biological approach. The diagnostic criteria of the DSM were elaborated, and as these essentially medicalised the emotional difficulties that often come with coping with adverse life events, they proved to be highly inclusive. In many cases, this led to healthy people being diagnosed with psychiatric disorders, which has led to the current epidemic of unhappy and sad people being labelled as affected by a mental disorder.

Antidepressant drugs have been widely used to treat these cases, and there was an astonishing increase in the prescription of these drugs in parallel with the explosion depression diagnoses. The problem was then exacerbated by the limited effectiveness of these drugs for treating mild or non-pathological mood disorders—and also by the adverse side-effects of the treatment.

At the same time, psychotherapies also transformed into the new world of biological psychiatry and neuroscience. Cognitive and cognitive-behavioural approaches were introduced and they became very popular and widespread. However, because the cognitively oriented psychotherapies used largely the same instruments as biological psychiatry, they were quickly affected by the same difficulties with diagnosis and the evaluation of medical effectiveness.

"Mindfulness" and the role it plays in cognitive therapy falls within this picture. Because of the large number of studies available now, it is possible to evaluate them with meta-analysis. The results of this can then be critically evaluated to begin to offer a comprehensive picture of the limits and drawbacks of the studies available. This book will look at the evidence of these studies in the chapter called "The Cases of US and UK, and the Marketing of Mindfulness." Considering the diffusion of "mindfulness" in the West, and how it has become less and less related to traditional forms of meditation. It will also examine how Kabat-Zinn's original eight-week structure became so pervasive in the practice of mindfulness.

As the popularity of mindfulness increased, it was included in a variety of interventions aimed at broadly improving "wellbeing" and enhancing people's performance in a whole variety of fields. It is amazing to consider how its remarkable popularity allowed it to become an enormous market, estimated to produce more than $1 billion a year for US businesses alone. Its popularity has also led to it being used for a whole range of new purposes—from enhancing the performance of businesspeople to improving the resilience and combat performance of US soldiers. In the UK, it is covered by National Health Service guidelines—which are elaborated on by the National Institute for Health and Care Excellence. These guidelines say mild forms of depression and anxiety should first be treated with psychological support and psychotherapy, with antidepressants proposed only when patients are unresponsive to these. A large national initiative, the Improving Access to

Psychotherapy programme, was organised and made available throughout the UK. This includes psychotherapeutic interventions, one of which is a mindfulness approach called Mindfulness-Based Cognitive Therapy (MBCT). The IAPT programme is a unique example of attempting an experiment like this with an entire nation. It is one of the largest-ever applied psychotherapeutic experiments, and focuses on cognitive (CT) and cognitive behavioural therapy (CBT), as well as MBCT.

During its diffusion across the US—and, later, into other parts of the world—mindfulness progressively lost its connection with the religious world and Buddhism, morphing as it was applied to psychology and medicine. A remarkable number of reports are still being published in scientific journals, aiming to show the effectiveness of "mindfulness" interventions for the treatment of an extensive range of mental and psychosomatic disorders. Most of the published studies report positive results on a relatively small—but statistically significant—scale. The majority also report results that were obtained using limited sample sizes, and the reproducibility of the results is poor.

Kabat-Zinn—and the many other researchers who followed him—made significant efforts to follow the methodological principles of "evidence-based medicine" when organising trials into the effectiveness of "mindfulness". Their protocols generally involved the careful selection of cases—strictly controlled for the nature of the condition considered—as well as the randomisation of subjects. A critical review of the articles published on these studies, however, shows that the criteria for including subjects are often questionable. In the case of mental conditions, they often use the diagnostic categories of the American Psychiatric Association (APA) and its Diagnostic and Statistical Manual of Mental Disorders (DSM), which are used widely but also seriously criticised—especially when they are applied to cases of minor mental suffering. Indeed, the diagnostic criteria of the DSM do not discriminate between morbid conditions and healthy reactions to adverse and stressful life events. One serious example is unhappiness and sadness, which are widely diagnosed as a "major depressive disorder" in mild, non-morbid cases.

In spite of the efforts made, a double blinding procedure is also never used in the interventions in these studies, and a placebo group is not included. The criteria for evaluating the outcome are often weak and based on small variations in the scoring of standard psychometric scales shortly after the end of the intervention. When mindfulness was integrated into cognitive psychotherapy, it was shown to be effective in controlling cases of depression that had responded poorly to antidepressant drugs. There was, however, no comparison to show that mindfulness-based cognitive therapy is more effective than cognitive psychotherapy alone.

It is generally acknowledged that one advantage of mindfulness-based interventions is that they do not involve the side-effects of drug treatment. There is, however, no evidence for this available, and concerns have been expressed.

Altogether, the studies on the effectiveness of mindfulness generally suffer from methodological limitations similar to those associated with the studies of antidepressant drugs. And on top of that, they also have their own particular limitations. The concern, therefore, is that mindfulness may simply become an alternative to the prescription of antidepressants—in the process also losing the advantages that might be obtained by following a meditative path. The chapter entitled "Methodological Flaws and the Evidence of Efficacy" scrutinizes the evidence available on this.

The last chapter of the book is called: "Future Perspectives on Mindfulness and Buddhism". As has been outlined above, "mindfulness" has progressively lost its connection with its Buddhist religious and philosophical roots. It has become a detached form of meditation more associated with a humanist perspective—with both mechanistic and reductionist strains.

Mindfulness has become one of the tools of psychotherapy, psychiatry and neuroscience. It is now a tool for intervention in a medicalised world. By this, I mean that in these fields, individual differences of emotional expression and in ways of coping with life events have been transformed into the manifestations of serious pathological conditions. These then have to be treated to bring the subject back within the uniform standards expected and defined by both medicine and society. Incidentally, the extraordinary diffusion of mindfulness and its acceptance into the world of evidence-based medicine did not occur at all in the disciplines grouped under "Complimentary Alternative Medicine" (CAM).

Important theoretical elements were overlooked when today's accepted mindfulness practices were established. In particular, the moral aspect of meditation—what is termed in the Noble Eightfold Path the "samadhi"—was neglected, and all attention was focused on the "sati". At the core of Buddhism is the complex articulation of a range of moral precepts. In particular, Buddhism sees the concept of the "self" as an illusion that is to be overcome in order to avoid existential suffering. Mindfulness as most people understand it in the West today overlooks this, and even uses it in relation to the completely contradictory concept of the "ego" in psychology. In fact, mindfulness has become progressively entwined with cognitive psychotherapy, which is mainly centred on strengthening a poorly functioning "self".

It is particularly remarkable that of all Buddhist practices meditation should have been adopted, when, in fact, it is not regularly practised in most Eastern Buddhist countries—except by monks.

Today, mindfulness has been enthusiastically integrated into cognitive psychotherapies. It is one of the many branches that have emerged of a field that is fundamentally based on aspects of neuroscience and biological psychiatry. Yet neuroscience still does not seem to have been able to reduce the problem of mental disease and of milder, non-morbid mood disorders (of both existential and reactive origins) to something fully understood by psychiatry and amenable to effective pharmacological and psychotherapeutic intervention.

Mindfulness has been used not only to treat mental disorders and suffering, but also to improve the performance of subjects. This application seems geared overall to nourishing individualism and individual narcissistic tendencies: a far remove from the Buddhist origins of meditation. In Buddhism, meditation is focused on helping to develop a person's resources to allow them to cope with the challenges of life. This may lead to individual empowerment, personal growth and the development of new ways to overcome the suffering of existential difficulties.

Buddhism has a long history, and only relatively recently has it begun to spread to the West. This was because of migrants, as well as the efforts of early scholars and determined pioneers who trained in monasteries in Eastern Buddhist countries. The efforts of these groups brought many new adepts and devotees—and even gave root to a new sort of Western Buddhism, known to some as "secular Buddhism", which is not immediately related to any of its historic forms in Eastern traditions. Only time will tell the path of Buddhism, meditation, and mindfulness in the future. Certainly, the idea of forging a means of personal development and empowerment in our globalised society is both interesting and appealing. It might even be an exceptional opportunity to integrate the West's astonishing scientific achievements with the extraordinarily sophisticated strands of thought developed by Buddhism during its twenty-five century-long history in the East.

## References

Booth, R. (2019). *Master of mindfulness, Jon Kabat-Zinn: 'People are losing their minds. That is what we need to wake up to'*. Retrieved from https://www.theguardian.com/lifeandstyle/2017/oct/22/mindfulness-jon-kabat-zinn-depression-trump-grenfell. Accessed 15 April 2019.

Burkeman, O. (2019). *Do we really need more guides to mindfulness?* Retrieved from https://www.theguardian.com/books/2016/jan/09/do-we-need-guide-to-mindfulness-oliver-burkeman. Accessed 15 April 2019.

Flood, A. (2019). *Sales of mind, body, spirit books boom in UK amid 'mindfulness mega-trend'*. Retrieved from https://www.theguardian.com/books/2017/jul/31/sales-of-mind-body-spirit-books-boom-in-uk-amid-mindfulness-mega-trend. Accessed 15 April 2019.

Joiner, T. (2017). *Mindlessness: The corruption of mindfulness in a culture of Narcissism*. New York: Oxford University Press.

Van Dam, N., van Vugt, M., Vago, D., Schmalzl, L., Saron, C., Olendzki, A., … Meyer, D. (2017). Mind the hype: A critical evaluation and prescriptive agenda for research on mindfulness and meditation. *Perspectives on Psychological Science, 13*(1), 36–61. https://doi.org/10.1177/1745691617709589.

Wieczner, J. (2016). *Meditation has become a billion-dollar business*. Retrieved from http://fortune.com/2016/03/12/meditation-mindfulness-apps/. Accessed 15 April 2019.

# 2
# What Is Mindfulness?

When considering the phenomenon of mindfulness, the first issue that needs attention is the definition of mindfulness, and how it shifted from its origins in Buddhist meditation to the form we see today. We also need to look more closely at how it is perceived and used today.

What we call mindfulness evolved from Buddhist meditation through a series of processes and practices related to awareness and acceptance. It was initially proposed and applied as an intervention for stress reduction. And from there, it was increasingly used for a range of other therapeutic applications. Mindfulness now pervades many aspects of contemporary society, and there has been more and more interest in what it is, who it could help and what effects it has on the mind and brain (Creswell, 2017; Wilson, 2014a).

The modern term mindfulness was first used by Jon Kabat-Zinn, referring to an approach he devised to bring the practice of meditation into Western culture. The idea was to give people a path that would allow them to attenuate the sufferings of life—particularly stress, through his Mindfulness-Based Stress Reduction (MBSR) programme. His proposal, as he recalled in a 2010 press release about the kickoff of National Breast Cancer Awareness Month at UCLA,



T. Giraldi, *Psychotherapy, Mindfulness and Buddhist Meditation*,
https://doi.org/10.1007/978-3-030-29003-0_2

offered: “the wisdom and the heart of Buddhist meditation without the Buddhism…” (Fisher, Fisher, & Staff, 2019). He defined mindfulness as the “awareness that arises through paying attention, on purpose, in the present moment, non-judgementally” (“Jon Kabat-Zinn: Defining Mindfulness—Mindful”, 2019). This definition is synthetic and appealing, and nobody could really object to it. It is not, however, this definition that should be questioned, but rather how these laudable goals are to be achieved—and whether Kabat-Zinn’s approach to mindfulness is an effective way to achieve them.

With time, the terms “mindfulness” and “meditation” have increasingly come to be used interchangeably. The word “mindfulness”, the state of mind attained through the practice of meditation, is now commonly used to mean meditation itself. Considering the definition of mindfulness therefore inevitably leads to an examination of its origins and connections with Buddhism and Buddhist meditation.

Mindfulness is the fundamental attentional stance underlying all the streams of Buddhist meditative practice developed over the 2500 years since the religion first emerged in Northern India. Buddhism diversified as it spread across Asia. The Theravada Hinayana tradition developed throughout Southeast Asia: Cambodia, Laos, Myanmar and Sri Lanka. The Mahayana Zen Schools developed in China, Japan, Vietnam and Korea. Meanwhile, the Vajrayana tradition of Tibetan Buddhism was established in Tibet, Mongolia, Nepal, Bhutan, Ladakh, and is now followed in the places where the Tibetan community lives in exile.

It is commonly held that mindfulness is the English translation of *sati* in the Buddhist scriptures, which were originally written in *pali*, the ancient language of the areas where Buddhism first emerged. But given the millennia-long life of Buddhism, the development of various forms of the faith, and their diffusion throughout Asia and across the world, it is now, unsurprisingly, quite difficult to untangle the complex relationships between meditation, mindfulness and the *sati* of Buddhist traditions.

Meditation is practised by the Hinayana, Mahayana and Vajrayana Buddhist traditions, and each one has its own meditation practices and texts. This will be examined in greater detail in a later chapter, but suffice it to say that until the end of the nineteenth century, few

Westerners had the opportunity for a first-hand experience of meditation as practised in Eastern cultures. Few had access to the basic texts of these traditions either. And as demand for translations of these texts progressively grew in later years, it emerged just how immense these scriptures were. In the case of the *Pali Texts* of the Theravada tradition, from the beginning of twentieth century until 2009, 188 volumes of text were translated and made accessible to scholars (Harvey, 2013a).

To have at least a vague understanding of the meaning of *sati*, it is essential to grasp the basic tenets of Buddhism, and these are the *Three Marks of Existence*, *Four Noble Truths* and the *Noble Eightfold Path*.

Buddhism emphasises that change and impermanence are fundamental features of everything, including existential suffering. There are fundamentally *Three Marks of Existence*: the impermanence of all conditioned phenomena (anicca), that they are painful (dukkha), and the non-existence of self (anattā).

The *Four Noble Truths* are:

> Suffering, Origin of suffering, Cessation of suffering, The path to the cessation of suffering.

The path leading to the cessation of the sufferings of life is the *Noble Eightfold Path*, also called *The Middle Way*. The *Noble Eightfold Path* comprises:

> Wisdom, differentiated into Right View and Right Resolve;
>
> Moral Virtue, differentiated into Right Speech, Right Action and Right Livelihood;
>
> Meditation, differentiated into Right Effort, Right Mental Presence and Right Concentration.

It is the *Right Mental Presence* of the *Eightfold Noble Path* which appears in the *Pali Texts* as *sati*, and has since been universally translated as mindfulness (Harvey, 2013b).

To attempt a clearer understanding of the Buddhist world, there are other issues that must be considered. Buddhism is substantially rooted in a moral base: one of the *Eightfold Noble Paths* is, indeed, the *Moral*

*Virtue*. Moreover, each of the articulations of the *Wisdom*, *Moral Virtue* and *Meditation* of the *Noble Eightfold Path* is characterised by the qualification of *Right.* This has obvious ethical implications, as in the case of *Right Mental Presence*, *samma-sati*. The *Right* (*samma*) attribute has, however, been disregarded in the process of translating *sati* into mindfulness (Harvey, 2013b, 2013c).

The significance of morality in Buddhism is also reinforced by the importance of the Five Precepts, the basic code of ethics for lay followers of Buddhism. The Five Precepts are: abstaining from killing living beings, stealing, sexual misconduct, lying and intoxication. These precepts are further extended for people entering monastic life (Harvey, 2013d). The Five Precepts are at the core of Buddhism and Buddhist morality, and they appear in the ancient texts of the various Buddhist traditions. They have also been referred to in relation to problems in modern society by contemporary personalities such as Thich Nhat Hanh, whose teachings on mindfulness will be explored later on. Overall, though, the practice of mindfulness in the West in recent decades has largely disregarded the moral associations of meditation, which are essential to Buddhist thought.

Additionally, the second component of meditation, *Right concentration* (*samadhi*, or rather *samma-samadhi*), has been lost in translation from Buddhist traditions to modern Western mindfulness. *Samma-samadhi* is, in fact, so important to Buddhist meditation that it is the foundation of the *Soto* Zen Japanese Buddhist tradition, and is practised as *shikantaza*, "just sitting". Here, meditation becomes the central core of the whole practice and path to enlightenment (Harvey, 2013e). The translation into English, and the exact meaning of *sati*, have also been debated in relation to *smrti*, the Hindu Sanskrit counterpart of *sati*. The term means "to remember", "to recollect" and "to bear in mind" rather than moment-to-moment awareness of whatever arises in the mind (Levman, 2017).

In the Zen tradition, the *Soto Zen* school focuses on "Zazen", sitting meditation where the individual concentrates on their own breathing to absorb themselves in emptiness. Another difficulty—or paradox, even—arises from the Buddhist texts on "Chan". This was the dominant form of Zen Buddhism in China before it migrated to Japan, and in this tradition the state of mind attained through Zen meditation is considered a form of *mindlessness* rather than of *mindfulness* (Sharf, 2014).

Some of the same difficulties to do with mindfulness also arise when considering meditation, and these have emerged more and more in publications from recent decades. For example, a search in the PubMed Archive of Biomedical and Life Sciences at the U.S. National Institutes of Health shows that in 2017 there were 912 articles related to "mindfulness", 439 connected to "meditation" and 22 relating to "mindfulness meditation." (It must, of course, be noted that there is a considerable overlap in the material because the terms used in the papers often differed slightly from the exact word searched.)

Meditation has different meanings for different observers and in different contexts. The various Buddhist schools developed different forms of meditation, where the meditator must silently focus their attention for relatively long periods of time on a particular mental task. There is no doubt that silently sitting cross-legged and concentrating on one's breathing—as in the "shikantaza" of the *Soto Zen* tradition—is the purest form of meditation. This is similar to the "koans" of Rinzai Zen, as well as the breathing and mental representation of mental and physical processes of vipassana meditation in the Therevada school. And this school, it should be remembered, is where you can find the original roots of the mindfulness movement. Tibetan Vairayana rituals involve developing complex visualisations during meditation. In mindfulness, however, meditation is generally accompanied and verbally guided by a therapist. The therapist also adds elements from other approaches that help patients into a state of consciousness different from sleeping or being awake: a state similar to hypnosis, auto-hypnosis and autogenic training.

Meditation is often seen as a great and mysterious subject, which in the past has always conjured up the image of a solitary Asian ascetic sitting in the lotus position in a deep trance. In American contemporary culture meditation perceived in a similar light to yoga classes, martial arts and medical programmes to control stress and hypertension. More recently, it has even been seen as a means to help top athletes prepare themselves for demanding competitions.

Academic and religious scholars often see meditation as one of the spiritual practices followed since ancient times as part of yoga and Hinduism in India, Taoism in China, then Buddhism in both China and India—and later in other countries in South-East Asia. They even see it in the context of the spiritual worlds of Christianity, Judaism and Islam (Eifring, 2013, 2015; Taylor 1999).

There is therefore clearly a need for accepted definitions, especially considering the transformation of meditation into the broader "mindfulness" we see today—and its widespread use as a mental health intervention. The term "meditation" may refer to both an action and a state (of a person absorbed in meditation). It may also refer collectively to the numerous different approaches to it that have been developed over the years (Bond et al., 2009). One accurate study of the use of meditation in healthcare is that produced by Ospina and her colleagues at the Agency for Healthcare Research and Quality, part of the US Department of Health and Human Services. It was a report of the results of an extensive search and detailed review of the literature available (Ospina, 2007).

Of the definition and types of meditation, the authors said that:

> Despite the lack of consensus in the scientific literature on a definition of meditation, most investigators would agree that meditation implies a form of mental training that requires either stilling or emptying the mind, and that has as its goal a state of "detached observation" in which practitioners are aware of their environment, but do not become involved in thinking about it. All types of meditation practices seem to be based on the concept of self-observation of immediate psychic activity, training one's level of awareness, and cultivating an attitude of acceptance of process rather than content. Meditation is an umbrella term that encompasses a family of practices that share some distinctive features, but that vary in important ways in their purpose and practice. This lack of specificity of the concept of meditation precludes developing an exhaustive taxonomy of meditation practices. However, in order to systematically address the question of the state of research of meditation practices in healthcare, we must attempt to identify the components that are common to the many practices that are claimed to be meditation or that incorporate a meditative component, and also clearly distinguish meditation

> practices from other therapeutic and self-regulation strategies such as self-hypnosis or visualization and from other relaxation techniques that do not contain a meditative component. Meditation practices may be classified according to certain phenomenological characteristics: the primary goal of practice (therapeutic or spiritual), the direction of the attention (mindfulness, concentrative, and practices that shift between the field or background perception and experience and an object within the field, the kind of anchor employed (a word, breath, sound, object or sensation), and according to the posture used (motionless sitting or moving). Like other complex and multifaceted therapeutic interventions, meditation practices involve a mixture of specific and vaguely defined characteristics, and they can be practiced on their own or in conjunction with other therapies.

This survey of the literature identified 1959 articles, and excluded 911 deemed inadequate to be included in the study for various reasons. Yet even this careful examination does not appear to have successfully identified a common definition of meditation for the purposes medical intervention and scientific study. In the end, the study concludes with an image of meditation not all that different from the stereotypical picture of the lone Asian ascetic sitting cross-legged in a trance-like state.

We might therefore tentatively accept the simplified image of a meditator as a person who adopts a specific relaxed posture—mainly sitting cross-legged. This is to minimise the proprioceptive messages coming from the body, and also to reduce as far as possible the neuromuscular, anti-gravity bodily responses needed to maintain a stable sitting position. The meditator stays in a quiet place, with limited sensory inputs from the surrounding environment, and remains there undisturbed for relatively long, continuous periods of time. No deliberate attention is given to the external world, and the meditator concentrates on their breathing and potentially also on their internal world. In this way, mental activity progressively calms down, and the turmoil of the everyday thoughts that usually crowd the mind is replaced by a quiet and deepening state of effortless concentration. As the meditator improves, they attain this state of calm concentration more and more easily. More practice also allows them to deepen their state of calm, and maintain it with less and less effort. They even gain the ability to attain it outside periods of meditation. The regular meditator is thus able to attain a new state of consciousness outside of the usual tumult of everyday, uncontrolled thoughts—which may be accompanied by sudden intuitive insights and a level comprehension beyond rational and dialectic reasoning. This is a simplified description, but it is broadly in accord with the vast variety of texts, images and statues of the Buddha and his various manifestations in Buddhist iconography (Harvey, 2013f).

After briefly considering meditation in relation to Buddhism, where the practice originated, it would be useful to examine the specific characteristics of "mindfulness"—both as it was initially proposed by Kabat-Zinn in his Mindfulness-Based Stress Reduction programme (MBSR), and as it has since developed and altered.

In 1990, John Kabat-Zinn published his book *Full Catastrophe Living* (Kabat-Zinn, 1990a), which gained enormous popularity, selling over 400,000 copies worldwide. It was even republished in a 15th anniversary edition with a slightly changed subtitle including the words "using mindfulness meditation" (Kabat-Zinn, 1990b)—and then again in a revised edition in 2013 (Kabat-Zinn, 2013). Kabat-Zinn published several other books on mindfulness, which were also widely popular; *Wherever You Go, There You Are,* for example, sold over 750,000 copies (Kabat-Zinn, 1994).

These books built an enormous worldwide reputation both for Kabat-Zinn and for the concept of mindfulness, and so certainly bear greater attention here. In the first edition of *Full Catastrophe Living,* the introduction is called *Stress, pain and illness: facing the full catastrophe,* offering a clue to the nature of the "catastrophe" referred to in the title. The succeeding sections are called: "I The Practice of Mindfulness: Paying Attention"; "II The Paradigm: A New Way of Thinking About Health and Illness"; "III Stress"; "IV The applications: taking on the full catastrophe", and "V The way of awareness".

Examining the text does not reveal any significant innovations. In particular, *Chapter I* mentions the power of breathing, sitting meditation, the body-scan technique, yoga as meditation, walking meditation and the importance of mindfulness. *Sub-chapter 10,* about getting started in the practice, is of central importance, and describes the eight-week programme over six pages. This same scheme would be adopted and used by practically all the studies and iterations of mindfulness after Kabat-Zinn's proposal.

The programme aims to help patients concentrate for about 45 minutes every day in a variety of suggested ways, such as "body scan", yoga and meditation. Meditation is practised in lying, sitting, standing and walking positions, as well as during yoga. The periods of meditation are regularly guided by vocal instructions and suggestions. Kabat-Zinn also provides audio CD recordings of a therapist with his books on mindfulness—which are available as MP3 files on the internet too. They are intended to be used for associated homework assignments ("Jon Kabat-Zinn Series I, II and II Digital MP3 Downloads", 2019).

The books on mindfulness that followed Kabat-Zinn's original *Full Catastrophe Living* follow the same eight-week programme, and are also accompanied by audio instructions; a good example of this is the book by Williams and Penman (2011). The aim of the programme is to develop the awareness of the subject—not only during the eight weeks, but also afterwards.

In Kabat-Zinn's book, there are more ways of addressing specific problems, such as physical symptoms, physical and emotional pain, fear, panic, anxiety—as well as various different types of stress—in *Chapter IV.* Then *Chapter V* focuses on the difficulties of beginning and keeping up formal and informal practices. To help readers keep to the mindfulness routine, at the end of the book there is an *Awareness of pleasant or unpleasant events calendar* agenda, which is meant to be filled in regularly.

The book considers a wide range of subjects, and deals with them in a popular but essentially superficial way. There are no references provided in the text, but there is a six-page list of reading recommendations. The main theme of the book is stress, and its negative effects on both physical and emotional wellbeing. It is therefore surprising that there is not at least some reference to the extensive literature on this matter that was available at the time of publication. The themes of stress, health and disease have been examined and popularised by excellent books such as *Why Zebras Don't Get Ulcers: Guide to Stress, Stress-Related Diseases and Coping* by Sapolsky (2004). It must be noted too that when Kabat-Zinn's book first appeared, there was also plenty of literature available on stress and other related issues—as well as a large amount of innovative research about the relationships between the mind, the central and peripheral nervous system, the endocrine organs and the immune system. New ideas and disciplines were being established in areas such as neuro-immuno-modulation and psycho-neuro-immunology. New scientific societies were being started, such as the *Psychoneuroimmunology Research Society (PNIRS)*, with eminent scholars as members, as well as excellent congresses ("PNIRS—Home", 2019). Valuable new journals were also being started, such as *Brain, Behaviour and Immunity* (Brain, Behaviour, & Immunity, 2019), and authoritative texts such as *Psychoneuroimmunology* were being published (Ader, Felten, & Cohen, 2006). There was also Herbert Benson, a pioneer of mind-body medicine from the Seventies: his book entitled *The relaxation response* (his own scientific term for meditation) (Benson, 1975) became a best-seller (Benson & Klipper, 2009), as did his other later works on the subject. These are not mentioned at all in the reading recommendations at the end of *Full catastrophe living*.

It is possible to better understand Kabat-Zinn's contributions to mindfulness by considering his biography. His family gave him a highly intellectual background, and he received formal training as a molecular biologist, gaining a Ph.D. in 1971 from the Massachusetts Institute of Technology. This intellectual and scientific background may have led him to apply develop mindfulness in a scientific rather than a religious framework.

Kabat-Zinn initially encountered meditation when he met Philip Kapleau, one of the first Western Zen teachers, who had gained formal training in the *Sanbo Kyodan* tradition. This is a blend of the traditional Japanese Sōtō and Rinzai Zen schools, formulated by the Japanese master Hakuun Yasutani roshi; it was popularised in the United States by Philip Kapleau (Sharf, 1995). Kabat-Zinn then studied meditation with Seung Sahn, a master who arrived in America from South Korea in 1972, and taught the Korean version of Zen. Kabat-Zinn also became a student of Thich Nhat Hanh's teachings. This last encounter deserves and needs significant attention because it was the basis for two diverging and radically different forms of mindfulness in the West.

One particular biography of Thich Nhat Hanh is accompanied by his poem "*Please Call Me by My True Names*". Thich Nhat Hanh is one of the best-known and most respected Zen masters in the world: he is also a poet, as well as a peace and human rights activist. In short, he is someone who has led an extraordinary life. Born in central Vietnam in 1926, he joined a Buddhist monastery at the age of sixteen. The Vietnam War confronted the country's monks with the question of whether they should adhere to the contemplative life and continue just meditating in their monasteries, or whether they should actively help the villagers suffering from the devastation of the war. Thich Nhat Hanh chose to do both, helping to found the "*Engaged Buddhism*" movement. His life since has been dedicated to the work of inner transformation for the benefit of individuals and society. During his travels in the U.S. at the time of Vietnam war, he met Martin Luther King, Jr. and persuaded him to publicly oppose the war, helping to galvanize the peace movement. And in fact, the following year, Martin Luther King, Jr. nominated him for the Nobel Peace Prize.

In 1982, Thich Nhat Hanh went on to found Plum Village, a Buddhist community in exile in France, where he continued his work to alleviate the suffering of refugees, political prisoners and hungry families in Vietnam and throughout the Third World. The Plum Village community later expanded to another eight monastic practice centres across Europe, the USA and Asia—and through them, welcomed many westerners interested in practising "engaged Buddhist" teachings.

Thich Nhat Hanh has published some 100 works of poetry, prose, and prayer—including more than 40 in English. Some have had a wide diffusion around the world and even become best-sellers. His teachings on the practice of Buddhism concentrate especially on mindfulness, and this can be seen immediately in the titles of several of his books, including: *The Miracle of Mindfulness*, *The Miracle of Mindfulness: A Manual on Meditation*, *The Path of Emancipation: Talks from a 21-Day Mindfulness Retreat* and *The Miracle of Mindfulness: The Classic Guide to Meditation* (Hahn, 1991). Thich Nhat Hanh's key teachings are strictly based on the ancient Buddhist scripture of Anapanasati sutta (Harvey, 2013g), as specifically seen in the *Mindfulness of Breathing*, as well as the Satipatthana sutta, as found in the *Four Establishments of Mindfulness* (Sayadaw, 1990).

Meditation practised according to these Buddhist teachings leads to mindfulness. It is a way of helping people to learn to live in the present moment instead of in the past and in the future. And according to these teachings, dwelling in the present moment is the only way to truly develop peace, both in one's self and in the world (Hahn, 2008).

Thich Nhat Hanh is widely regarded as one of the great spiritual teachers of the twentieth century, and he belongs to the tradition of Vietnamese Zen. Aged 16, he entered Tu Hieu monastery, where he trained in the Mahayana school of Vietnamese Zen Buddhism. His teacher was the 41st generation Master of the Lieu Quan School of Vietnamese Zen Buddhism, who formally ordained him in 1949. He spent much of his life travelling and teaching throughout Vietnam, but was expelled from the country in 1965. He continued teaching elsewhere, however—particularly in the Plum Villages he founded in France and other parts of the world ("Community of Interbeing", 2019).

Considering the life of Thich Nhat Hanh offers the opportunity to focus on some of the essential aspects of traditional Buddhist monk training, which are relevant here because of their implications for the training of contemporary mindfulness and meditation practitioners.

In various different Buddhist traditions, teachers and masters receive the "*Dharma transmission*" from a teacher who will, in turn have received it from their master. The "*Dharma transmission*", also called "*mind to mind transmission*" and "*transmission without reliance on words*", gives a student the formal recognition that they can teach others. This transmission is traceable through an unbroken succession of teachers and disciples—a spiritual 'bloodline' theoretically traceable back to the Buddha himself. It is called the "*lineage*" and is a highly revered feature of Buddhist tradition.

The "*Dharma transmission*", and the "*lineage*" through which it was transmitted and received, are crucial qualifications of a Buddhist teacher (Harvey, 2013h). Buddhist monks train under the guidance of a master in a temple belonging to a recognized "*lineage*" and doctrine. It is a demanding and extensive process that involves a substantial amount of meditation (Harvey, 2013i). Through the process, disciples may be ordained as monks and may even pass through further training stages.

To be recognised as having experienced the first instance of "*awakening*" (*kensho* in the Zen tradition), disciples must go through a lengthy period of hard study, practice and training. Then they must go through an even more arduous and lengthy process to be recognised as a master. The whole process usually takes decades.

These practices have been followed for centuries and centuries in the East, and only a small number of people are motivated enough to undergo the hardships of the time-consuming and rigorous training process. Meditation is an essential part of the training process, and is practised by aspiring monks in a monastery (Harvey, 2013j; Sharf, 1995). Outside of this, however, even devoted laypeople closely involved with the community of a Buddhist temple do not usually practise meditation. Most Buddhists generally only come into contact with monasteries for liturgies—mainly related to deaths and also less frequently for other spiritual reasons or in the case of a personal crisis (Bodiford, 1992).

Given the rigour of traditional Buddhist monk training, it is understandable that many people over the years have sought to find alternatives: less arduous ways to teach Buddhist principles and practices—and which also forego the less relevant aspects of the original traditions. One example is *Sanbo Kyodan Zen*, which was developed in the late twentieth century by the Japanese master Hakuun Yasutani roshi. *Sanbo Kyodan* later reached the US thanks to the efforts of Yasutani's disciples such as Philip Kapleau, who was one of the first people to introduce Kabat-Zinn to Buddhism (Bodiford, 2008; Sharf, 1995). Another example is the Therevada tradition, in which meditation was abandoned in the 10th century. In the nineteenth and twentieth centuries, however, a new *Vipassana* meditation practice developed, based on a contemporary reading of the ancient Therevada texts. This practice then spread widely in the West (McMahan, 2008; Sharf, 1995).

In Thich Nhat Hahn's Plum Villages, he promoted a form of mindfulness based on ancient Buddhist texts and essentially involving meditation practised in a serene, quiet and concentrated environment. It is the essence of traditional Buddhist meditation transposed into a contemporary Western context. The Plum Villages also emphasise the connection with traditional Buddhism and the "*lineage*" of teachers.

In the Plum Villages, monks and nuns are only officially authorised to teach eight years after their ordination, through a ceremony where the *Dharma Lamp* is "transmitted". The rules for lay followers are more variable: they can choose to go on spiritual retreats of different lengths, from daily and three-month "Winter Retreats", all the way up to a "Five-Year Monastic Programme" ("Plum Village", 2019).

Overall, the spiritual practices of the Plum Villages are essentially stripped down Buddhism, which focus on calming and pacifying the mind through periods of silent meditation. Their teachings, mainly focused on the direct and non-intellectual awareness of the here and now, are grounded in early Buddhism, and particularly on two forms of meditation originally taught by the Buddha: "*Mindfulness of Breathing*" and the "*Four Establishments of Mindfulness*". This is clearly seen in the writings of Thich Nhat Hahn. The 2017 film "*Walk with me*" also offers a delicate and moving picture of a monastic community of Zen Buddhist monks and nuns who have dedicated their lives to mastering the art of mindfulness with Thich Nhat Hanh ("Walk with Me [2017]—IMDb", 2019).

The life and works of Thich Nhat Hanh and Jon Kabat-Zinn are examples of two very popular—and very different—ways that meditation and mindfulness have spread in the West in the second part of the twentieth century. In the case of Thich Nhat Hanh, the teachings are profoundly rooted in Buddhism and early Buddhist doctrines. They follow the basic practices of Buddhist meditation, which are based on wordless direct experience and extended periods of sitting in silent meditation.

Jon Kabat-Zinn, on the other hand, started with an early interest in Buddhism after he was exposed to the teachings of the *Sanbo Kyodan*, Korean Zen and Thich Nhat Hanh himself, later in his life when he began teaching Zen at the Cambridge Zen Centre. Unlike practitioners in Thich Nhat Hanh's school of mindfulness, however, he did not gain formal recognition as a teacher of Buddhism through transmission and the "*lineage*" (Wilson, 2014b). Despite this, however, he had great success popularising mindfulness in psychological, medical and scientific contexts. His scientific training was undoubtedly very important in this—particularly when establishing his "*Stress Reduction Clinic*" and the "*Center for Mindfulness in Medicine, Health Care, and Society*" at the University of Massachusetts Medical School, based on his programme "*Mindfulness-Based Stress Reduction*" (MBSR). Kabat-Zinn also put significant effort into establishing the effectiveness of his eight-week MBSR programme as a medical intervention.

When others adopted Kabat-Zinn's approach to mindfulness later, the vast majority also used his eight-week programme. An excellent example of that is Williams's book "*Mindfulness: Diverse Perspectives on Its Meaning, Origins and Applications*", which applies Kabat-Zinn's programme to depression and general unhappiness—both using mindfulness alone and also combining it with cognitive psychotherapy (Wlliams & Kabat-Zin, 2013).

In 2011, Kabat-Zinn and Mark Williams also invited a select group of experts to discuss "state-of-the-art" mindfulness. Their contributions were collected in a single issue of *Contemporary Buddhism: An Interdisciplinary Journal* (Mindfulness: Diverse Perspectives on Its Meaning, Origins, and Multiple Applications at the Intersection of Science and Dharma, 2011). These same contributions were also published by Piatkus as the book entitled "*Mindfulness: Diverse Perspectives on Its Meaning, Origins and Applications*" (Wlliams & Kabat-Zin, 2013).

The editors of the book attribute many of its ideas to the close collaboration over two decades between Jon Kabat-Zinn and Mark Williams—as well as Zindel Segal and John Teasdale. Mark Williams founded the *Centre for Mindfulness Research and Practice* at Bangor University, North Wales, as well as the *Oxford Mindfulness Centre* at the University of Oxford. Both have produced a wealth of investigations and reports about mindfulness and its application in psychology, psychiatry and medicine.

Mindfulness was ultimately integrated into cognitive psychotherapy not only because of Kabat-Zinn's approach, but also because of the work of Zindel Segal at the University of Toronto, Mark Williams at the Universities of Bangor and Oxford and also John Teasdale at the University of Cambridge. As a result, "*Mindfulness-Based Cognitive Therapy*" (MBCT) was developed. An improved version of it is now used, described by its creators as "*a new and turbocharged version of MBCT, which we might call MBCT 2.0*" (Williams & Segal, 2012).

There are several things to consider here. In *Mindfulness-Based Cognitive Therapy of Depression*, Segal, Williams and Teasdale go into much more detail about the integration of mindfulness into therapy. Williams's expectations of the effectiveness of mindfulness are particularly interesting because he believes it can tackle not only depression, but also unhappiness and stress together with their bodily consequences (Williams & Penman, 2011). He suggests, too, that it could target not only the initial appearance of depression, but also prevent relapses. The idea of combining it with medication and antidepressant drugs is also broached (Segal, Williams, & Teasdale 2012).

There is no doubt that MBCT as presented in the book by Segal, Williams and Teasdale is impressive. Their work puts Jon Kabat-Zinn's original eight-week MBSR programme in a richer context. They give proper attention to the "*Challenges of depression*" in *Part I*, its treatment with "*Mindfulness-based cognitive therapy*" in *Part II*, and "*Evaluation and dissemination*" in *Part III*. Part III is particularly interesting because it directly addresses questions about the effectiveness of the intervention, how it actually works and how practitioners—called "instructors"—are trained. They make a concerted effort to use the best protocols available to assess the effectiveness of MBCT interventions, including ensuring participants are given different treatments and examined using a randomised procedure. The delicate issue of the training of the "instructors" is mentioned at the end of the book in "*Chapter 21. Moving the Programme Off the Page and into the Clinic: Supports for Mindfulness-Based Cognitive Therapy Instructors and Their Patients*". In the UK, the authors mention, there is postgraduate training leading to a master's degree in MBCT available at Oxford University and the University of Exeter. Bangor University also offers a Master's in mindfulness, with a major focus on both MBSR and MBCT (Segal et al., 2012).

Kabat-Zinn has also addressed the issue of teachers' education, and as a result there is currently a programme at the University of Massachusetts that gives trainees a Certification in MBSR Teacher Education ("MBSR Teacher Training", 2019). In certain other countries, there are also recognised MBSR training providers who follow the same theory and practices as the original founders of the approach.

That, then, is how MBSR was developed and how it evolved into MBCT. It is impressive not only because of how far the practice has spread, but also because of the persuasive and extensive work that has gone into substantiating the theory and practice of mindfulness-based interventions.

This, however, is not the only way to see the history of mindfulness-based interventions. It is also worth considering mindfulness and its applications in relation to its origins in Buddhist history and culture.

Meditation has been practised in all known historical schools of Buddhism, and there is little doubt about the exact meaning of "meditation" in this context. Over time, however, the practice diversified based on local cultural influences and scholarly strands of thought. The variations, however, do not seem to conflict with the simple picture of a meditator as someone sitting in a quiet and silent place, focusing on their breathing and calming their mind by concentrating on their inner mental activities. This was the case with the "*koans*" of the Rinzai Zen—and also with the breathing and mental representation of both mental and physical processes in the Vipassana meditation of the Therevada school. (This, of course, is also the school to which the roots of the mindfulness movement can be traced.) And the Tibetan Vairayana practice also involves various complex mental visualisations during meditation.

The meditation used in mindfulness is largely verbally guided by a therapist. It has also acquired some of the characteristics of other approaches developed in West, which have some elements in common with meditative practices, and similarly bring patients into a specific state of consciousness different to either sleeping or being awake. Examples of this include hypnosis, auto-hypnosis and autogenic training, and it is not clear how much of the effect of mindfulness application can be attributed to these.

Although there were many variations of meditation based on different local cultural influences and scholarly strands of thought, the simple picture in all is still of a meditator sitting in a quiet place focusing on their breathing and calming their mind. Because mindfulness has become detached from its Buddhist beginnings, however, it is difficult to draw out a similarly clear and simple picture of it. Attempts to define it in such an elemental way lead to widespread debate between experts in several different fields, including psychology, psychotherapy, Buddhism, philosophy and others.

The diverging picture appearing here between meditation and mindfulness leads onto the question of the nature of Buddhism. The Buddhist scriptures, attributed to the original, historical Buddha, admonish speculation as a time-wasting diversion from spiritual practice and attempts to grasp the true meaning of the Teachings. One example provided in the scriptures is of a man shot by a poisoned arrow, who then refuses to let a doctor cure him until he knows everything about who shot the arrow and what the arrow was made of (Harvey, 2013k). There is also a speech given to the Kalama population stressing the need to reject teachings based on authoritative tradition and rational speculation, instead emphasising the importance of examining and analysing actual experience (Harvey, 2013l). From this perspective, Buddhism is properly understood when one avoids scriptures, priests and masters and instead follows the *Noble Eightfold Path*—including meditation. One could interpret this now as a caution against focusing excessively on rationally defining meditation and mindfulness.

The application of mindfulness involves a certain amount of meditation. But then there is the question of how this meditation is practised—particularly considering the many and varied religious traditions that used it in the past. At present, meditation, as seen in both MBSR and MBCT, is generally guided by the voice of an "instructor". And as well as the issue of the "quality" of meditation, there is also the question of the "quantity" of meditation. In Buddhist tradition, monastic training was generally characterised by extended periods of meditation, whereas lay devotees did not practise meditation at all, no matter how sincere their faith. In modern mindfulness applications, there has been less and less meditation after MBSR was initially proposed. It has become progressively less significant in relation to the other actions of the "instructor" who accompanies it. Then when mindfulness was included in cognitive psychotherapy in the MBCT approach, it was more like a homework assignment than the millennia-old practice upon which it was originally based.

There is similar uncertainty about just how much meditation is involved in the programmes to train certified mindfulness practitioners and "instructors". People gain these qualifications at the end of a formal period of training—a matter of weeks—in which meditation is only part of the course. This is in stark contrast to Buddhist tradition, in which someone is recognised as a teacher after years of training in which meditation is the dominant feature. In other words, in MBCT for example, although practitioners are certainly experienced cognitive psychotherapists who have undergone prolonged and specific training, it is far less clear how much experience they have of practising and teaching meditation.

The integration of mindfulness into psychotherapeutic intervention also raises the general issue of the relationship between Buddhism and meditation and the world of psychotherapy. This is something examined by an excellent panel of experts in a special issue of *Contemporary Buddhism* devoted to mindfulness (Mindfulness: Diverse Perspectives on Its Meaning, Origins, and Multiple Applications at the Intersection of Science and Dharma, 2011). The aims of the guest editors (Richard Davidson, Zindel Segal and Amishi Jha) are to "*explain its rationale, aims, and intentions. Integrating mindfulness-based approaches into medicine, psychology, neuroscience, healthcare, education, business leadership, and other major societal institutions has become a burgeoning field*". The different contributions are mainly scholarly, and are accompanied by those of contributors with formal religious training such as Ven. Bhikkhu Bodhi. There are also contributions from people like Martine Batchelor, who has extensive experience practising Korean Zen meditation in a monastic context. The main Buddhist perspective offered, however, comes from people from the Therevada Hinayana tradition, while other Buddhist schools are hardly considered. Overall, the main psychological framework is provided by the cognitive sciences and cognitive psychotherapy. The rich and complex world of psychodynamic experiences—which may, in fact offer vital clues about the world of mindfulness—is largely ignored.

Exploring how Buddhism could potentially help to understand and alleviate mental suffering is not a new idea in the world of psychology and medicine: in fact, it has been considered from many different perspectives. Indeed, cognitive science and the psychotherapies are a recent part of the worldwide study of the human mind that flourished from the end of the nineteenth century—particularly after Sigmund Freud's seminal psychoanalytical work. Serious examination of the mind, psyche and basis of mental suffering then became possible, and was developed and advanced in both the East and the West. And when ancient Buddhist texts were translated, it quickly became possible to incorporate an understanding of Buddhism into these scholarly endeavours. Westerners were able to gain first-hand experience and understanding of Buddhism and the practice of meditation. This, however, was early in the development of the study of the human mind—before the cognitive sciences fully came into their own. By the time the cognitive sciences became an advanced field, there was already widespread interest in Buddhism and there had been numerous contributions on the subject by eminent personalities. As both fields advanced, interventions based on meditation also began to emerge. Today, the psychodynamic, humanist and interpersonal perspectives that fuelled these developments are still alive and well—and pushing new advances in humanist psychotherapeutic avenues.

These themes will be further explored in the following chapters. The next will focus on how Buddhism became more and more widely known in the West, and how that led to new attempts to alleviate suffering based on Buddhist practices.

## References

Ader, R., Felten, D. L., & Cohen, N. (2006). *Psychoneuroimmunology* (4th ed.). New York: Academic Press.

Aitken, R. (1988). *The mind of clover: Essays in Zen Buddhist ethics*. New York: North Point Press.

Benson, H. (1975). *The relaxation response*. New York: Avon Books.

Benson, H., & Klipper, M. (2009). *The relaxation response*. New York: HarperCollins.

Bodiford, W. (1992). Zen in the art of funerals: Ritual salvation in Japanese Buddhism. *History of Religions, 32*(2), 146–164. https://doi.org/10.1086/463322.

Bodiford, W. M. (2008). Dharma transmission in theory and practice. In *Zen ritual: Studies of Zen Buddhist theory in practice* (pp. 261–282). Oxford: Oxford University Press.

Bond, K., Ospina, M., Hooton, N., Bialy, L., Dryden, D., Buscemi, N., et al. (2009). Defining a complex intervention: The development of demarcation criteria for "meditation". *Psychology of Religion and Spirituality, 1*(2), 129–137. https://doi.org/10.1037/a0015736.

Brain, Behavior, & Immunity. (2019). Retrieved from https://www.journals.elsevier.com/brain-behavior-and-immunity. Accessed 16 April 2019.

Community of Interbeing. (2019). Retrieved from https://web.archive.org/web/20080102023137/http:/www.interbeing.org.uk/teachers/thay.html. Accessed 16 April 2019.

Creswell, J. (2017). Mindfulness interventions. *Annual Review of Psychology, 68*(1), 491–516. https://doi.org/10.1146/annurev-psych-042716-051139.

Eifring, A. (2015). *Meditation and culture: The interplay of practice and context.* London: Bloomsbury Academic.

Eifring, A. (Ed.). (2013). *Meditation in Judaism, Christianity and Islam: Cultural histories*. London: Bloomsbury Academic.

Fisher, D., Fisher, A., & Staff, L. (2019). *Mindfulness and the cessation of suffering: An exclusive new interview with mindfulness pioneer…* Retrieved from https://www.lionsroar.com/mindfulness-and-the-cessation-of-suffering-an-exclusive-new-interview-with-mindfulness-pioneer-jon-kabat-zinn/. Accessed 16 April 2019.

Hahn, T. N. (1991). *The miracle of mindfulness.* New Delhi, India: Rider Books.

Hahn, T. N. (2008). Please call me by my true names. *Human Architecture: Journal of the Sociology of Self-knowledge, VI*(3, Summer), 3–6. Retrieved from https://www.okcir.com/Articles%20VI%203/TNHCallMEByMyTrueNames-FM.pdf. Accessed 16 April 2019.

Harvey, P. (2013a). *An introduction to Buddhism* (p. 422). New York: Cambridge University Press.

Harvey, P. (2013b). *An introduction to Buddhism* (pp. 56–87). New York: Cambridge University Press.

Harvey, P. (2013c). *An introduction to Buddhism* (pp. 264–286). New York: Cambridge University Press.

Harvey, P. (2013d). *An introduction to Buddhism* (pp. 298–308). New York: Cambridge University Press.

Harvey, P. (2013e). *An introduction to Buddhism* (p. 362). New York: Cambridge University Press.

Harvey, P. (2013f). *An introduction to Buddhism* (pp. 20–21, 105–108). New York: Cambridge University Press.
Harvey, P. (2013g). *An introduction to Buddhism: History and practices* (p. 328). New York: Cambridge University.
Harvey, P. (2013h). *An introduction to Buddhism: History and practices* (pp. 194–235). New York: Cambridge University.
Harvey, P. (2013i). *An introduction to Buddhism: History and practices* (pp. 287–375). New York: Cambridge University.
Harvey, P. (2013j). *An introduction to Buddhism: History and practices* (pp. 194–236). New York: Cambridge University.
Harvey, P. (2013k). *An introduction to Buddhism: History and practices* (p. 78). New York: Cambridge University.
Harvey, P. (2013l). *An introduction to Buddhism: History and practices* (p. 30). New York: Cambridge University.
Jon Kabat-Zinn Series I, II and II Digital MP3 Downloads. (2019). Retrieved from https://www.betterlisten.com/pages/jonkabatzinnseries123. Accessed 16 April 2019.
Jon Kabat-Zinn: Defining Mindfulness—Mindful. (2019). Retrieved from https://www.mindful.org/jon-kabat-zinn-defining-mindfulness/. Accessed 16 April 2019.
Kabat-Zinn, J. (1990a). *Full catastrophe living: Using the wisdom of your body and mind to face stress, pain, and illness*. New York: Dell Publishing.
Kabat-Zinn, J. (1990b). *Full catastrophe living: Hot to cope with stress, pain and illness using mindfulness meditation*. London: Piatkus.
Kabat-Zinn, J. (1994). *Wherever you go, there you are*. Piatkus: London.
Kabat-Zinn, J. (2013). *Full catastrophe living (revised edition): Using the wisdom of your body and mind to face stress, pain, and illness*. New York: Bantam.
Levman, B. (2017). Putting smrti back into sati. *Journal of the Oxford Centre for Buddhist Studies, 2017*(13), 121–149.
MBSR Teacher Training. (2019). Retrieved from https://www.umassmed.edu/cfm/training/MBSR-Teacher-Education/. Accessed 16 April 2019.
McMahan, D. (2008). *The making of Buddhist modernism*. Oxford: Oxford University Press.
Mindfulness: Diverse Perspectives on Its Meaning, Origins, and Multiple Applications at the Intersection of Science and Dharma. Special Issue. (2011). *Contemporary Buddhism: An Interdisciplinary Journal, 12*(1), 1–306.
Ospina, M. B. et al. (2007, June). *Evidence report/technology assessment number 155 meditation practices for health: State of the research*. AHRQ Publication

No. 07-E010. Retrieved from https://archive.ahrq.gov/downloads/pub/evidence/pdf/meditation/medit.pdf. Accessed 16 April 2019.

Plum Village. (2019). Retrieved from https://plumvillage.org/. Accessed 16 April 2019.

PNIRS—Home. (2019). Retrieved from https://www.pnirs.org/index.cfm. Accessed 16 April 2019.

Sapolsky, R. (2004). *Why zebras don't get ulcers*. New York: Holt.

Sayadaw, M. (1990). *Satipatthana Vipassana*. Kandy, Sri Lanka: Buddhist Publication Society.

Segal, Z. V., Williams, J. M. G., & Teasdale, J. D. (2012). *Mindfulness-based cognitive therapy of depression* (2nd ed.). London: Guilford Press.

Sharf, R. (1995). Sanbōkyōdan: Zen and the way of the New Religions. *Japanese Journal of Religious Studies, 22*(3–4). https://doi.org/10.18874/jjrs.22.3-4.1995.417-458.

Sharf, R. (2014). Mindfulness and mindlessness in early Chan. *Philosophy East and West, 64*(4), 933–964. https://doi.org/10.1353/pew.2014.0074.

Taylor, E. (1999). Introduction. In M. Murphy & S. Donovan (Eds.), *The physical and psychological effects of meditation: A review of contemporary research: With a comprehensive bibliography, 1931–1996* (pp. 1–30). Sausalito, CA: Institute of Noetic Sciences.

Walk with Me (2017)—IMDb. (2019). Retrieved from https://www.imdb.com/title/tt2331100/. Accessed 16 April 2019.

Williams, J., & Segal, Z. (2012). *Mindfulness-based cognitive therapy for depression* (2nd ed.). London: Guilford Press.

Williams, M., & Penman, D. (2011). *Mindfulness: A practical guide to finding peace in a frantic word*. London: Piatkus.

Wilson, J. (2014a). *Mindful America: Meditation and the mutual transformation of Buddhism and American culture*. Oxford: Oxford University Press.

Wilson, J. (2014b). *Mindful America: Meditation and the mutual transformation of Buddhism and American culture* (p. 35). Oxford: Oxford University Press.

Wlliams, J. M. G., & Kabat-Zinn, J. (Eds.). (2013). *Mindfulness: Diverse perspectives on its meaning, origins and applications*. Abingdon, Oxon: Routledge.

# 3

# The Spread of Buddhism from East to West

This chapter will examine how it happened that aspects of Buddhism, a religion with a long history in Asia, came to be adopted in the West. In particular, it will chart how they came to be used to treat a host of different psychological, psychiatric and medical disorders, improve general wellbeing—and how they even, in a strangely narcissistic and cosmetic turn, came to be used as a way to improve personal performance in a range of fields.

Mindfulness-based medical interventions spread so remarkably in the last thirty years—particularly in America and Europe—essentially because Jon Kabat-Zinn's original programme proposed using meditation to attenuate the strains of a stressful life in modern Western society. Thinking back to the USA in the 90s, it is easy to imagine how Kabat-Zinn might have had doubts about suggesting an ancient Asian religious ritual to his patients. But then, not that long before, in the 50s and 60s of the Beat Generation, there had already been considerable interest in Zen Buddhism. Rather than laying the groundwork for it, however, it is easy to see how the association of Buddhism with this small intellectual niche of American society could actually have made it harder for the rest of the population to take meditation seriously.


T. Giraldi, *Psychotherapy, Mindfulness and Buddhist Meditation*,
https://doi.org/10.1007/978-3-030-29003-0_3

Kabat-Zinn appears to have taken two key steps to popularise meditation or "mindfulness". First, he relied on the core Buddhist teaching of the "Middle Way", through which one can overcome the suffering that is inextricably linked with the passage of life. Looking at the whole complex framework of Buddhism, Kabat-Zinn pulled out just one element, *sati* or "mindfulness", overlooking both *smrti* and *Samadhi.* In the process, he ignored several key aspects of Buddhism, such as the fact that however devoted the population of a Buddhist country may be, meditation is still only practised by a small number of monks residing in monasteries. He also seems to have disregarded the deep moral values that are meant to underpin Buddhism (Foulk, 2008; Harvey, 2000).

Second, Kabat-Zinn believed that he could get people to accept meditation by transforming it into "mindfulness", and then by shearing it of its connection to Buddhism as part of his stress-reduction MBSR programme. Based on these two ideas, at the Stress Reduction Clinic at the University of Massachusetts Medical School, he proposed using "mindfulness" as a new way to grapple with suffering, following "*the wisdom and the heart of Buddhist meditation without the Buddhism…*" (Fisher, Fisher, & Staff, 2019).

When Kabat-Zinn developed and announced his approach, he largely neglected to mention the fact that over the course of many years, Buddhism had already attracted the attention of a large number of Western thinkers. Here, then, it may be worthwhile to actually trace how thinkers and scholars in the West first engaged with Buddhism—and how many of them actually began developing new approaches to mental health based on its practices and principles (Aich, 2013). But first, before exploring this, there are a few things to consider.

Buddhism is often seen as comparable to other great global religions such as Judaism, Christianity and Islam, and it may be useful to consider the similarities and differences between these different creeds. They all evidently have some remarkably similar features, which raises the question of whether religions have similar traits because they share a common supernatural origin, or because they all based on similar mechanisms of the human mind. The American philosopher and psychologist William James—particularly based on his 1902 book *The Varieties of Religious Experience*—is considered an early expert in this field.

After him there was also a host of other eminent psychoanalysts, psychologists and thinkers who made important contributions to this fascinating, complex and contradictory field—particularly on Buddhism (James, 2012; Kato, 2016; Spilka, 2012).

There is one very interesting case study to consider here. During and immediately after the Second World War, a large number of Melanesian islanders became involved in what has come to be known as the "cargo cult". The name derives from the belief of these islanders that a range of ritualistic acts, such as building of an airplane runway, would result in the appearance of material wealth on their islands—especially highly desirable Western goods ("cargo")—via Western airplanes. The "cult" had a "vision" of the future, particularly in times of crisis, as well as a charismatic figure who was the custodian and minister of its rituals.

The origin of the "cargo cult" is not unique. Another similar example is the John Frum cult formed on the island of Tanna, Vanuatu. This movement started before the war, and worshiped an unspecified American with the name "John Frum", who, it was claimed, had brought cargo to the island during World War II. He was seen as the spiritual entity who would provide cargo in the future.

The characteristics of these cults are so peculiar that they have become key talking points in debates about religion and morality. Richard Dawkins has even suggested that religion is evolutionarily imprinted in our minds and that, in this context, the "cargo cults" might be seen as the origins of a religion unfolding before our eyes (Attenborough, 1983; Dawkins, 2006).

These facets of the debate about religion have obviously not been exhausted. In terms of the differences and similarities between religions, while Judaism, Christianity and Islam share some common features, Buddhism—including all the variations in its schools and traditions—can be seen as much more distinct from the others.

Whereas the other great religions are essentially based on the revelation of a supernatural power, the beliefs and spiritual practices of Buddhism are based on the teachings of Siddharta Gautama, the real, historical Buddha, who lived in Ancient India some time between the sixth and fourth centuries BCE. Buddhism later spread out through much of Asia, and is now the world's fourth-largest religion, with more than 520 million followers—over 7 per cent of the global population. During its diffusion over the last 2500 years, Buddhism absorbed different characteristics from the countries it spread to. The major traditions that have developed are the Theravāda tradition of Southeast Asia (Thailand, Burma, Cambodia, and Vietnam); the Mahayana (Zen) schools of Vietnam, China, Japan, and Korea, and the Vajrayana tradition of Tibetan Buddhism, found in Tibet, Mongolia, Nepal, Bhutan, Ladakh and, more recently, in the Tibetan community in exile (Snelling, 1998; Trainor, 2004).

It is believed the words originally preached by the historical Buddha are not directly preserved. What is available today, therefore, is an extremely large collection of scriptures which were written afterwards in a range of different periods—depending on the Buddhist tradition that maintains them. The texts are collections from orally transmitted traditions, which naturally grew in number through centuries of practice. The sermons actually attributed to the historical Buddha are referred to as the Sutra Discourses (Batchelor, 2013; Harvey, 2013). The amount of Buddhist literature available today is immense. Take the example of the Theravāda tradition. The Pali Text Society was founded in 1881 by Thomas William Rhys Davids "*to foster and promote the study of Pali texts*" (*Pali* being the language in which the texts of the Theravāda tradition were written). By 1922, when Rhys Davids died, the Pali Text Society had issued 64 separate texts in 94 volumes exceeding 26,000 pages—as well as a wide range of articles by English and European scholars; this gigantic project still continues ("Pali Text Society Home Page", 2019).

The idea of finding what "what Buddha really taught" is compelling, and there was a recent attempt at this by, among others, Stephen Batchelor. Batchelor had, for a long time, been practising Tibetan Buddhism at Dharamsala in northern India, at the headquarters of the Dalai Lama after the Chinese annexation of Tibet. He then continued in Tibetan missions established across Europe and, after that, in Korea with the late Zen Master Kusan Sunim. Most recently, Batchelor became a renowned proponent of agnostic or secular Buddhism, and published numerous books on the subject (Batchelor, 1997, 2010, 2015a, 2015b, 2017). After an extensive study of the earliest Buddhist scriptures, Batchelor became convinced that the essence of Buddha Siddharta Gautama's original teachings was in the "The Setting in Motion of the Wheel of the Dharma Sutra". This is an account of discussions he is believed to have had in Varanasi (today Benares), where he moved after attaining enlightenment through prolonged and exhausting meditation under the Bodhy tree (Batcheor, 2010).

In this sutra, he discusses the so-called "Four Noble Truths". An essential part of this is the idea that the suffering of life is caused by the impermanence of the objects of our attachment. We have to be aware of existential pain (Sufferance), its causes (Cause of sufferance), that it can be overcome (Cessation of sufferance), and that to achieve this, one has to follow "the Middle Way" (the Noble Eightfold Path), which will bring freedom from the pains of existence and final enlightenment. The steps of The Eightfold Path are Moral Virtue (right speech, action and livelihood), Meditation[1] (right effort, mental presence[2] and concentration) and Insight and Wisdom (right view and resolve).

As has already been discussed, the *Pali* term "sati" is translated in English as "mindfulness", a word apparently so compelling that it has gained universal acceptance and is used in most other foreign languages—taking on a sort of life of its own (Van Dam et al., 2017). Sati (mindfulness) is one of the components of meditation (samadhi), and samadhi and sati (mindfulness and meditation) are both parts of a complex framework of ideas that is grounded in morality (as in the Moral Virtue). The adjective "*right*", with its clear moral meaning, is repeated in all the descriptions of "Moral Virtue", "Meditation" and "Insight and Wisdom" in the Eightfold Path (Snelling, 1998).

Morality is not just a crucial component of the Four Noble Truths of the Eightfold Path; it also recurs in relation to many of the other main Buddhist values, such as the precepts, which require devoted lay Buddhists to refrain from killing living creatures, stealing, unchastity (sensuality, sexuality, lust), incorrect speech and taking intoxicants.

[1]"samadhi", the original *Pali* word commonly translated as "meditation".

[2]"sati", the original *Pali* word for the active watchful and constantly present mind, commonly translated as "mindfulness".

Added to this, ordained monks also have to refrain from eating at inappropriate times, singing (dancing, playing music), using perfumes, cosmetics and decorative accessories, sleeping on luxurious soft beds and accepting money (Aitken, 1984).

The teachings of "The Setting in Motion of the Wheel of the Dharma Sutra", are accompanied by another extraordinary sutra, the Kālāma Sutra. It is believed to recount Siddharta Gautama's lesson to the people of the village of Kesaputta, the Kalamas. They were asking for his advice because they were confused by the many wandering holy men and ascetics claiming to offer their own spiritual path and way of living, while denouncing the teachings of others. Who, the Kālāmas asked, should they believe? In response, Siddharta Gautama delivered a sermon for those who were unconvinced by mere claims and revelations. It is often termed the Buddha's "charter of free inquiry ("Kalama Sutta: The Buddha's Charter of Free Inquiry", 2019).

The Kālāma Sutra highlights the importance of prudence when seeking truth, wisdom and knowledge—whether religious or not. It opposes blind faith, dogmatism and beliefs spawned from specious reasoning. The sermon includes which sources of knowledge should not immediately be seen as truthful without further investigation, covering oral history, traditional and new sources, scriptures and other official texts, suppositional reasoning, philosophical dogmatism, common sense, personal opinions, experts, authorities and even one's own teacher. Instead, the Kālāma Sutra calls on people to ground their knowledge in their own direct experience. Buddhism overall proposes not passive acceptance, but a constant questioning and personal testing to identify the truths that will verifiably reduce one's stress or misery. According to Buddhism, any sensible person should not go on what has been acquired by repeated hearing, tradition or rumour—or anything that is based on scriptures, surmise, axioms, specious reasoning, bias or another's apparent ability. Instead, the Buddha says, one should only accept a teaching when one personally knows that it is skilful, blameless, praiseworthy and conducive to happiness—and that it is praised by the wise. The sermon to the Kālāmas is therefore justly famous for its commitment to free inquiry, and for arguing against fanaticism, bigotry, dogmatism and intolerance ("Kalama Sutta: The Buddha's Charter of Free Inquiry", 2019).

The contents of the Kālāma Sutra, together with "The Setting in Motion of the Wheel of the Dharma Sutra", are extraordinarily important, and they are probably the basis for the singular unity of Buddhism. In spite of the long life of Buddhism, its extensive area of diffusion and the different cultures of the peoples who practised it, the core of the religion has remained remarkably unchanged. Indeed, the main traditions today largely maintain and share the same basic teachings. In stark contrast to the other great religions, Buddhism is characterised by the absence not only of a supernatural revelation, but also of schisms, proselytising and support for violence and war. In fact, it may be these unusual features that explain the widespread interest in Buddhism in the West—and also, therefore, the popularity of "mindfulness", in which aspects of Buddhism took on a life of their own.

When considering the spread of Buddhism to the West, it is important to remember that the Far East, the treasures of its cultures and, indeed, Buddhism, were largely unknown in Europe until the great voyages of discovery in the fifteenth century. These travels allowed the Europeans to gain a comprehensive geographical picture of our planet; they enabled new commercial ventures—and they laid the foundations for enormous colonial empires. But at the same time, the culture of Asia and the sub-continent—and of the countries of the South and Far-East was largely shunned—based on a Eurocentric sense of superiority. Instead, Europe saw these countries mainly in terms of simple commercial gain. Among intellectuals, however, 'Orientalism' did take on a certain appeal. And, before long, because of the presence of religious missionaries, scholars and imperial civil servants, Buddhism came to the attention of Western intellectuals like Nietzsche and Hesse, who found in it the inspiration for their books *The Anti-Christ* and *Siddharta*, which are still widely read (Said, 2014).

Buddhism first came to be truly understood in the West through scholarly study and the actual practice of the religion at around the beginning of the nineteenth century. It was a time of increasing and more complex contact between Eastern and Western cultures, and in this time several key developments planted the seeds that would allow Buddhism to flourish more widely in the West.

In America, immigration was actively encouraged because there was a need for large numbers of workers to complete the vast construction projects sprawling across the country in the second half of the nineteenth century. And, indeed, the poverty and war dominating so many countries around the world at the time meant there were many who were more than willing to uproot to the USA. Buddhism was therefore introduced to the USA by Asian immigrants. Immigration from China first began in earnest around 1820, and the number of Chinese migrants increased rapidly with news of the 1849 California Gold Rush. The first Buddhist temple in America was then built in 1853 in San Francisco by the Sze Yap Company, a Sino-American fraternal society.

Large-scale immigration from Japan began in the late 1880s, and from Korea in around 1903. The Japanese settlements were established initially in Hawaii, where the first temple was built in 1896. The first Japanese Buddhist temple in continental USA was built in San Francisco in 1899. The first Buddhist clergy to take up residence there were Shuye Sonoda and Kakuryo Nishimjima, missionaries from Japan, who arrived in 1899 (Fields, 1992).

Zen, one of the Japanese Buddhist Schools, was introduced to the United States by Japanese priests who were sent there to serve local immigrant groups; a small group also came to study the American culture and way of life. The first Zen Buddhist priest to teach in North America was Soyen Shaku, who, in 1905, was invited to stay in the United States by a wealthy American couple. For nine months, he lived near San Francisco, where he established a small meditation hall (zendo). His pioneering work led to the development of the Japanese Rinzai Zen School, which would later flourish, spread to the rest of continental America, and make an important contribution to the spread of Rinzai Zen worldwide.

The Soto Zen School was also developed in the USA, but later, when Soyu Matsuoka-roshi was sent to America to establish the Chicago Buddhist Temple in 1949, before relocating to establish another temple at Long Beach in 1971. Shunryu Suzuki was also sent to San Francisco in the late 1950s to teach meditation, and soon attracted American students and "beatniks". The growing group around him went on to form a network of highly influential Zen centres across the country—largely thanks to the innovation and creativity of the 60s San Francisco counter-cultural movement (Ford, 2006; Seager, 1999).

The two other main schools that spread to the West were Theravāda and Tibetan Buddhism. In the nineteenth century, a sort of process of cultural exchange began between the Theravadins in Asia and Western audiences who were interested in ancient wisdom. Helena Blavatsky and Henry Steel Olcott, founders of the Theosophical Society, played an important part in this process. By this time, the lay Vipassana practice of meditation had also developed in many Theravāda countries, and from the 1970s onwards, a widespread Vipassana movement emerged in the West (McMahan, 2008).

Tibetan Buddhism is based on the form of Buddhism that emerged in Tibet, the Himalayas and a large part of Central Asia, where it is still practised. It can be traced back to the last stages of Indian Buddhism, when the religion was introduced into the Tibetan Empire (roughly the seventh to nineth centuries CE). In 1950, however, Tibet was famously annexed by the Chinese People's Republic. Then in 1959, the 14th Dalai Lama, Tenzin Gyatso, and a great number of clergy fled the country to settle in India and other neighbouring regions. After the Tibetan diaspora, Tibetan Buddhism gained many new adherents in the West and all around the world. Now many new monasteries have been established and are run by fully ordained Tibetan Buddhist Lamas (Polichetti, 1993; White, 2000).

Two other traditional Buddhist movements also gained a foothold in the US before spreading to other Western countries: both the Korean and the Vietnamese Zen Schools. Thich Nhat Hanh is a widely known Vietnamese Buddhist master and peace activist, who attracted large numbers of followers in the USA and Europe—and whose teachings emphasise the importance of mindfulness (in the pure, traditional Buddhist sense) as the most important practice in daily life (Hanh, 2008).

One key part of the spread of Buddhism from East to West was the London Buddhist Society. It was founded in 1924 by Christmas Humphreys, a British judge and a convert to Buddhism, as an offshoot from a Theosophical Lodge. Humphreys remained the president of the society from 1924 right up until his death in 1983. The Buddhist Society was one of the first Buddhist organisations outside Asia, and remains one of the oldest in Europe. It has held many talks and classes on the teachings and practice of the Zen, Theravāda and Tibetan traditions. The premises of the society also house one of the leading British libraries on Buddhism—which includes many works published by the society itself ("The Buddhist Society: Home", 2019).

Christmas Humphreys was a prolific writer, and published an impressive number of books on the various traditions of Buddhism. They have made a remarkable contribution to the understanding of Buddhism in the English-speaking world. These books were also made possible by Humphreys' personal acquaintance with many of the other leading figures of the day trying to make Buddhism accessible to westerners ("The Blavatsky Trust: Christmas Humphreys", 2019; Humphreys, 1978).

One of these extraordinary personalities, who made unique and invaluable contributions, is Daisetsu Teitaro Suzuki. It is not easy to offer a concise summary of this remarkable individual and his contribution to the field. In the course of his long and fruitful life, Suzuki became the first authoritative voice of Japanese Buddhism—especially Zen—in the Western World. He travelled and lectured right across the globe, and his lectures and writings had a major impact on religious, artistic and philosophical thinking that continues to this day.

Daisetsu Teitaro Suzuki (1870–1966) was a Japanese translator, teacher, and constructive interpreter of Zen Buddhist thought for the West. He was born in Kanazawa in Western Japan, where he was descended from a long line of physicians of the samurai class. He was, of course, expected to follow in their footsteps, but his family could not afford to pay for the young Suzuki to go to medical school. Pondering the financial misfortunes of his family, he turned to the Rinzai temple where they were registered.

Unable to go to medical school, Suzuki pursued other avenues, eventually becoming an English teacher. Meanwhile, he grew more and more interested in Buddhism and decided to enlist as a novitiate at the Engakuji Rinzai Zen monastery in Kamakura, where his master gave him his Buddhist name, Daisetsu, meaning "great humility."

Suzuki had excellent language skills, and as early as 1893, he translated a sermon by Shaku Soyen into English for the World's Parliament of Religions in Chicago. Soyen was the successor of the Zen master Imakita Kosen, and his sermon was called "The Law of Cause and Effect, as Taught by Buddha". The Parliament of Religions for which he translated it turned out to be an extremely important event not only for developing inter-faith dialogue in general, but also for establishing Buddhism in the West. It was organised in Chicago at the same time as the World Columbian Exposition in 1893, an early world's fair. Several Buddhist personalities were invited to participate, including Shaku Soyen, touted as the "First American Ancestor" of zen, as well as Anagarika Dharmapala, introduced as a representative of "Southern Buddhism" (the term used for Theravada at the time). And although the Japanese Pure Land master Kiyozawa Manshi could not attend, one of his essays was read in his absence. It was a whole century before the Parliament met again in Chicago in 1993 (Fields, 1992).

In Chicago, Shaku Soyen met Paul Carus and recommended Suzuki as a translator for Carus's firm, the "Open Court Publishing Company" of La Salle, Illinois. From 1897 to 1909, Suzuki lived in the United States and translated Sanskrit, Pali, Chinese, and Japanese texts for Open Court. Suzuki then returned to Japan in 1909 and went on to hold various academic positions, including professor of English and Buddhist philosophy at Otani University. He built up a growing scholarly reputation in the West, based on his many published works, such as the three-volume *Essays in Zen Buddhism* (Suzuki, 1927, 1933, 1934), *The Training of the Zen Buddhist Monk* (Suzuki, 2007), and his book *Zen Buddhism and Its Influence on Japanese Culture* (Suzuki, 1959). He travelled and lectured extensively at universities in the United States and Europe during the 1950s, and in this time was visiting professor at Columbia University, where his open lectures attracted many members of the intellectual elite. He died in Kamakura in 1966, leaving numerous unpublished manuscripts (Abe, 1986; Snelling, 1985).

Suzuki' opened up a large body of Japanese literature to the West, not only through his own English language translations, but also through the many other translations he inspired. Suzuki's own works are particularly interesting not only because of his linguistic talents, but also because of the evidence they show of his ongoing study of Buddhism and Rinzai Zen. Suzuki's books have been read and commented on many notable figures; one particular example is Carl Jung's 30-page commentary on *An introduction to Zen Buddhism.* It is an important example of an early expert on the human mind engaging with Zen Buddhism from what we might call today a humanistic psychodynamic perspective (Suzuki, 1974; Suzuki & Jung, 2007). Suzuki's studies showed the deep influence that Zen exerted on Japanese culture, and are the basis of the extraordinary diffusion of Zen in the USA.

The life of Daisetsu Teitaro Suzuki is covered in a fascinating 2006 documentary, which includes interviews and testimonies by figures such as the psychoanalyst Erich Fromm, the theologian Thomas Merton, the musician John Cage and Robert Aitken, a Zen teacher who was one of first to be ordained by Japanese Master Koun Yamada ("A Zen Life—Film", 2019). This documentary shows how Zen was embraced in the Fifties by artists and intellectuals like Jack Kerouac, Allen Ginsberg and Alan Watts, who formed the Beat Zen Generation. It also charts how the counter-revolution of the Sixties established Zen in the Western cultural and spiritual landscape. Japanese Zen masters (roshis) came to teach in the West, such as Yasutani, Maezumi, Shunryu Suzuki and Sasaki. Their many Western students became teachers and were recognised as roshis in their own right, including Richard Baker, Robert Aitken, Philip Kapleau, Dennis Merzel, Bernie Glassman and Daido Loori. Then, in the Seventies and Eighties, the rise of humanist and transpersonal psychology helped Zen become even more popular (Ford, 2006; van der Braak, 2008).

It was in the soil of post-war America that the seeds planted by the early missionaries first really began to flourish. Temples were established in various parts of the USA, with resident masters and monks with proper, formal training from their home countries. At the same time, after the Second World War and the Korean War, many soldiers returned home with first-hand experience of the Buddhist traditions of Japan and Korea. Other courageous pioneers, including some from Europe, also trekked to Asia to gain first-hand experience of Buddhism after reading English translations of the religion's ancient scriptures. Many even sought formal training in Asia's Buddhist temples.

Buddhism, therefore, gained a foothold in the West in no small part thanks to the pioneers who first made it possible for westerners to read translations of the religion's basic texts. Buddhism also gained traction in the west because of a courageous few who had formally trained for years in Buddhist temples in the East, and chose to bring the traditions and ideas of the faith to the West.

One formally trained Buddhist who particularly helped to spread the religion to the USA is Hakuun Yasutani, who founded his own school called Sanbo Kyodan in 1954 in an attempt to make Zen Buddhism easier for westerners to follow. He had many followers, who also, in turn, became influential teachers, such as Philip Kapleau and Robert Aitken. After 13 years' training, Kapleau was ordained by Yasutani in 1965 and given permission to teach. He then wrote his seminal work *The Three Pillars of Zen* and founded the Rochester Zen Center in New York in 1965. Robert Aitken, known as the "dean of American Zen", received Dharma transmission from Hakuun Yasutani's master Koun Yamada in 1985. He then decided to live as a layperson, translating numerous Zen texts and also founding the Diamond Sangha in Hawaii in 1959 which soon grew into a network of affiliated centres (Seager, 1999).

Two other people who had a major influence on the spread of Buddhism were Ruth Fuller Sasaki and Irmgard Schlögl. Ruth Fuller Sasaki met and studied with Daisetz Teitaro Suzuki in Japan in 1930. In 1938, she became a key supporter of the Buddhist Society of America, later known as the First Zen Institute of America, in New York. Then, in 1944 she married Sokei-an, the Zen priest in residence there. In 1949, she went to Kyoto where she stayed for most of the rest of her life, becoming in 1958 the first foreigner to be a priest of Daitoku-ji, a Rinzai Zen temple (Sterling, 2006). Sasaki played an important role in encouraging and facilitating the practice and study of Zen in America, and was instrumental in translating many Zen texts into English. One of her most important works was *Zen Dust*, a highly accurate and comprehensive book that is still considered an essential text book today (Miura & Sasaki, 1966).

Irmgard Schlögl was born in Austria in 1921, where she obtained a Ph.D. in Geology. Then in 1950, she joined the Zen Group at the

Buddhist Society, led by Christmas Humphreys. In 1960, she went to Japan and trained at Daitoku-ji monastery, where she stayed until 1972; it was in this time that she was ordained and given authorisation to teach in the Rinzai lineage. Given the name Myokyo-ni, she founded two temples in the UK, which were inhabited by a group of Japanese Zen monks: the Shobo-an in London, and later the Fairlight in Luton. She taught in these until her death in 2007, and her ordained successors continue to teach in both to this day ("Obituary: The Venerable Myokyo-ni", 2019).

These are the main factors and developments in the early spread of Buddhism to the West: an in-depth discussion of what followed is outside the scope of this chapter. Essentially, however, after almost half a century of diffusion and consolidation in the USA and Europe, there are now numerous firmly established Buddhist communities in various countries in the West, following a range of different traditions.

Tibetan Vairajana Buddhism has an especially strong presence because of the Tibetan communities in exile, with Dzogchen teachings receiving particular attention ("International Dzogchen Community", 2019; Norbu, 2006). The Hinayana tradition has also gained a notably strong foothold, largely because of the growing interest in vipassana meditation (Coleman, 2001; McMahan, 2008).

Various zen traditions have also gained a strong foothold in many parts of the world. The Soto school of zen is firmly established in Japan and abroad, and as a result, the Sōtō Zen International Association was founded in Japan ("Sotozen-net", 2019). In Europe, the followers of the teachings of Taisen Deshimaru also established the International Zen Association ("International Zen Association", 2019).

In terms of Rinzai Zen, Harada Shodo Roshi is a descendant of Yamada Mumon Roshi who was abbot of Shōfuku-ji in Kobe, and head of the Myōshin-ji branch of the Rinzai school in Japan. Harada Shodo Roshi is an influential master in Japan, where he is the abbott of Sogen-ji in Okayama; he also founded One Drop Community, which is active in the US and Europe ("OneDropZen: Home", 2019). Someone else who is particularly active today is another teacher of Yamada Mumom Roshi descent, Engaku Taino, who founded a temple and a community called Zenshi-Ji Scaramuccia in central Italy ("Scaramuccia", 2019).

The London Buddhist Society still continues its traditional initiatives to help people of various levels of experience with their practice of Therevada, Tibetan and Zen Buddhism ("The Buddhist Society: Home", 2019). Zen Buddhism is also practised at two temples, the Fairlight in Luton, and the Shobo-an temple in central London. They both still follow the teachings and lineage of Myokyo-Ni, the Abbott of the temples until her death. Myokyo-Ni trained extensively in Japan with Sōkō Morinaga Rōshi, her teacher and the head monk at Daitoku-ji (Obituary: The Venerable Myokyo-ni, 2019; Rizai Zen Center, 2019). The Plum Villages, which are based on the teachings of Thich Nhat Hanh, are another example of a community following the teachings of a highly esteemed and recognised master from an established traditional lineage.

The traditions in these places are strictly maintained, which has been essential for preserving and disseminating the traditional practices pf various Buddhist schools in the West. These communities are taught by masters with formal, traditional training and who have received the "Dharma transmission" from their predecessors: the continuation of a lineage that goes back through a long line of enlightened masters. Many of the Buddhist communities now extant in the West were established after the end of the Second World War, and with time, the religion adapted to new times and circumstances in the West (Watts, 1996). Buddhist teachings had to be made accessible to contemporary citizens of America and Europe. A new generation of teachers had to be trained and recognized in innovative new ways, since "Dharma transmission" from the original temples in Asia became less and less practical. These processes are still under way, and it is still hard to tell how they will transform the practice of traditional Buddhism in the West.

There are, of course, other Buddhist traditions out there, but these have not been considered here because they have had less of an impact on the West. This is the case with the Nichiren, Pure Land, Shingon and Tendai sects (Buswell & Lopez, 2003). More recently, other new approaches and sects have also appeared in the East, such as Sokagakkai in Japan ("Soka Gakkai", 2019) and Falun Gong in China (Lu, 2005). Transcendental meditation is another form, but it has not been considered here because it is not related to Buddhism. I mention it simply because its core teachings are based on meditation and it is widely practiced in the USA and other Western countries (Horgan, 2019).

Another ongoing trend is the secularisation of the developed world, where more and more people are losing interest in the main religions. As a result, secular Buddhism (also known as 'agnostic', 'atheist' and 'pragmatic') is becoming increasingly popular. It is an emerging form of Buddhism based on humanist, sceptical and agnostic values—as well as pragmatism and naturalism, rather than religious or supernatural beliefs. The aim of this approach is to avoid traditional beliefs that could be considered superstitious: for example, the existence of supernatural beings such as devas, bodhisattvas, nāgas, pretas and Buddhas, as well as merit and its transference, rebirth and Buddhist cosmology including the existence of pure lands and hells (Batchelor, 2013, 2015a, 2015b; McMahan, 2017).

In recent decades, globalisation has led to the wide diffusion and digitisation of information. An essential part of this was the rise of the internet, the great technological advance of the modern age, which has made it possible to exchange and share information with astonishing speed and ease. It has, it need hardly be said, had a number of profound effects on society. The internet also coincided with the rise of a number of other revolutionary technologies, including mobile phone networks, which led to the development of smart phones, affordable, powerful and tiny computers that connect us in real time to the rest of the world. These developments are driving profound changes in our society, and are, therefore, necessarily influencing religion and the religiosity of entire communities. Buddhism is inevitably affected by these transformations (Grieve & Veidlinger, 2018).

There are now an astonishing amount of sites related to Buddhism on the internet. A Google search for "Buddhism" comes up with 86,300,000 finds, which rises to 98,500,000 for "mindfulness". "Meditation" comes up with 343,000,000 which falls to 70,000,000 for "Buddhist meditation". Evidently, it can be difficult to get your bearings in this ocean of information—especially if you are not experienced at navigating it. There are many important and useful websites out there, which are run by serious organisations. With just one internet search coming up with so much information, however, it can be difficult to sift reliable sources from the rest. The enormous diffusion of information has also led to commercialisation in many quarters, with a large number of websites calling for direct payments and fees—as well as high volumes of advertising (Wallinder-Pierini, 2018).

The "Tricycle Foundation" is a good example of a not-for-profit educational organisation in this field. Established in 1990, it publishes "Tricycle: The Buddhist Review", an independent, non-sectarian Buddhist quarterly that publishes Buddhist teachings, practices and critiques. Many remarkable individuals have contributed to it over the years including, among others, the Dalai Lama, Thich Nhat Hanh, Jon Kabat-Zinn, Joseph Goldstein, Jack Kornfield, Curtis White, Jack Kerouac, Allen Ginsberg, Gary Snyder, Stephen Batchelor, Robert Aitken, Alice Walker and John Cage. It also offers a a wide variety of online courses, which range from "Buddhism for beginners" to "Korean Buddhist Cooking" and "Mindfulness: Its Origins, Purpose, and Transformational Power" ("Tricycle: The Buddhist Review", 2019). In Europe, The Bodhi College, a faculty that includes Steven Batchelor, offers "fresh ways of understanding the Dharma today through rediscovering the core insights of early Buddhist teachings". The college has a range of online and residential courses of various lengths and in a number of different languages. These range from different levels of Buddhist teaching to the online course "Buddhist Foundations of Mindfulness". As with the courses on the Tricycle Foundation's website, of course, all of these require a paid subscription ("Bodhi College", 2019).

Given the connectivity the internet has enabled, it is not surprising that mental health interventions have been developed that replace direct meetings between therapists and patients with an internet connection and a computer screen: even mindfulness did not escape this phenomenon (Wahbeh & Oken, 2016).

Computer programme-based therapeutic interventions are now widespread, and many positive results reported (Andersson, 2009; Hedman et al., 2014). It is conceivable that this could allow therapists to work with more individual patients (Wright et al., 2005). It is also possible that in cases where patients live far away from their care institutions, a computer-based psychotherapeutic programme could be useful in the hands of a specially trained therapist (Luz, Gagliani, & Romano, 2015).

As the internet has risen, so too has social media, and it was inevitable that mindfulness would become involved in this phenomenon too. There are now a vast amount of Facebook pages and Twitter posts on the subject of mindfulness, and these also allow the exchange of information and online interactions between followers (Shonin, 2014). Similarly, many "apps" for smartphones have also been developed to help with mindfulness and meditation. These are changing the perception of mindfulness and meditation, and their effects must be carefully evaluated (Mani, Kavanagh, Hides, & Stoyanov, 2015).

As well as smartphone "apps", there are also devices specifically devoted to mindfulness and meditation. These are basically Electro Encephalographic (EEG) devices, now produced as affordable consumer appliances, which are capable of collecting the electrical signals generated by brain activity—in a much simpler way than usually required in medicine (Ratti, Waninger, Berka, Ruffini, & Verma, 2017). One of these devices is the Neurosky Mindwave, which can be connected to a smartphone through a downloadable app, and can then perform various—sometimes gamified tasks related to education, wellness, meditation and even Zen (Neurosky—Art of Zen—PC., 2019).

It is clear that in many instances, remarkable technological developments can be put to positive use as tools in the armoury of mental health. It is also clear, however, that some of these technological tools may impoverish the therapeutic relationship between patients and therapists. This impoverishment may also be exacerbated by the accompanying individual isolation—and the loss of the positive effects of group therapy. When Buddhism is taught through the internet, and there is no longer any form of communion between teachers and trainees, it is hard not to conclude that the "Sangha"—the "community", which along with the "Buddha" and the "Dharma", constitutes one of the "Three Jewels" of Buddhism—has been lost (Dawson & Cowan, 2004). This may also be said to apply to "mindfulness", which is still essentially, if not overtly, rooted in Buddhist teachings.

This is a necessarily limited outline of some of the most significant steps along the road that brought Buddhism, an ancient Eastern tradition, to the contemporary West. During this process, however, something unexpected happened, and the specific Buddhist practice of meditation took on a life of its own. Meditation, transformed into mindfulness, not only flourished unexpectedly widely; it also entered the world of medicine and psychology as a means of intervention. It came to be widely accepted as one of the tools that could be used to intervene in the world of mental health—and even in physical diseases. Mindfulness came to prominence in the modern age of scientific medicine, and because of this there have been many studies to attempt to demonstrate its efficacy.

This, however, was not the case for other Eastern practices such as yoga. This fact, and the studies to prove the efficacy of mindfulness, will be considered in greater detail in later chapters.

## References

A Zen Life—Film. (2019). Retrieved from http://www.azenlife-film.org/top.htm. Accessed 17 April 2019.

Abe, M. (1986). *A Zen life: D.T. Suzuki remembered*. New York: Weatherhill.

Aich, T. (2013). Buddha philosophy and Western psychology. *Indian Journal of Psychiatry, 55*(6), 165. https://doi.org/10.4103/0019-5545.105517.

Aitken, R. (1984). *The mind of clover: Essays in Zen Buddhist ethics*. New York: North Point Press.

Andersson, G. (2009). Using the Internet to provide cognitive behaviour therapy. *Behaviour Research and Therapy, 47*(3), 175–180. https://doi.org/10.1016/j.brat.2009.01.010.

Attenborough, D. (1983). *David Attenborough's travel book Journeys to the past: Travels in New Guinea, Madagascar, and the northern territory of Australia*. London: Penguin Books.

Batchelor, S. (1997). *Buddhism without beliefs*. New York: Riverhead Books.

Batchelor, S. (2010). *Confession of a Buddhist atheist*. New York: Spiegel & Grau.

Batchelor, S. (2013). *Confession of a Buddhist atheist*. New York: Spiegel & Grau.

Batchelor, S. (2015a). *After Buddhism: Rethinking the dharma for a secular age*. New Haven: Yale University Press.

Batchelor, S. (2015b). A secular Buddhism. *Journal of Global Buddhism, 13*, 87–107.

Batchelor, S. (2017). *Secular Buddhism: Imagining the dharma in an uncertain world*. New Haven and London: Yale University Press.

Bodhi College. (2019). Retrieved from https://bodhi-college.org/. Accessed 17 April 2019.

Buswell, R. E., Jr., & Lopez, D., Jr. (2003). *The Princeton dictionary of Buddhism* (pp. 430–435). Princeton: Princeton University Press.

Coleman, J. W. (2001) *The new Buddhism: The Western transformation of an ancient tradition*. Oxford: Oxford University Press.

Dawkins, R. (2006). *The god delusion*. London: Bantam Press.

Dawson, L., & Cowan, D. (2004). *Religion online*. New York: Routledge.

Fields, R. (1992). *How the swans came to the lake: A narrative history of Buddhism in America*. Boulder, CO: Shambala Boulder.

Fisher, D., Fisher, A., & Staff, L. (2019). *Mindfulness and the cessation of suffering: An exclusive new interview with mindfulness pioneer….* Retrieved from https://www.lionsroar.com/mindfulness-and-the-cessation-of-suffering-an-exclusive-new-interview-with-mindfulness-pioneer-jon-kabat-zinn/. Accessed 17 April 2019.

Ford, J. I. (2006). *Zen master who?* Boston: Wisdom Publications.

Foulk, T. G. (2008). Ritual in Japanese Zen Buddhism. In S. Heine & D. S. Wright (Eds.), *Zen ritual studies of Zen Buddhist theory in practice*. Oxford: Oxford University Press.

Grieve, G., & Veidlinger, D. (2018). *Buddhism, the Internet, and digital media: The pixel in the lotus*. London: Routledge.

Hanh, T. N. (2008). *The miracle of mindfulness: The classic guide to meditation by the world's most revered master*. London: Rider.

Harvey, P. (2000). *An introduction to Buddhist ethics, foundations, values and issues*. Cambridge: Cambridge University Press.

Harvey, P. (2013). *An introduction to Buddhism* (pp. 459–462). New York: Cambridge University Press.

Hedman, E., Ljótsson, B., Kaldo, V., Hesser, H., El Alaoui, S., Kraepelien, M., et al. (2014). Effectiveness of Internet-based cognitive behaviour therapy for depression in routine psychiatric care. *Journal of Affective Disorders, 155*, 49–58. https://doi.org/10.1016/j.jad.2013.10.023.

Horgan, J. (2019). *Research on TM and other forms of meditation stinks*. Retrieved from https://blogs.scientificamerican.com/cross-check/research-has-not-shown-that-meditation-beats-a-placebo/. Accessed 17 April 2019.

Humphreys, C. (1978). *Both sides of the circle: The autobiography of Christmas Humphreys*. Boston: Allen & Unwin.

International Dzogchen Community. (2019). Retrieved from https://dzogchen.net/. Accessed 17 April 2019.

International Zen Association. (2019). Retrieved from https://www.zen-azi.org/en. Accessed 17 April 2019.

James, W. (2012). *The varieties of religious experience: A study in human nature*. Oxford World's Classics. Oxford: Oxford University Press.

Kalama Sutta: The Buddha's Charter of Free Inquiry. (2019). Retrieved from https://web.archive.org/web/20130204141603/, http://www.accesstoinsight.org/lib/authors/soma/wheel008.html. Accessed 17 April 2019.

Kato, H. (2016). The relationship between the psychology of religion and Buddhist psychology. *Japanese Psychological Research, 58,* 70–84. https://doi.org/10.1111/jpr.12121.

Lu, Y. (2005). Entrepreneurial logics and the evolution of Falun Gong. *Journal for the Scientific Study of Religion, 44*(2), 173–185. https://doi.org/10.1111/j.1468-5906.2005.00274.x.

Luz, P., Gagliani, M., & Romano, B. (2015). Distance psychotherapy—New reality. *Arquivos Brasileiros De Cardiologia*. https://doi.org/10.5935/abc.20150067.

Mani, M., Kavanagh, D., Hides, L., & Stoyanov, S. (2015). Review and evaluation of mindfulness-based iPhone apps. *JMIR Mhealth and Uhealth, 3*(3), e82. https://doi.org/10.2196/mhealth.4328.

McMahan, D. L. (2008). *The making of Buddhist modernism*. Oxford: Oxford University Press.

McMahan, D. L. (2017). Buddhism and global secularisms. *Journal of Global Buddhism, 18,* 112–128.

Miura, I., & Sasaki, R. (1966). *Zen dust: The history of the koan and koan study in Rinzai (Linji) Zen*. New York: Harcourt.

Neurosky—Art of Zen—PC. (2019). Retrieved from https://store.neurosky.com/products/art-of-zen. Accessed 17 April 2019.

Norbu, C. N. (2006). *Dzogchen teachings*. Ithaca, NY: Snow Lion Publications.

Obituary: The Venerable Myokyo-ni. (2019). Retrieved from https://www.theguardian.com/news/2007/apr/23/guardianobituaries.religion. Accessed 17 April 2019.

OneDropZen: Home. (2019). Retrieved from http://onedropzen.org/home. Accessed 17 April 2019.

Pali Text Society Home Page. (2019). Retrieved from http://www.palitext.com/. Accessed 17 April 2019.

Polichetti, M. (1993). The spread of Tibetan Buddhism in the West. *The Tibet Journal, 18*(3), 65–67. Retrieved from http://www.jstor.org/stable/43302254. Accessed 17 April 2019.
Ratti, E., Waninger, S., Berka, C., Ruffini, G., & Verma, A. (2017). Comparison of medical and consumer wireless EEG systems for use in clinical trials. *Frontiers in Human Neuroscience, 11*. https://doi.org/10.3389/fnhum.2017.00398.
Rizai Zen Center. (2019). Retrieved from http://www.rinzaizencentre.org.uk/. Accessed 17 April 2019.
Said, E. (2014). *Orientalism*. New York: Knopf Doubleday.
Scaramuccia. (2019). Retrieved from https://www.zenshinji.org/home/. Accessed 17 April 2019.
Seager, R. H. (1999). *Buddhism in America*. New York: Columbia University Press.
Shonin, E. (2014). Mindfulness and the social media. *Journal of Mass Communication & Journalism, 4*(5). https://doi.org/10.4172/2165-7912.1000194.
Snelling, J. (1985). *D.T. Suzuki: A biography*. London: The Buddhist Society.
Snelling, J. (1998). *The Buddhist handbook*. Rochester, VT: Inner Traditions.
Soka Gakkai—Buddhism—Oxford Bibliographies—Obo. (2019). Retrieved from http://www.oxfordbibliographies.com/view/document/obo-9780195393521/obo-9780195393521-0053.xml. Accessed 17 April 2019.
Sotozen-net. (2019). Retrieved from https://global.sotozen-net.or.jp/eng/index.html. Accessed 17 April 2019.
Spilka, B. (2012). Psychology of religion, history of. In R. W. Rieber (Ed.), *Encyclopedia of the history of psychological theories* (pp. 923–933). New York: Springer.
Sterling, I. (2006). *Zen pioneer: The life and works of Ruth Fuller Sasaki*. Shoemaker & Hoard. http://www.shoemakerhoard.com. Accessed 17 April 2019.
Suzuki, D. (1959). *Zen Buddhism and its influence on Japanese culture*. London: Routledge and Kegan Paul.
Suzuki, D. (2007). *The training of the Zen Buddhist monk*. New York: Cosimo Classics.
Suzuki, D. T. (1927). *Essays in Zen Buddhism: First series*. New York: Grove Press.
Suzuki, D. T. (1933). *Essays in Zen Buddhism: Second series*. New York: Samuel Weiser.
Suzuki, D. T. (1934). *Essays in Zen Buddhism: Third series*. York Beach, ME: Samuel Weiser.

Suzuki, D. T. (1974). Lectures on Zen Buddhism. In D. Suzuki, E. Fromm, & R. De Martino (Eds.), *Zen Buddhism and psychoanalysis* (pp. 1–59). London: Souvenir Press.

Suzuki, D., & Jung, C. (2007). *An introduction to Zen Buddhism* [Place of publication not identified]. Grove/Atlantic.

The Blavatsky Trust: Christmas Humphreys. (2019). Retrieved from http://www.blavatskytrust.org.uk/html/c_humphreys.htm. Accessed 17 April 2019.

The Buddhist Society: Home. (2019). Retrieved from http://thebuddhistsociety.org/. Accessed 17 April 2019.

Trainor, K. (2004). *Buddhism: The illustrated guide*. Oxford: Oxford University Press.

Tricycle: The Buddhist Review—The Independent Voice of Buddhism in the West. (2019). Retrieved from https://tricycle.org/. Accessed 17 April 2019.

Van Dam, N., van Vugt, M., Vago, D., Schmalzl, L., Saron, C., Olendzki, A., et al. (2017). Mind the hype: A critical evaluation and prescriptive agenda for research on mindfulness and meditation. *Perspectives on Psychological Science, 13*(1), 36–61. https://doi.org/10.1177/1745691617709589.

van der Braak, A. (2008). Zen spirituality in a secular age. *Studies in Spirituality, 18,* 39–60. https://doi.org/10.2143/sis.18.0.2033282.

Wahbeh, H., & Oken, B. (2016). Internet mindfulness meditation intervention for the general public: Pilot randomized controlled trial. *JMIR Mental Health, 3*(3), e37. https://doi.org/10.2196/mental.5900.

Wallinder-Pierini, L. S. E. (2018). The Buddhist dharma for sale: Who owns the past? The Internet and objects of worship. *Journal of Global Buddhism, 19,* 95–111.

Watts, A. (1996). Beat Zen, square Zen, and Zen. *Chicago Review, 42*(3). Retrieved from http://www.thezensite.com/ZenEssays/Miscellaneous/Beat_Zen_Square_Zen.html. Accessed 15 January 2019. Accessed 17 April 2019.

White, D. G. (2000). Introduction. In D. G. White (Ed.), *Tantra in practice* (p. 21). Princeton: Princeton University Press.

Wright, J., Wright, A., Albano, A., Basco, M., Goldsmith, L., Raffield, T., & Otto, M. (2005). Computer-assisted cognitive therapy for depression: Maintaining efficacy while reducing therapist time. *American Journal of Psychiatry, 162*(6), 1158–1164. https://doi.org/10.1176/appi.ajp.162.6.1158.

# 4

# Psychologists and Psychiatrists Became Interested in Buddhism

The great voyages of exploration made from the sixteenth century onwards allowed for an ever-better understanding of global geography.

Communities of Europeans began to establish settlements in many parts of the world, which allowed European states to build up huge intercontinental colonial empires, which would reshape the world forever.

European powers began to export their culture, influencing countries across the globe. Initially, it was a distinctly one-way relationship, with colonial dominions exerting little cultural influence on European imperialists. Generally, this was because European cultures held them to be inferior, even when, as in the case of India, they had ancient and extremely sophisticated cultures. With time, however, this began to change and the traditions of the East began to receive more attention. This was nourished by the beauty and richness of many of the cultural artefacts that became available to the Europeans (Macfie, 2009). Soon the religions of the East also began to draw the attention of Western scholars—especially as translations of ancient scriptures became more widely available (King, 2009).


T. Giraldi, *Psychotherapy, Mindfulness and Buddhist Meditation*,
https://doi.org/10.1007/978-3-030-29003-0_4

Buddhism was one of the religions that drew the attention of Western scholars, even though the complexity of its teachings and its wide variety of forms made it somewhat more difficult for them to grapple with.

There is, however, a general consensus that American Spiritualism played a major part in the diffusion of Buddhism in the West—particularly the work of Colonel Olcott, Madame Blavatsky and the Theosophical Society (Fields, 1992). In Europe, early devoted pioneers and translators such as Edward Conze (Sangharakshita, 1996) played a similar role. Reginald Horace Blyth also produced an amazingly varied and extensive series of works on Zen and *haiku* poetry (Reginald Horace Blyth [1898–1964], "Chronology, Bibliography, Links, Quotes, Resources", 2019). As mentioned in the previous chapter, Conze and Blyth were significantly influenced by the work by Daisetz T. Suzuki. Suzuki played a central part in the diffusion of Mahayana Buddhism, analysing and translating texts that had previously been inaccessible in the West. His work and thought deeply inspired the study and practice of Buddhism in America and Europe. The Pali Text Society also played a vital role by translating and popularising the fundamental texts of Theravada Buddhism.

These exceptional endeavours gave Westerners access to a host of traditional Buddhist texts and the teachings and ideas within them. Considering the remarkable and unique features of Buddhism, it is not surprising that as soon as they were available, they attracted the attention of intellectuals, including eminent psychologists. Before considering their work on meditation and mindfulness, however, it is also worthwhile considering why exactly they were drawn to Buddhism.

Central to all Buddhist traditions is the Varanasi discourse *Setting in Motion the Wheel of Dharma*. It is believed to be by the historic Buddha, Siddhartha Gautama, when he attained enlightenment after strenuous meditation. Here we find the *Four Noble Truths*: suffering exists, suffering has an identifiable cause, and the cause may be terminated. The way to terminate it is the *Noble Eightfold Path*. The sufferings of life are caused by the *Three marks of existence*: the unsatisfactoriness (*Dukkha*), the impermanence (*Anicca*) of composite things and the inexistence of the self (*Anatta*). Through the *Middle Way* of the *Noble Eightfold Path*, one of the facets of which is meditation, people can overcome the sufferings of life and attain *Nirvan*a (Snelling, 1998).

These ideas were especially interesting to scholars at the end of nineteenth century and beginning of the twentieth, and in particular to psychoanalysts in a time when psychology and its therapeutic applications were largely based on psychoanalysis. Since this period, a psychodynamic approach has been prevalent in psychoanalysis: the mental problems it addresses are believed to be caused by reactions to life experiences, and psychoanalysis seeks to correct them with analytical "talk therapy". In the late nineteenth and early twentieth centuries, then, a parallel was identified between the life sufferings of Buddhism and the mental suffering addressed by psychoanalysts. They were also greatly drawn to Buddhist ideas about the "self".

In psychology, the idea of the "self" is at the heart of mental suffering. In Buddhism, the "self" is an illusion produced by the mind, and it is the attachment to self that causes the sufferings of life (Albahari, 2006).

As interest in Buddhism grew in the West, so too did the availability of translated religious literature, including not only traditional texts, but also works on the training and life of Buddhist monks (Suzuki, 2007), as well as the influence of Buddhism on Eastern culture (Suzuki, 2010). Western thinkers were certainly most drawn to works on Zen. One major factor behind the extraordinary popularity of this branch of Buddhism was the work of Daisetz Suzuki and the many who were inspired by his lectures and writings. Zen was also especially popular because of several innate features that are extremely attractive to westerners.

Imagine for a moment the evocative and, to Western eyes, peculiar atmosphere of a Japanese monastery. Several centuries old, it is the home of a group of ordained monks who have been training for many years under the guidance of the *Master* of the place, the *Roshi*. The *Master* belongs to a lineage of previous masters, which in theory goes back to the original Buddha, Siddhartha Gautama. From his predecessor, the *Master* received the certification of his "enlightenment" and his authorisation to teach (in the Rinzai Zen tradition, it is the *inka shōmei*, but there are variations in other traditions). Under the guidance of the

*Master*, the monks follow a strict daily routine of silence and concentration, always respecting their precepts and vows. They spend a long time in 'zazen', sitting deeply absorbed in silent meditation. They maintain the same silent concentration in all their daily tasks to keep the monastery running in perfect order (*samu*). At certain times of year, Zen monks have a week of even more focused concentration, the *sesshin*. The aim of the training is to reach *nirvana*, the awakening or enlightenment. In Zen tradition, the first glimpse of enlightenment is called the *kensho*, and the general term for it is *satori*. Sitting meditation, *Zazen*, is common in both main forms of Zen Buddhism, *Soto* and the *Rinzai*. In *Rinzai*, monks practise zazen by meditating on the *Koan* they have received from the master. The *Koan* is a problem that cannot be answered rationally, and monks show the *Master* they have answered it in a personal interview called the *Sanzen* (Suzuki, 1960)

It is easy to understand the attraction of an exotic and beautiful ancient temple, where one seeks "awakening" guided by an enlightened master who has been "certified" with a Satori. For this reason, generations of Americans and Europeans moved to Japan to undertake years of training in Zen monasteries. At the same time, scholars in the West produced an amazing number of studies and books on the central themes of Zen: predominantly meditation, *Koan* and enlightenment. Psychologists were similarly attracted by these subjects, which have an obvious relevance to their field, adaptation to difficult life events and the overcoming of human existential suffering. This connection is well illustrated by the fact that in Buddhism, enlightenment is associated with the experience of awakening—just as with the attainment of a profound insight in psychoanalysis.

Psychologists were also interested in the state of consciousness during meditation, and its comparisons with the mental states induced with psychedelic drugs and other hallucinogens. When experimentation with these substances first became popular in the fifties and sixties on the west coast of the USA, many drew comparisons between Buddhism and the effects of psychedelic drugs (Millière, Carhart-Harris, Roseman, Trautwein, & Berkovich-Ohana, 2018; Osto, 2018).

One great psychoanalyst who was attracted to Buddhism and the orient was Carl Gustav Jung. Jung had very many and varied interests, including everything from paranormal beliefs and alchemy to quantum mechanics and oriental culture (McLynn, 1998). He was particularly interested in spirituality and the psychology of spirituality, and his studies included the comparative analysis of Western and Eastern religions. His pre-WWII writings of this are collected in his book *Psychology and Religion: West and East*, which was published in 1958 (Jung, 1958). In terms of Eastern religions, the book covers topics such as the *Tibetan book of the dead*, *Yoga and the West*, the *Psychology of Eastern Meditation*, the *Holy men of India* and the *Foreword to the I Ching*. One work that is particularly relevant here is the *Foreword to Suzuki's Introduction to Zen Buddhism* (Jung, 1958).

The book is extremely interesting, written as it is by a psychoanalyst who shows a profound and complex understanding of the themes and theory of Zen. This is particularly remarkable because at that time, little was known about Zen in the west outside of a very restricted circle of intellectuals and converts to Buddhism. He thus became a pioneer in this field, making vital early contributions to Western understanding of it. The text is so rich and varied that it is impossible to give a representative sample here. Suffice it to say that the main themes he analyses and comments on relate to both East and West. These include mysticism and the great mystics, their spiritual exercises and meditative practices, the self and its role in Zen and psychology, the nature of consciousness, the naturalness of spiritual experiences, enlightenment and *satori*, meditation and *koans*, and the role of masters in guiding devotees.

One important bridge between East and West was built by a major international conference on Zen Buddhism and Psychoanalysis, which was organized under the auspices of the Autonomous National University of Mexico in the first week of August 1957 in Cuernavaca, Mexico. It was attended by about fifty psychiatrists and psychologists (the majority of them psychoanalysts) from both Mexico and the United States. There was even an outstanding contribution made by Daisetz Suzuki. The well known psychoanalyst Eric Fromm was also among the participants, and after the conference a classic book was produced called *Psychoanalysis and Zen Buddhism* (Suzuki, Fromm, & De Martino, 1970) which included contributions from Fromm, Suzuki and

De Martino. Zen Buddhism and psychoanalysis were widely discussed from a variety of different perspectives. In the words of Fromm:

> Each is a characteristic expression of Eastern and Western thought, where Zen Buddhism is a blending of Indian rationality and abstraction with Chinese concreteness and realism, and psychoanalysis is as exquisitely Western as Zen is Eastern, being the child of Western humanism and rationalism, and of the nineteenth-century romantic search for the dark forces which elude rationalism. Zen is a theory and technique to achieve "enlightenment," an experience which in the West would be called religious or mystical. Psychoanalysis is a therapy for mental illness; Zen a way to spiritual salvation. Can the discussion of the relationship between psychoanalysis and Zen Buddhism result in anything but the statement that there exists no relationship except that of radical and unbridgeable difference? (Suzuki et al., 1970)

After the sixties, there were also more direct reports on meditation when Western pioneers started to seek authentic training in the monasteries of Japan and South Asia. They had to overcome the considerable challenge of adapting to a radically different culture and also undergo the hardships of monastic life. Until they returned to the West—some as fully ordained monks—there was almost no first-hand knowledge of the experiential practice of traditional Buddhist meditation.

A unique contribution in this area was made by Tomio Hirai, a Japanese psychiatrist who was interested in Zen and its possible implications for mental health. Hirai was born in Tokyo in 1927, and graduated from the Medical School of the University of Tokyo in 1950. He became an outstanding authority in psychiatry in his country, and came to lead Japanese research into psychophysiology. Eventually, he was also elected president of the Japanese Society of Psychiatry and Neurology, as well as the Japan Mental Health Association (Tomio Hirai [1927–1993], 2019).

During his professional life, he became more and more interested in the applications of Zen and meditation in mental health. As a respected Japanese professor, by the 60s, he was able to draw the attention of a number of Zen masters, and soon became the first lay scholar in history to be given access to Zen monasteries.

Hirai wrote extensively, and part of his work has been translated for English readers. His contributions are particularly interesting because he was a clinician who trained in Japan, where psychiatry was uniquely influenced by the country's culture and history (Totsuka, 1990), and yet considered the possible applications of Zen in mental health from a broadly Western perspective.

One of the first articles published by Hirai is called *An electroencephalographic study on Zen meditation (zazen)*. The introduction to this article includes a description and definition of Zen meditation that is extremely precise and concise (Kasamatsu & Hirai, 1966):

> Zazen (Zen meditation) means the sitting meditation which is a kind of religious exercise in Zen-Buddhism. In Japan there are two Zen sects named Soto and Rinzai. Both sects regard Zazen as the most important training method of their disciples to enlighten their minds. Zen sitting is performed in two basic meditation forms: A full cross-legged sitting and a half cross-legged sitting. During the Zen sitting, the disciples' eyes must be open and look downward about one meter ahead and his hands generally join. In a quiet room the disciple sits on a round cushion and practises the meditation for about 30 minutes. Sometimes the intensive Zen training is performed 8 to 10 times a day for about one week. This is called Sesshin in Zen Buddhism. The disciples do not engage in daily activities but live the religious life following a strict schedule. By practising Zen meditation it is said that man can become emancipated from the dualistic bondage of subjectivity and objectivity, of mind and body, and of birth and death. And he can be free from lust and self-consciousness, and be awakened to his pure, serene and true-self. This mental state (Satori or enlightenment) will often be misunderstood as trance or hypnosis. It is said that Satori is not an abnormal mental state but one's everyday mind in the Zen sense. Dr. Erich Fromm describes "If we would try to express enlightenment in psychological terms, I would say that it is a state in which the person is completely tuned to the reality outside and inside of him, a state in which he is fully aware of it and fully grasps it. He is aware of it – that is, not his brain, nor any other part of his organism, but he, the whole man. He is aware of it not as of an object

> over there which he grasps with his thought, but it, the flower, the dog, the man, in its or his full reality. He who awakes is open and responsive to the world, and he can be open and responsive because he has given up holding on to himself as a thing, and thus has become empty and ready to receive. To be enlightened means 'the full awakening of the total personality to reality'. If one asks how this state of mind is concerned with psychotherapy, it may be said that Zen meditation is the method through which we can communicate with the unconscious. In this context, however, the unconscious does not mean Freud's "unconscious". Rather, "the unconscious" in Zen is closely related to the unconscious which was described by Jung, C. G. or Fromm, E. In regard to this problem Dr. Daisetsu Suzuki states the meaning of it as "the Cosmic unconscious. At any rate the Zen meditation influences not only the mind but also the body of the whole organism". (Kasamatsu & Hirai, 1966)

The experiment was organized using the psychophysiological techniques available in the 60s, and involved recording the electroencephalogram (EEG), the heart pulse rate, respiration and galvanic skin response (GSR), as well as the responses to sensory stimuli. It also recorded the ECG's alpha pattern blocking time using repeated click auditory stimulations. The experiment involved 48 subjects belonging to the Soto and Rinzai sects, classified according to their experience of meditation. Some were disciples with 1–5 or 5–20 years of experience, while others were priests with over 20 years' experience.

There was also a control group of 18 lay subjects with matching characteristics.

The experiment found that there were specific ECG changes during meditation, such as an increase in the amplitude and decrease in the frequency of alpha waves. The records from some priests also showed a rhythmical theta train. These changes were different to those observed during sleep and hypnotic trances, and were accompanied by a dehabituation of the alpha blocking caused by repeated auditory clicks (Kasamatsu & Hirai, 1966) Hirai's experiment has been explored in greater detail in two books: *Zen and the Mind: A Scientific Approach to Zen Practice* (Hirai, 1978) and *Zen Meditation Therapy* (Hirai, 1975).

This research is of particular interest because it takes us back to the Japan of the early 60s. It was performed in Japanese Zen monasteries, where daily practices had remained unchanged for centuries—and unobserved by Western disciples and visitors, who were only admitted later.

The subjects chosen for the study had different levels of experience of meditation, ranging from 1 to 5 years among less advanced disciples and over 20 years among experienced priests. Although the results are limited by the techniques available at the time, they definitely suggest that meditation—at least the Zazen practised in Zen monasteries—induces specific mental states that differ from those observed during hypnosis and sleep. Interestingly, these results chime with the body of evidence that has been gathered on the subject since. However, it is important to remember, of course, the specific nature of the meditative experience examined—especially its duration.

The contributions of Hirai are not limited to psychophysiological studies of Zen meditation; in his books, he also examines Zen meditation and therapy in relation to yoga, hypnosis and the autogenic training that was gaining prominence in the West at the time. He also examines Morita therapy, which was reasonably widespread in Japan at the time (Hirai, 1978). Hirai later returned to these subjects in a revised and enlarged edition published in 1989—which also included his examination of consciousness and psychedelic drugs, as well as the applications of Zen meditation for psychotherapy, psychiatry and good health (Hirai, 1989).

When considering psychologists' past attempts to build a bridge between Buddhist meditation and mental health, it is also important to remember practices that originated in Japan and still continue to this day, interwoven as they are, into the fabric of Japanese culture. Morita Therapy is one such, and was developed by Japanese psychiatrist Shoma Morita in the early part of the twentieth century under the influence of Zen. It was initially developed as a treatment for a type of anxiety neurosis called "*shinkeishitsu*". Over time, the principles of his approach were adapted to outpatient settings and expanded to address not only emotional wellbeing but also to improve people's function in many other aspects of daily life. In the traditional inpatient approach, there is a period of isolated bed rest before the patient is given counselling, instruction and occupational therapy. Now, Morita principles are also increasingly being applied in outpatient settings (The Morita School of Japanese Psychology, 2019).

The other approach worth considering here is Naikan, which was developed in Japan in the 1940s by Ishin Yashimoto, a devout Buddhist of the Pure Land (Judo Shinshu) sect. His strong religious spirit led him to practise "*mishirabe*", an arduous and difficult form of meditation and self-reflection (Reynolds, 1989).

In the case of both Morita and Naikan therapy, it is clear that, at least in their original from, they require a strong commitment from patients that is unlikely to be found in the West (Chervenkova & Krishnan, 2017). Remarkably, practitioners of Morita therapy also recently devised Acceptance and Commitment Therapy (ACT), which involves integrating principles of cognitive and behavioural psychotherapy with Morita therapy, leading to a significant improvement in the latter (Kitanishi & Mori, 1995; Murase, 1974).

Transcendental meditation (TM) is a form of silent mantra meditation that was developed in India in the mid-1950s by Maharishi Mahesh Yogi, who later taught thousands of people during a series of world tours from 1958 to 1965. TM became popular in the 1960s and 1970s when the meditation technique was adopted by numerous celebrities such as the Beatles. Since then, TM has been taught to millions of people through a worldwide organisation that includes educational programmes, health products and related services. It has become a phenomenon that is so widespread as to deserve special attention ("How the Offshoot of an Ancient Hindu Practice Popularized by the Beatles Made Its Way to Wall Street", 2019). Its teachers claim that the practice of TM will lead to gains in the realms of spirituality, psychology, wellbeing, physical health and even society (Forem, 2012). Not all of those who have experienced it are happy, however (Hoffman, 2017). Numerous studies were possible thanks to the large number of people practising TM, but their quality was poor and firm conclusions on the impact of this form of meditation in healthcare could not be drawn (Ospina et al., 2007).

A simple, secular version of TM was devised for people in the West by Herbert Benson, a Harvard physician. It was presented in 1975 in the book *The Relaxation Response*, which became a bestseller in the

US (Benson & Klipper, 2001). Benson, a pioneer of mind-body medicine, has done extensive research and published widely on this subject, founding and heading up the Benson-Henry Institute (BHI) as Professor of Medicine at the Harvard Medical School (Herbert Benson—Benson-Henry Institute, 2019). Joan Borysenko, herself a pioneer of the mind-body connection in integrative medicine, began her studies under Herbert Benson, and subsequently became a leading authority in this field. Her book *Minding the Body, Mending the Mind* also became a classic bestseller (Borysenko, 2007; Joan Borysenko, 2019).

Another major contribution to the study of Zen, meditation and mental health was made by James H. Austin, an American neurologist who developed a strong interest in Zen Buddhism when he was stationed in Japan in 1950 and 1951 during the Korean War. Then, in 1974, he took sabbatical leave in Kyoto at the same institution where Shuji Takaori, a Japanese colleague who gained a Ph.D. in neuropharmacology from Austin's University, was working. Takaori introduced him to Nanrei Kobori Roshi, the Zen master of Daitoku-ji, the main Rinzai Zen Temple in Kyoto. Under Roshi's guidance, Austin was thus able to directly experience Zen practices at Ryoko-in, a sub-temple of Daitoku-ji.

Austin met another noted Zen master during a second sabbatical in 1982 in London: Irmgard Scloegel, known by her Buddhist name Myokyo-ni. He practised Zen under her guidance at the Shobo-an Temple in London (Shobo-an Zen Centre, About Us, 2019). In 1999, Austin published an 844-page book called *Zen and the Brain: Toward an Understanding of Meditation and Consciousness*, which reviewed the available literature and attempted to connect Zen Buddhism and neuroscience (Austin, 2001). Austin went on to publish more books on Zen and neuroscience, including the 2006 work *Zen-Brain Reflections: Reviewing Recent Developments in Meditation and States of Consciousness* (Austin, 2010), which is a 586-page-long sequel to *Zen and the Brain*. He has written five more works on the subject: *Selfless Insight* (Austin, 2009), *Meditating Selflessly* (Austin, 2011), *Zen-Brain Horizons* (Austin, 2014) and *Living Zen Remindfully* (Austin, 2016).

Alan Wilson Watts, a British-born philosopher and writer, is another incisive scholar of Eastern and Western psychology and philosophy. He received a Master's degree in theology and became an Episcopal priest in 1945, then left the ministry in 1950 and moved to California, where he joined the faculty of the American Academy of Asian Studies. Watts gained a large audience, and wrote extensively on Eastern and Western religion, introducing the then burgeoning youth culture to *The Way of Zen* (1957), one of the first bestselling books on Zen Buddhism (Furlong, 2010; Watts, 1989). He also wrote *Psychotherapy East and West* (1961), in which he proposed that Buddhism could be considered a form of psychotherapy and not a religion. For Watts, humans live in a seemingly hostile universe where social norms and illusions bind and constrict them. He believed that if the profound insights of Freud and Jung could be melded with Eastern traditions, they could help to free humans from this and their battle with the self (Watts, 2017).

After the 50s and 60s, the cultural and spiritual influence of the East continued to grow in the West. In his book *Awakening the Heart*, John Welwood collected contributions on the role of Buddhist meditation and spirituality in human growth, well-being and psychotherapy. The chapter by Eric Fromm is called *The nature of well-being*. Another chapter, entitled *Where is the self?* is written by Joshu Sasaki Roshi, who played a major role in the diffusion of Zen throughout the US and attracted famous followers such as Leonard Cohen (Ford, 2006; Welwood, 1985).

*Beyond Therapy: The Impact of Eastern Religions on Psychological Theory and Practice*, a book edited by Guy Claxon, collected a range of different perspectives on the relationship of Buddhist psychology and meditation to psychotherapy (Claxton, 1996). The contributions in it are from experts with a deep, direct knowledge of the various fields considered, such as David Brandon and Susan Blackmore. Brandon has a background both as a social worker and the director of a government-sponsored research project on homeless young people in the UK. He has also published extensively about his experiences with homeless people (Brandon, 1974). An ardent convert to Buddhism, he put Zen teachings into the practice in his social work (Brandon, 1990). Blackmore, on the other hand, is a British psychologist who in the last part of her career shifted her attention from the psychology of "memes" (Blackmore, 2000), a evolutionary idea originally proposed by the noted biologist Richard Dawkins, to consciousness and its relationship to Zen (Blackmore, 2005a, 2005b, 2009a, 2009b).

In his book *Zen Therapy*, David Brazier made a concerted effort to put the basic Buddhist teachings relevant to psychotherapy into a frame that would be accessible to non-specialist Western audiences (Brazier, 2012).

The case of Ainslie Meares is a little more unusual. Ainslie Dixon Meares was an Australian psychiatrist, scholar of hypnotism, psychotherapy and stress and also a prolific author, who lived and worked in Melbourne ("Biography—Ainslie Dixon Meares—Australian Dictionary of Biography", 2019). Meares created "atavistic regression", a system of relaxing meditation (Meares, 1984), which he claimed could be used to help cancer patients (Meares, 1977a, 1977b, 1978). One of his patients who practised atavistic regression was reportedly cured after his leg had been amputated for metastatic osteogenic sarcoma. He became an ardent proponent of meditation for cancer patients (Gawler & Bedson, 2011). Recently, however, it has been suggested that the patient may not have had cancer but systemic tuberculosis, since the diagnostic techniques available at the time could not clearly distinguish between the two (Haines & Lowenthal, 2012).

From the 60s onwards, there were remarkable changes both in Buddhism and in psychology and psychotherapy. More and more determined pioneers from the West were making the journey to the East to undertake meditation training in Buddhist monasteries in Japan and South Asia. They had to overcome the considerable challenge not only of the training itself, but also of adapting to a very different world. Some of them succeeded and were ordained as monks, before many returned to teach alongside the Eastern masters who first brought Buddhism to the West.

Eventually, then, the authorisation to teach and recognition of awakening—the 'lineage'—passed down lines that were developed entirely in the West. During this time, while positive changes were happening, new challenges were also rising. People began to question traditional aspects of Buddhist schools that were deeply rooted in ancient scriptures and complex rituals—not least Tibetan Buddhism. People began to ask whether it would be possible to develop Buddhist practices free from the religious traditions of the various sects. This question is still very much open, and has become more pressing because of movements such as the secular or agnostic Buddhism mentioned in the previous chapter. Western mindfulness itself is one example of the practice of meditation detached from Buddhist traditions.

Psychiatry and clinical psychology also underwent profound changes in the twentieth century and particularly after the 60s. Kraepelin's contributions at the end of the nineteenth century had helped to position psychiatry as a medical specialism. Despite the medical classification of the discipline, however, there were still disappointingly few therapeutic interventions available to psychiatrists. Worst of all, few of them were remotely effective. For much of the twentieth century, those who could afford it treated less severe disorders, which were often deemed to have "neurotic" origins, with psychoanalysis.

The Second World War only extended the influence of psychoanalysis on psychiatry in the US as large numbers of European psychiatrists of Jewish origin fled there from the Nazis. With the development of psychopharmacology in the late 50s, however, the situation began to change. The arrival of psychopharmacology gave psychiatrists an entire new armoury of psychotropic agents that were effective against the symptoms of even the most severe mental conditions. Psychiatry used the opportunity to shore up its status as a scientific medical discipline. The idea of "biological psychiatry" was even developed to offer a new perspective on diagnosis and treatment. And, as new pharmacological treatments became more and more easily available and effective, so psychoanalysis became less and less relevant to psychiatry and clinical psychology. Psychoanalysis and other similar pshychodynamic therapies for mental suffering were increasingly superceded by behavioural and cognitive psychology and psychotherapy (Wallace & Gach, 2011).

During the course of the twentieth century, then, both Buddhism and psychoanalysis underwent a sort of agnostic transformation. In Buddhism, there were concerted attempts to detach it from its formal traditions and rituals, while clinical psychology was transformed by the rise of behavioural and cognitive psychotherapies based in neuroscience and biological psychiatry.

Overall, then, the idea of engaging with Buddhist ideas and meditation for psychology and psychotherapy in the West is not new or original, and has in fact come up many times in the last century. The results of these engagements with Buddhism and meditation may be seen as generally positive (Murphy, Donovan, & Taylor, 1999; Sampaio, Lima, & Ladeia, 2016)—even when reviewed later in the context of "evidence-based medicine" (Goyal et al., 2014). Although biological psychiatry and cognitive and behavioural psychotherapies undoubtedly had a transformational effect on psychology and psychotherapy, Buddhism and Eastern traditions also had a vital and distinct influence on these disciplines (Schneider, 2003; Scotton, Chinen, & Battista, 2009; Turner, Lukoff, Barnhouse, & Lu, 1995).

Unlike these influences, however, mindfulness is unique because it was accepted into the world of "evidence-based medicine". Previous similar interventions had always been deemed "alternative" to biologically-grounded treatments. How this came to be will be examined in the following chapters.

## References

Albahari, M. (2006). *Analytical Buddhism: The two-tiered illusion of self.* Basingstoke: Palgrave Macmillan.

Austin, J. (2001). *Zen and the brain.* Cambridge, MA: MIT Press.

Austin, J. (2009). *Selfless insight: Zen and the meditative transformations of consciousness.* Cambridge, MA: MIT Press.

Austin, J. (2010). *Zen-brain reflections.* Cambridge, MA: MIT Press.

Austin, J. (2011). *Meditating selflessly.* Cambridge, MA: MIT Press.

Austin, J. (2014). *Zen brain horizons.* Cambridge, MA: MIT Press.

Austin, J. (2016). *Living zen remindfully—Retraining subconscious awareness.* Cambridge, MA: MIT Press.

Benson, H., & Klipper, M. (2001). *The relaxation response.* New York, NY: Quill.

Biography—Ainslie Dixon Meares—Australian Dictionary of Biography. (2019). Retrieved from http://adb.anu.edu.au/biography/meares-ainslie-dixon-14944. Accessed 20 April 2019.

Blackmore, S. (2000). *The meme machine.* Oxford, UK: Oxford University Press.

Blackmore, S. (2005a). *A very short introduction*. Oxford: Oxford University Press.
Blackmore, S. (2005b). *Conversations on consciousness*. Oxford: Oxford University Press.
Blackmore, S. (2009a). *Consciousness*. London: Hodder Education—An Hachette UK Company.
Blackmore, S. (2009b). *Ten Zen questions*. Oxford: Oneworld.
Blyth, Reginald Horace (1898–1964). *Chronology, bibliography, links, quotes, resources*. (2019). Retrieved from http://www.gardendigest.com/zen/blyth.htm. Accessed 20 April 2019.
Borysenko, J. (2007). *Minding the body, mending the mind*. New York: Da Capo Press.
Borysenko, Joan. (2019). Retrieved from https://www.joanborysenko.com/about-joan/. Accessed 20 April 2019.
Brandon, D. (1974). *Homeless*. London: Sheldon Press.
Brandon, D. (1990). *Zen in the art of helping*. London, UK: Arkana.
Brazier, D. (2012). *Zen therapy*. London: Constable & Robinson.
Chervenkova, V., & Krishnan, J. (2017). *Japanese psychotherapies*. Osaka: Springer Nature Singapore.
Claxton, G. (1996). *Beyond therapy*. Sturminster Newton: Prism.
Fields, R. (1992). *How the swans came to the lake*. Boston: Shambhala.
Ford, J. (2006). *Zen master who?* Boston: Wisdom Publications.
Forem, J. (2012). *Transcendental meditation*. Carlsbad, CA: Hay House.
Furlong, M. (2010). *Zen effects*. Woodstock, VT: Sklylight Paths.
Gawler, I., & Bedson, P. (2011). *Meditation*. New York: Jeremy P. Tarcher/Penguin.
Goyal, M., Singh, S., Sibinga, E., Gould, N., Rowland-Seymour, A., Sharma, R., et al. (2014). Meditation programs for psychological stress and well-being. *JAMA Internal Medicine, 174*(3), 357. https://doi.org/10.1001/jamainternmed.2013.13018.
Haines, I., & Lowenthal, R. (2012). Hypothesis: The importance of a histological diagnosis when diagnosing and treating advanced cancer. Famous patient recovery may not have been from metastatic disease. *Internal Medicine Journal, 42*(2), 212–216. https://doi.org/10.1111/j.1445-5994.2011.02686.x.
Herbert Benson—Benson-Henry Institute. (2019). Retrieved from https://www.bensonhenryinstitute.org/about-us-dr-herbert-benson/. Accessed 20 April 2019.

Hirai, Tomio (1927–1993). (2019). Retrieved from https://terebess.hu/zen/mesterek/HiraiTomio.html. Accessed 20 April 2019.
Hirai, T. (1975). *Zen meditation therapy*. Tokyo: Japan Publications.
Hirai, T. (1978). *Zen and the mind: A scientific approach to Zen practice*. Tokyo: Japan Publications.
Hirai, T. (1989). *Zen meditation and psychotherapy*. Tokyo: Japan Publications.
Hoffman, C. (2017). *Greetings from Utopia Park: Surviving a transcendent childhood*. New York: Harper.
How the Offshoot of an Ancient Hindu Practice Popularized by the Beatles Made Its Way to Wall Street. (2019). Retrieved from https://www.businessinsider.com/history-of-transcendental-meditation-2016-11?IR=T. Accessed 20 April 2019.
Jung, C. G. (1958). *Psychology and religion: West and East*. Bolligen Series XX. Princeton: Princeton University Press.
Kasamatsu, A., & Hirai, T. (1966). An electroencephalographic study on the Zen meditation (zazen). *Psychiatry and Clinical Neurosciences, 20*(4), 315–336. https://doi.org/10.1111/j.1440-1819.1966.tb02646.x.
King, R. (2009). *Orientalism and religion*. London: Routledge.
Kitanishi, K., & Mori, A. (1995). Morita therapy: 1919 to 1995. *Psychiatry and Clinical Neurosciences, 49*(5–6), 245–254. https://doi.org/10.1111/j.1440-1819.1995.tb01896.x.
Macfie, A. (2009). *Orientalism*. Edinburgh: Edinburgh University Press.
McLynn, F. (1998). *Carl Gustav Jung*. New York: St. Martin's Griffin.
Meares, A. (1977a). Atavistic regression as a factor in the remission of cancer. *Medical Journal of Australia, 2*(4), 132–133.
Meares, A. (1977b). Follow up: Regression of cancer of the rectum after intensive meditation. *Medical Journal of Australia, 2*(10), 539–540.
Meares, A. (1978). Regression of osteogenic sarcoma association with intensive meditation. *Medical Journal of Australia, 2*(9), 433.
Meares, A. (1984). *The wealth within*. Bath: Ashgrove Press.
Millière, R., Carhart-Harris, R., Roseman, L., Trautwein, F., & Berkovich-Ohana, A. (2018). Psychedelics, meditation, and self-consciousness. *Frontiers in Psychology, 9*. https://doi.org/10.3389/fpsyg.2018.01475.
Murase, T. (1974). Naikan, Morita, and Western psychotherapy. *Archives of General Psychiatry, 31*(1), 121. https://doi.org/10.1001/archpsyc.1974.01760130091016.
Murphy, M., Donovan, S., & Taylor, E. (1999). *The physical and psychological effects of meditation*. Sausalito, CA: Institute of Noetic Sciences.

Ospina, M. B., Bond, K., Karkhaneh, M., Tjosvold, L., Vandermeer, B., Liang, Y., … Klassen, T. P. (2007). *Meditation practices for health: State of the research*. Evidence Report/Technology Assessment, No. 155, pp. 1–263.

Osto, D. (2018). *Altered states: Buddhism and psychedelic spirituality in America*. New York: Columbia Press.

Reynolds, D. (1989). *Flowing bridges, quiet waters: Japanese psychotherapies, Morita and Naikan*. SUNY Series in Transpersonal and Humanistic Psychology. Albany: State University of New York Press.

Sampaio, C., Lima, M., & Ladeia, A. (2016). Meditation, health and scientific investigations: Review of the literature. *Journal of Religion and Health, 56*(2), 411–427. https://doi.org/10.1007/s10943-016-0211-1.

Sangharakshita. (1996). *Great Buddhists of the twentieth century*. Birmingham: Windhorse Publications.

Schneider, K. (2003). *The handbook of humanistic psychology*. Thousand Oaks, CA: Sage.

Scotton, B., Chinen, A., & Battista, J. (2009). *Textbook of transpersonal psychiatry and psychology*. New York: Basic Books.

Shobo-an Zen Centre, About Us. (2019). Retrieved from http://www.rinzaizencentre.org.uk/our-lineage.php. Accessed 20 April 2019.

Snelling, J. (1998). *The Buddhist handbook*. Rochester, VT: Inner Traditions.

Suzuki, D. (1960). *Manual of Zen Buddhism*. New York: Grove Press.

Suzuki, D. (2007). *The training of the Zen Buddhist monk*. New York: Cosimo Classics.

Suzuki, D. (2010). *Zen and Japanese culture*. Princeton, NJ: Princeton University Press.

Suzuki, D., Fromm, E., & De Martino, R. (1970). *Zen Buddhism & psychoanalysis*. New York: Harper & Row.

The Morita School of Japanese Psychology. (2019). Retrieved from http://www.moritaschool.com/read-me/. Accessed 20 April 2019.

Totsuka, E. (1990). The history of Japanese psychiatry and the rights of mental patients. *Psychiatric Bulletin, 14*, 193–200.

Turner, R. P., Lukoff, D., Barnhouse, R. T., & Lu, F. G. (1995). A culturally sensitive diagnostic category in the DSM-IV. *The Journal of Nervous and Mental Disease, 183*(7), 435–444. https://doi.org/10.1097/00005053-199507000-00003.

Wallace, E., & Gach, J. (2011). *History of psychiatry and medical psychology*. New York: Springer.

Watts, A. (1989). *The way of Zen*. New York: Vintage Books.
Watts, A. (2017). *Psychotherapy East and West*. [Place of publication not identified]: New World Library.
Welwood, J. (1985). *Awakening the heart*. Boston, MA: Shambhala.

# 5
# The Applications of "Mindfulness" in Psychology and Medicine

Existential suffering is an unavoidable fact of human life, and the core of ancient Buddhist ideology is that it can provide a path to overcome this. Recently, however, psychiatrists and psychotherapists have started to approach this matter from a medical perspective. From the beginning, they found it difficult to draw a clear distinction between normal, healthy responses to life events and pathological conditions. In fact, to this day, the distinction remains unclear.

There have always been mental disorders, manifesting themselves differently depending on sufferers' social milieu. And, at the end of the nineteenth century, psychiatry was established as a medical speciality to deal with them. Diagnostic categories, which are still the basis of how we classify mental disorders today, were clearly defined for the first time and rapidly adopted. In terms of interventions, the treatments available at this time were largely ineffective—without conceptual grounds or empirical evidence of efficacy.

Things began to change dramatically with the rapid scientific and clinical developments at the end of the Second World War. A basic mechanism of the human brain, "neurotransmission", was discovered and scientists quickly came to understand that neurons in the brain



T. Giraldi, *Psychotherapy, Mindfulness and Buddhist Meditation*,
https://doi.org/10.1007/978-3-030-29003-0_5

communicate mainly through the exchange of neurotransmitters such as dopamine and serotonin. A new group of medicines, psychotropic drugs, was developed, laying the foundations of psychopharmacology. These new drugs, which modified neurotransmission in the brain, were able to markedly reduce the symptoms of even the most serious mental diseases. Through these, it became possible to treat anxiety, psychosis, schizophrenia, maniac-depressive psychosis, as well as melancholia and depression.

These therapeutic breakthroughs had a profound impact on the whole field of mental health, radically changing the lives of patients and how mental institutions were organised. Psychiatry finally came to rely on a properly defined set of diagnostic and therapeutic principles and was soon treated with the same respect as other medical specialisms. The new therapeutic pharmacological interventions, in particular, led to the birth and rapid growth of biological psychiatry. In the 60s, the rise of biological psychiatry was greatly aided by the development of a new diagnostic system, the Diagnostic Statistical Manual. Although it was seriously criticised at the time, the Diagnostic Statistical Manual would become extremely influential (Lieberman & Ogas, 2015; Shorter, 2005, 2015).

There is a continuous spectrum between the extremes of serious mental diseases ("pathologies") and milder cases of natural existential suffering. In many cases, in fact, both conditions are present in a person at the same time. Traditionally, severe "psychotic" cases were always approached differently to milder "neurotic" cases, which were potentially reversible and could be treated with interventions such as hypnosis and psychoanalysis. When the world of Buddhism suddenly became accessible to Western researchers at the end of the nineteenth Century, some curious minds were immediately drawn to the idea of adding Buddhist meditation to the toolkit of mental health interventions available to psychiatrists.

Much varied and complex evidence about the effects of Buddhist meditation started to accumulate in the West. This is hardly surprising, given the many and varied forms of meditation practice in Buddhism. The studies on Buddhism also involve a wide variety of different research methods. A very large number of studies accumulated over the years, and as a result it is now possible to perform a meta-analysis of them.

When considering the ever-greater attention given to meditation by Western psychiatrists, it is important to consider just how much Western medicine as a whole changed during the course of the nineteenth and twentieth Centuries—in no small part because of the development and refinement of the scientific method by clinical researchers (Le Fanu, 2014). A crucial factor in this was the adoption of rational protocols for clinical trials, which led to so-called "*evidence-based medicine*". As a result, the effectiveness of medical procedures could finally be empirically and objectively verified (Howick, 2011).

As it became possible to scientifically test medical procedures, so new regulatory agencies began to emerge, beginning with the US Food and Drug Administration, founded in 1906. At the beginning, the main impetus behind them was the drive to stop a wave of fatal poisonings because of toxic pharmaceutical products on the market. Soon, however, the agencies were also charged with testing the efficacy of prescription medicines. Eventually, they were also tasked with applying the same standards to medical devices and procedures (Rägo & Santoso, 2008).

After Kabat-Zinn's original proposal, mindfulness-based interventions became increasingly widespread, and came to be used for improving wellbeing as well as treating a number of mental and physical ailments. Unsurprisingly, therefore, it was not long before health authorities became interested in the idea of using mindfulness and meditation as health interventions. While there was justifiable concern about the efficacy of these interventions, little consideration was given to their safety, which should have been monitored—even if it was assumed mindfulness interventions were harmless.

In 2007, the *U.S. Department of Health and Human Services' Agency for Healthcare Research and Quality* published a report on this subject called *Evidence Report/Technology Assessment. Number 155. Meditation Practices for Health: State of the Research.* It was prepared at the *University of Alberta Evidence-based Practice Center* by Ospina and her co-workers (Ospina, 2007). In total, it runs to almost five hundred pages, covering a wide range of topics. It includes, as a background, the definition and types of meditation, as well as a summary of the various kinds of meditation practices used in healing and healthcare. The key questions addressed in this research are to do with the practice of meditation, the state of research on the therapeutic use of meditation and the evidence available of its efficacy and effectiveness. It also covers the physiological and neuropsychological effects of meditation.

The practices considered in the book include transcendental meditation, Benson's relaxation, Vipassana meditation, Zen Buddhist meditation, Mindfulness-Based Stress Reduction (MBSR), Mindfulness-Based Cognitive Therapy (MBCT), Yoga, Tai Chi and Qi Gong. The book carefully considers the 1031 scientifically rigorous studies available, examining the diseases treated and the types of meditation used and applying meta-analytic techniques. The results cover five broad categories of meditation practices: mantra meditation, mindfulness meditation, Yoga, Tai Chi, and Qi Gong. The three most studied conditions were hypertension, other cardiovascular diseases and substance abuse. There were sixty-five intervention studies examining the effects of meditation on these conditions. Overall, the studies that were used for meta-analysis were not high-quality and were often based on small numbers of participants. Nevertheless, rigorous meta-analysis found that transcendental meditation, Qi Gong and Zen Buddhist meditation significantly reduced blood pressure. Yoga also helped to reduce stress, but was no better than MBSR at reducing anxiety in patients with cardiovascular diseases.

The discussion of the results of this study is necessarily complex, and the authors made this conclusion:

> The field of research on meditation techniques and their therapeutic applications has been clouded by confusion over what constitutes meditation and by a lack of methodological rigor in much of the research. Further research needs to be directed toward distinguishing the effects and characteristics of the many different techniques falling under the rubric "meditation." The single and multimodality meditation practices included in this report were categorized for pragmatic reasons, but specific attention must be paid to developing definitions for these techniques that are both conceptually and operationally useful. Such definitions

> are a prerequisite for scientific research of the highest quality. Research of higher quality is vital to respond appropriately to the many persistent questions in this area. The dearth of high-quality evidence highlights the need for greater care in defining and choosing the interventions and in choosing controls, populations, and outcomes that permit comparison of studies across techniques regarding their therapeutic effects. More care in these choices will allow effects to be estimated with greater reliability and validity. More randomized trials that draw on the experience of investigators or consultants with a strong background in clinical and basic research should be conducted. As a whole, firm conclusions on the effects of meditation practices in healthcare cannot be drawn based on the available evidence. However, the results analysed from methodologically stronger research include findings sufficiently favourable to emphasize the value of further research in this field. It is imperative that future studies on meditation practices be more rigorous in design, execution, and analysis, and in the reporting of the results. Greater importance should be placed on the reporting of study methods and providing detailed descriptions of the training of the participants, qualifications of meditation instructors, and on reporting the criteria and methods used to determine a successful meditation practice.

Broadly speaking, the authors seem to conclude that the issue of meditation being used in mental health interventions is complex because both subjects are in themselves extremely complex. What emerges clearly, however, is just how difficult it is to bring meditation into the realm of science, where widely hugely different practices are compared and the individuality of subjects is lost or at best reduced to rigidly standardised categories. This rigidity and standardisation also causes problems when attempting to examine and evaluate the effects of meditation as an intervention. The impact of meditative intervention, indeed, seems to progressively fade away the more you attempt to bring them into the rigorous restrictions of *evidence-based* medicine.

Nevertheless, despite the caution one must apply when attempting to draw objective conclusions from scientifically rigorous evidence, many of the published studies leave the impression that meditation has had a positive effect of the lives of some of the people who have practised it. In some cases, people's health has improved or they have even recovered from illnesses entirely. In many other cases, people have learned to cope better with their difficulties. These impressions are consistent with the conclusions of *Meditation Practices for Health*, as well as many other research papers on the subject.

The idea of using meditation as a therapeutic tool is not new, and how psychoanalysts and psychologists first became interested in it has already been examined. More recently, in 1991, Bogart prepared a review of the available literature on the introduction of meditation into therapy based on his own psychoanalytic background. In his work, he considered the views of proponents and critics of the relaxation model of meditation, as well as theories about the cognitive changes induced in meditators. He summarized psychoanalytic and Jungian arguments, as well as the views of transpersonal psychologists about meditation.

He concludes that the effectiveness of meditation depends on what specific therapeutic goals have been set. In some cases, he believes meditation may indeed further the aims of psychotherapy. It is important to note, however, that he does believe there are also many contrary cases, especially when the aim of therapy is to strengthen ego boundaries, release powerful emotions or work through complex relational dynamics (Bogart, 1991).

As behavioural and cognitive psychologies and psychotherapies have become more widespread, psychoanalysis has received less and less attention (Aflalo & Price, 2005). Psychoanalysts, however, continue to examine interesting new humanistic and spiritual approaches based on meditation and Zen Buddhism (Magid, 2002; Moncayo, 2012).The irresistible growth of mindfulness did not happen in a void, and started among a multitude of interventions, both old and new, such as Qi Gong and Zen Buddhist meditation, transcendental meditation, as well as a many more minor practices such as autogenic training, relaxation techniques, hypnosis and auto-hypnosis.

As therapeutic meditation became more widespread, however, it was increasingly criticised and many new concerns were raised about it. Meditation came to be used as an intervention, it was claimed, because of myopic rhetoric that distorted the meaning and practices of Buddhism. More people also began to criticise its removal from the moral foundations of Buddhism, and also questioned how far it could be translated into a modern medical framework (Hickey, 2010).

The mindfulness boom began in the 70s, as we have already seen, when Kabat-Zinn developed the idea of using Buddhist meditation as a therapeutic tool, and attempted to bring meditation into the mainstream of scientifically and objectively grounded medicine. Kabat-Zinn's legitimate concerns about bringing mindfulness into the realm of medicine and science clearly appear from the very first papers he published on the matter. The intervention he devised, however, came to have a huge influence on later applications of mindfulness, including its integration into different psychotherapies. It now seems right, therefore, to examine his work in more detail now.

The first thing to consider is the name he gave his structured eight-week course, MBSR, which then inspired the name of his *Stress Reduction Clinic*, founded in 1979 at the University of Massachusetts Medical School. His use of the term 'stress' is interesting because it leads us to the earlier work of Hans Selye, a Hungarian physiologist who trained in Europe before moving to Canada ahead of the outbreak of the Second World War. Selye is seen as the father of the concept of 'stress'. He developed the idea based on the influence of Claude Bernard's 'milieu intérieur' (our inner composition) and 'homeostasis' (the equilibrium of a person's internal composition and functions).

As a physiologist, Selye conceptualized stress as having two components: a set of responses which he called the 'general adaptation syndrome', and the onset of a pathological state of exhaustion after ongoing, unrelieved stress. The 'general adaptation syndrome' consists of a uniform set of responses when an organism is subjected to a range of physical external challenges, the 'stressors'. These responses are the activation of the sympathetic autonomic nervous system and the neuroendocrine system, also involving the release of epinephrine. These responses allow the organism to adapt to the stressors and maintain its usual composition and bodily function. Pathological consequences only arise when the organism is exposed to stressful conditions for so long that the body is exhausted and certain tissues and functions are harmed because of excessive stimulation (Selye, 1956).

In humans, not only physical, but also psychological factors may act as stressors. In fact, it is psychological rather than physical factors that have come in for the most academic and popular interest. One particularly popular book on the subject is *Why Zebras Don't Get Ulcers,* which was first published in 1994, then re-released in two best-selling editions. This book shows just how important stress is in allowing us to cope with the external world. You can get a gist of this just from the chapter titles: Glands, Gooseflesh and Hormones; Stroke, Heart Attacks and Voodoo Death; Stress, Metabolism and Liquidating Your Assets; Ulcers, the Runs and Hot Fudge Sundaes; Dwarfism and the Importance of Mothers; Sex and Reproduction; Immunity, Stress, and Disease; Stress and Pain; Stress and Memory; Stress and a Good Night's Sleep; Ageing and Death; Why Is Psychological Stress Stressful?; Stress and Depression; Personality, Temperament, and Their Stress-Related Consequences; and Junkies, Adrenaline Junkies and Pleasure (Sapolsky, 2004).

Experiencing serious life events may be associated with the appearance of pathological conditions, and Eugene S. Paykel has made essential contributions to this subject. The studies he carried out allowed him to create a scale of the most stressful life events. At the top of the list were catastrophic events like the death of a child, a spouse or a close family member, a jail sentence, an unfaithful spouse, major financial difficulties, business failure, being fired, miscarriage or stillbirth, and divorce. The list of life events then moves down to less catastrophic ones, listing them all the way down to the 61st: a child getting married with the respondent's approval. It is worth noting that some of the stressful life events included into this list are actually of a positive nature, such as marital reconciliation, the birth of a live child, a wife becoming pregnant, marriage, promotion and engagement (Paykel, Prusoff, & Uhlenhuth, 1971).

These findings were found to be consistent with the responses of a number of samples and a *Social readjustement rating scale* was prepared, which gave a score to each of the life events. Again, the death of spouse was at the top, with a score of 100, while a minor violation of the law was at the bottom, with 11. In between was a whole range of ordered events—both negative and positive (Holmes & Rahe, 1967).

These studies were based on the finding that a number of life events that require change and ongoing life adjustment are also associated with the onset of various diseases. Paykel was particularly interested in mood disorders, and thus studied the relationship between life events and depression. Paykel found that it was life events connected with leaving social fields, family, health and employment that were most closely associated with the onset of depression. The specific events Paykel found most often among depressed patients were: arguments with a spouse, marital separation, serious personal illness, the death of an immediate family member, a family member leaving home, the start of a new type of work and a change in the type of work a person is doing (Paykel, 1969).

These studies were performed in the 60s in the US, and their results must be considered in this specific cultural context. At the same time, however, they do seem to show, using sound methodology an statistical procedures, that a number of defined life events can cause an increased susceptibility to bodily diseases and depression. The individual coping mechanisms of a person do not seem to matter so much as the nature of the event: the stress of certain life events is the essential factor. Theoretically, then, it is not possible to devise an intervention to reduce the 'stress' that a major life event provokes in a subject. It is only possible to devise interventions to attenuate the *consequences* of the stress suffered.

The situation is different, however, when you consider the individual difficulties people face when *coping* with life events. In a population exposed to the same stressful life events, some subjects may be more vulnerable and may have a particularly existential and emotional response. It may be useful here to consider the current depression epidemic (World Federation for Mental Health, 2012). Of course, one factor behind the prevalence of this mood disorder is the inclusiveness of the US Diagnostic Statistic Manual's diagnostic criteria (Giraldi, 2017; Whitaker, 2010). There has been much authoritative criticism of their failure to differentiate between healthy responses to social stressors and pathological conditions that require medical attention (Frances, 2014; Horwitz & Wakefield, 2012).There are many mentally healthy subjects who have probably been identified as having a mental disorder because of a significant but non-pathological mood change, and they may benefit from an intervention that gives them new and more effective tools to cope with stressful life events.

It is also important to note that stress is not necessarily detrimental to health and wellbeing. Only prolonged exposure to stressful or unpleasant conditions generally leads to negative reactions. The term '*dis*tress' may be more appropriate for these specifically negative and prolonged conditions. It should also be noted that conditions that cause distress in some subjects may be positive and pleasurable to others. Instead of potentially harming health, they could actually improve it. This positive influence has sometimes been termed '*eu*stress' (McLean, 2010; Ohayashi & Yamada, 2012).

Over the course of the 1970s, Benson developed his "relaxation response" as an answer to the stressful life common in America at the time. He was critical of the idea of reframing meditation as a simple health practice. Kabat-Zinn called his new programme MBSR, but, unlike Benson, he didn't believe the medical language of stress reduction captured the complexity of what he intended to do for his patients. He did, however, accept the need to medicalise—at least in part—what he was devising.

MBSR was not just a stress-reduction programme, at least not in the sense that Benson had proposed, and was instead a melding of various different meditative traditions. MBSR was a therapeutic practice targeted at laypeople whose problems, at least in part, were the result of excessive self-critical rumination. For Kabat-Zinn, the suffering associated with illness was the result of one's attitude to one's condition. If this could be improved through practices that involved accepting individual experience without reaction or judgement, it might lead to the alleviation of various symptoms—especially pain and anxiety. In the end, patients might still need medical management, but they could be relieved of the mental suffering of anxiety, excessive self-criticism and judgment. They might also find themselves mentally transformed in ways that allowed them to cope more effectively with their infirmities (Harrington & Dunne, 2015).

In 2003, Kabat-Zinn published a commentary in the Journal of the American Psychological Association that reflected on the past, present and future of mindfulness-based interventions (Kabat-Zinn, 2003). It accompanied a review by Baer of a number of investigations into the clinical effectiveness of MBSR for patients with a wide range of medical conditions (Baer, 2006). Kabat-Zinn is particularly concerned with the study his group carried out into the use of MBSR as part of the treatment of patients with psoriasis (Kabat-Zinn et al., 1998). He particularly focuses on this study despite the fact that many others have already been published and reviewed by Baer. In his words:

> In the psoriasis study we asked if mindfulness could influence a healing process that we could see and photograph in people with a skin disease that has a strong relationship with psychological stress, namely, psoriasis. Thirty-seven patients with moderate to severe psoriasis who were candidates for treatment with phototherapy (UVB) or photochemotherapy (PUVA) were randomized into two groups. One group (meditators) followed guided mindfulness meditation instructions delivered by audiotape during their ultraviolet (UV) treatments (either PUVA or UVB) on a 3-times-per-week protocol. This tape included a guided visualization in which the subject visualized the ultraviolet light slowing down and then stopping the rapidly growing cells in the epidermis. The other group (usual care) received the light treatments (either PUVA or UVB) without listening to a tape. The skin status of each patient was monitored by clinic nurses at each treatment session and documented periodically by photography. The photographs were rated in terms of skin status by dermatologists blind to the identity and group assignment of the patients. These ratings were then used to validate or invalidate the nurses' necessarily unblinded ratings. A Cox proportional hazards analysis of the photographically validated data showed that the meditators' skin cleared at about 4 times the rate of the nonmeditators' (usual care group) during the 12-week study period. An earlier and smaller study also found that the meditators' skin cleared more rapidly than that of the nonmeditators. Although both studies suffer from a small sample size, the replicability of the finding suggests that the effect is real and merits further research. We cannot conclude from these observations that it is the mindfulness practice per se that is responsible for the fourfold rate of skin-clearing in the meditation cohort, although that is our hypothesis. However, the finding does lead to a number of potentially important, if currently tentative conclusions.

These results may be summarised simply: a group of 37 patients were divided into two sub-groups, where, as well as their conventional medical treatment, 19 received MBSR and 18 did not. The subjects were randomly assigned to the two experimental groups to ensure a lack of bias. The photographs of the effects were rated by dermatologists who were unaware of the different group treatments. A careful analysis of the results suggests the MBSR intervention had a significant effect. The meditators' skin cleared at about four times the rate of the non-meditators' Treated As Usual (TAU) care group during the 12-week study period.

In Kabat-Zinn's words:

> Although both studies[1] suffer from a small sample size, the replicability of the finding suggests that the effect is real and merits further research. We cannot conclude from these observations that it is the mindfulness practice per se that is responsible for the fourfold rate of skin-clearing in the meditation cohort, although that is our hypothesis.

Kabat-Zinn felt this study to be so significant that he described it in detail in his commentary. If we analyse the study in a little more detail, however, we uncover the following issues:

- It is replicated on two occasions. One is reported and one previous even smaller study is mentioned in the literature, which apparently suggested that the effect observed was real and merited further research.
- Evidence of the effect was found based on a comparison of two small patient groups (of 18 and 19 people).
- The patients in both groups recovered from their lesion suffered. The benefit of the treatment is apparently an increase in the rate at which skin heals from the psoriatic lesion.
- The patients knew whether they were receiving the intervention or not: they were *unblinded.*

[1]An earlier and smaller study also found that the meditators' skin cleared more rapidly than that of the non-meditators.

- The *blinded* dermatologists' ratings were used to validate the nurses' ***necessarily***[2] *unblinded* ratings.
  - The meditators followed guided mindfulness instructions on audiotape, which were delivered three times a week during their ultraviolet treatments. The tape included a guided visualization in which the subject visualized the ultraviolet light slowing down and then stopping the rapidly growing cells in the epidermis. The other group received the light treatments without listening to a tape. Visual imagery is a widespread intervention, which many have claimed is effective in its own right (Hall, 2006). It has not been determined how much of the reported effect was caused by meditation and how much it is attributable to guided meditation.
- Stress was not considered, and the level of stress experienced by the subjects before and after the interventions was not measured.

10 years later, Kabat-Zinn published a commentary in the Journal of the American Medical Association called *Mindfulness in Medicine*, in which he updates his definition of mindfulness, considers possible mechanisms, explores clinical applications of mindfulness and identifies the challenges to the field. He states his view again, saying:

> The relationships of mindfulness to medicine, since the original purpose of mindfulness in Buddhism—to alleviate suffering and cultivate compassion—suggests a potential role for this practice with medical patients and practitioners. Much cardiovascular disease, diabetes, cancer, and other chronic illness is caused or exacerbated by modifiable lifestyle factors, and lifestyle modification constitutes primary or ancillary treatment for most medical conditions. An aim of mindfulness practice is to take greater responsibility for one's life choices. Thus, mindfulness may promote a more participatory medicine by engaging and strengthening an individual's internal resources for optimizing health in both prevention of and recovery from illness. For intractable disease, meditative techniques that

[2] Bold italic added by the Author.

alter and refine awareness may modulate the subjective experience of pain or improve the ability to cope with pain and disability.

After reviewing the literature available on the mechanism of mindfulness, he turns his attention to its clinical applications. He recalls that pain, stress, coping, and quality of life were the first focus of medical research into mindfulness, referring to his own 1982 study. This work took descriptive data from medical patients who had been living with chronic pain for between six months and 48 years and who received MBSR in . Among the 51 participants who completed the program (88% of the 58 total enrolled), perceived pain decreased significantly, with half reporting a reduction of at least 50 per cent.

Kabat-Zinn also mentions a study of a larger number of cancer patients, some of whom were randomly assigned to a mindfulness group, while the others were put in a waiting list control group; in some of the mindfulness patients, there was a reduction in mood disturbance and the symptoms of stress. Others saw improvements in terms of accepting pain, the severity of general medical symptoms, physical functioning, and the ability to cope with daily life. There is also preliminary evidence of the effectiveness of mindfulness in alleviating the symptoms of a number of other medical conditions: depression, psoriasis, type two diabetes, sleep disturbance, attention-deficit hyperactivity disorder, obesity and over-eating. Researchers are also investigating the impact of mindfulness on pain, hypertension, myocardial ischemia, inflammatory bowel disease, human immunodeficiency virus and substance abuse.

The limitations of the research, as perceived at the time when the commentary was published, are not minor, however:

> The available research on mindfulness has major limitations, precluding any definitive assessment of effectiveness at this time. Published clinical studies frequently have small numbers of participants, lack an active control group, and include only subjective end points. Most of these studies do not adequately consider participant characteristics (making it difficult to generalize the effects to other groups), treatment methods (relating to reproducibility), study staff protocol adherence and participant skill acquisition (treatment fidelity), and relevant covariates (confounders and

mediators). Moreover, the lack of consensus about working definitions of mindfulness and other meditative practices impedes comparative studies. These limitations, although not unusual in a nascent field, need to be addressed in future research.

There is clearly an emerging gap between the extremely positive impression given by the results and the limitations of the research, which seems to affect the overall claim that mindfulness is clinically effective. Indeed, the final words of the commentary state that: "high quality, mechanism oriented studies and randomized controlled trials of mindfulness in medicine are needed." There is no reference, however, to the problem of blinding the interventions to the participants and therapists—or to the need for an appropriate placebo and actively treated controls groups (Ludwig, 2008).

Most of the limitations that emerge upon an attentive reading of the commentary are also present in many of the 29 studies included in Baer's 2003 literature review. The participants suffer from a wide range of different conditions, including: chronic pain, anxiety, depression, fibro-myalgia, psoriasis and cancer. The participants also varied and included medical patients, students and community volunteers. The number of subjects in each study ranged from 18 to 142. The assignment of the treatment group was randomised in only seven of the total 29 studies. A Treatment As Usual (TAU) control group was present in four, a Waiting List control group was present in another four and a non-meditator group was in one. There was no control group at all in 12 of the studies.

Baer's studies seem to have been chosen to provide evidence of the efficacy of MBSR according to the methodological procedures of evidence-based medicine. Nevertheless, they are characterised by a number of problems that limit the validity their conclusions. Most of their protocols do indeed include randomly selecting subjects for the control and treatment groups. They do not, however, use a blinding procedure when applying the interventions. In other words, the patients (and the staff applying the intervention) know whether they belong to the group receiving MBSR or to a control group with a different intervention or no intervention at all.

Another difficulty is the nature of the control group when the principles of evidence-based medicine are followed. Among the experimental groups, one section should be treated with an inactive *placebo* intervention, blinded to the patients as well as the staff administering the treatments and evaluating their effects—the so-called 'double blind' procedure. Together these form the double blinded 'Randomized Controlled Trial' (RCT) with a placebo control, which is considered the gold standard of modern clinical investigation. It is the procedure accepted by the scientific medical community for ascertaining the efficacy (and safety) of clinical interventions (Howick, 2011).

The authors of the studies examining mindfulness intervention evidently had difficulty organising trial protocols with appropriate control groups and placebos. This problem is not new when examining the efficacy of psychotherapies. One recent paper reviews the history and controversies associated with the use of placebos in psychotherapy, noting that unlike in the double-blinded randomised trials used in medicine, there is no such thing as *inert psychotherapy* to be used for controls (Wampold, Frost, & Yulish 2016).

Some researchers have expressed distinctly pessimistic views on this matter. One group concluded their analysis of psychotherapy and placebo studies by claiming that there is no evidence that psychotherapy is more beneficial than placebo treatment (Prioleau, Murdock, & Brody 1983). In 2010, Justman wrote in a paper that it might be vain to hope that something with as long-a history as the placebo effect might disappear from healing practices (Justman, 2010). These are the difficulties researchers face when trying to provide evidence of the efficacy of MBSR using the tools deemed necessary for studying somatic diseases and *physical* medical treatments. And these difficulties are similar to those faced by researchers attempting to assess the efficacy of any mental disorder treatments.

We shall temporarily leave aside a discussion of these problems in order to continue assessing the literature on the efficacy of MBSR and mindfulness.

A brief examination of the PubMed database suggests that a remarkable number of papers have been published and indexed since 1982 relating to the term 'mindfulness'. A search using the key word 'mindfulness' shows that 95 papers were published before 2003. Between 2004 and 2018, however, this number rose to a staggering 5845. The combination of 'mindfulness' and 'meditation' as keywords gives a figure of 48 before 2003, and 1718 between 2004 and 2018. 'Mindfulness based stress reduction' brings up 28 and 871 respectively. It should, of course, be noted that there is a certain degree of overlap in these papers. The numbers are nevertheless impressive, and include clinical studies that report that there are both physical and mental benefits to mindfulness in a range of different patient categories, as well as in healthy adults and children.

In 2016, Cresswell conducted a review of this vast literature. In it, he observes the remarkable increase in the number of randomised controlled trials (RCTs) of mindfulness interventions over the preceding two decades (Creswell, 2017). His review evaluates the growing body of evidence about the effects of mindfulness interventions on health, cognitive, affective and interpersonal outcomes. He also examines the applications of mindfulness for the workplace, the military and schools. As well as the applications of mindfulness, Cresswell also considers its psychological and neurobiological mechanisms, its dosage and its potential risks. There is also an assessment of how the methodology of mindfulness interventions could be improved for better results in areas such as chronic pain, depression relapses and addiction. Finally, Cresswell is also aware of and discusses the challenges of researching the community applications of mindfulness.

Cresswell writes in his review that in terms of physical health effects:

> Several large RCTs provide evidence that mindfulness interventions improve chronic pain management relative to TAU, with some initial evidence that mindfulness interventions may be superior to some active treatments (support groups, health education programs) but not to other treatments (CBT). There is also promising initial evidence that mindfulness interventions may reduce immune markers of proinflammation among stressed individuals and buffer declines in CD4+T lymphocytes in HIV-infected adults, although large well-controlled trials are needed to evaluate the links between mindfulness and immunity. Mindfulness interventions may reduce symptoms and improve quality of life across a broad

range of stress-related conditions (e.g., fibromyalgia, IBS, breast cancer, psoriasis).

For mental health effects:

Strong RCT evidence indicates that mindfulness interventions reduce depression relapse rates in at-risk individuals and improve the treatment of drug addiction. Specifically, multiple large RCTs indicate that MBCT reliably reduces the risk of depression relapse during follow-up periods among at-risk individuals and that MBRP (relative to standard relapse prevention programs) improves substance abuse outcomes. There are also several well-controlled studies showing that mindfulness interventions can reduce anxiety, depression, and PTSD symptomatology. In the mindfulness interventions literature, the research on mental health outcomes has made the most progress in comparing mindfulness interventions to other gold-standard clinical treatments, and there are some initial suggestions of contexts in which mindfulness interventions offer similar or additional long-term benefits compared to gold standard treatments (e.g., antidepressant medication, relapse prevention programs, CBT).

Cresswell also considers the question of control groups:

It is important to consider the comparison groups used in RCT studies of mindfulness interventions, and most published mindfulness intervention RCTs use TAU or wait-list controlled comparison groups. These studies provide a valuable initial evaluation of whether mindfulness interventions have an impact on outcomes above and beyond standard care or no treatment. Researchers have made impressive efforts to develop active treatment comparison programs that control for non-mindfulness-specific treatment factors (e.g., group support, home practice exercises, relaxation, placebo expectancies). These programs provide opportunities to evaluate whether mindfulness interventions have unique treatment effects above and beyond non-mindfulness-specific factors and whether mindfulness interventions can outperform gold-standard active pharmacological or behavioural treatments.

In terms of cognitive and affective outcomes, Cresswell notes:

> Among healthy young adult samples, mounting RCT evidence indicates that mindfulness interventions can improve attention-related outcomes (e.g., sustained attention, working memory) and affective outcomes (e.g., reducing rumination). (Creswell, 2017)

There are a number of other interesting subjects to consider in the review. The dosing, for example, seems to be an important matter: i.e. the amount of mindfulness practice that is necessary to see benefits and how dependent the effects are on the dose. It seems that there is a dose-response relationship in mindfulness interventions, whereby greater doses of mindfulness produce larger, scalable effects over the course of an eight-week treatment. Cresswell also examines the risks of mindfulness intervention, which are certainly present since it is not uncommon for participants to report a range of unpleasant reactions such as agitation, anxiety, discomfort or confusion. There have been even more adverse effects among patients who have suffered traumatic experiences or are at risk of psychosis or seizures. Some studies have also suggested that severe adverse reactions occur more frequently in more intensive mindfulness programmes. Among conventional eight-week programmes, however, evidence-based research suggests there is less of a risk of significant adverse effects.

Finally, the review also considers the explosion of internet- and smartphone-based mindfulness programmes that has hit the market in the last few years. These mindfulness intervention programmes have the tremendous advantage that they are inexpensive, portable and are more accessible for harder-to-reach populations. Given that so many people are using these programmes without a well-trained mindfulness teacher, however, there are serious questions that need answering about their safety and efficacy. There has been no rigorous research into their effectiveness compared to in-person, group-based mindfulness programmes, but initial studies do suggest they may have some positive effects for users (Creswell, 2017).

Kabat-Zinn's optimism and confidence in the medical effectiveness of mindfulness interventions was, at first, supported by little evidence. His work induced remarkable enthusiasm in many researchers and instigated a great many articles about the results of their work. The many published works about mindfulness interventions provided more and more evidence of its efficacy, and this became progressively more concrete as evidence-based medicine called for evermore rigorous protocols and RCT clinical trials. Cresswell's review offers a detailed examination of the best evidence available in 2017. It is, of course, a predominantly *psychological* perspective because of the author's own background and its publication in the Annual Review of Psychology.

The medical community was also aware of the phenomenon of mindfulness. Many reports on the subject have been published in medical journals, and one example worth considering comes from the *Journal of the American Medical Association's Medical News & Perspectives.* In it, an article called *Exploring the Promise of Mindfulness as Medicine* examines the reasons for the growing prominence of mindfulness and puts the practice under the microscope. It particularly examines the challenges of studying mindfulness as its practical applications. It raises the notion that physicians often do not accept mindfulness not only because of questions about its efficacy, but also because of economic considerations and personal views. It concludes:

> Whether physicians choose to recommend mindfulness practices to their patients may ultimately depend not just on accessibility, but on their willingness to incorporate mindfulness approaches into their clinical toolbox that are supported by the evidence base. (Buchholz, 2015)

Most of the reports published on the subject use the powerful tool of meta-analysis, which is the best possible way of analysing the evidence of the effectiveness of mindfulness interventions. It should be noted, however, that the results of meta-analysis may depend on the methods used, and particularly on the criteria for including or excluding studies.

Two large studies deserve consideration here. One is a 2014 study of meditation programmes and the other is a 2015 examination of mindfulness-based interventions. The 2014 study was carried out by researchers at Johns Hopkins University with the aim of determining how effective meditation programmes were at improving stress-related outcomes (anxiety, depression, stress/distress, positive moods, mental health–related quality of life, attention, substance use, eating habits, sleep, pain, and weight). The meta-analysis, after reviewing 18,753 publications, was made using 47 trials that included a total of 3515 participants. The results offer some evidence that mindfulness meditation programmes attenuate the symptoms of anxiety, depression and pain. The study, however, found that there was limited evidence that meditation improved stress/distress and mental health–related quality of life. Little or no evidence was found that meditation programmes affected positive mood, attention, substance use, eating habits, sleep and weight. No evidence was found that meditation programmes were better than active treatment (such as drugs, exercise, and other behavioural therapies). The authors concluded that meditation programmes can have a small to moderate effect on a number of the negative aspects of psychological stress, and that better studies will need to be designed to determine whether they can improve mental health and stress-related behaviour (Goyal et al., 2014).

The 2015 article was an overview of the systematic reviews and RCT meta-analysis available on how mindfulness-based therapies can be used to treat and prevent a range of common chronic conditions. The authors noted that one of the main reasons for the study is the fact that despite the growing prevalence of MBSR and MBCT, there is still much debate about the evidence of their efficacy. The aim of the study was therefore to provide a systematic overview of the effectiveness of MBSR and MBCT in different patient populations. A survey and meta-analysis of all the available RCT systematic reviews found 187. Of these, 23 were included, covering 115 unique RCTs and a total of 8683 unique subjects with various conditions. The results suggest that compared to Waiting List control groups and TAU groups, MBSR and MBCT significantly improve the symptoms of depression, anxiety, stress, quality of life and physical functioning.

There are significant limitations to many of the studies considered, including heterogeneity within patient categories, the risk of publication bias and limited long-term follow-up. Overall, the authors concluded that the available evidence justifies the use of MBSR and MBCT to alleviate both mental and physical symptoms during the treatment of cancer, cardiovascular disease, chronic pain, depression, anxiety disorders and to prevent a range of conditions in healthy adults and children (Gotink et al., 2015).

The positive results of the meta-analyses are based on the available studies, and therefore depend on the quality of the methodology used in them. There is ongoing concern about the methodological quality of research into the efficacy of mindfulness. At present MBSR is commonly used to manage the stress associated with chronic illness, as well as for treating some psychiatric conditions. Claims about its efficacy may, however, be exaggerated because the published literature was found to be "rife with methodological problems". The concerns include a lack of active comparison groups (which could allow the evaluation of non-specific benefits such as social support), as well as controls for time and attention, relatively little follow-up assessment of outcomes and little measurement of response set biases (social desirability, for example) (Bishop, 2002).

Treatment As Usual controls were used in many instances. Although these account for changes because of the passage of time, active control groups are needed to counteract the influence of non-specific factors such as demand characteristics and placebo effects. Moreover, in many of the trials, mindfulness is compared with other treatments such as cognitive behavioural psychotherapy and small sample sizes are used. Methodological concerns are therefore valid and continue to be voiced. The difficulty of introducing the vital double-blind placebo-controlled design has also not yet been resolved. What is more, researchers are still not paying enough attention to treatment fidelity, instructor training, instructor credibility and the idea of including *intent-to-treat* (ITT) analysis in the trial protocols (Baer, 2006; Bishop, 2002).

A systematic review of the methodology of mindfulness research reveals that in the 142 studies published between 2000 and 2016, there is no evidence of an overall increase in any study quality indicator. This is despite the fact that most changes in this time have been aimed at improving quality. If the sample is restricted to Europe and North America (the continents with the longest history of scientific research in this area), there is, however, an increase in the number of reported ITT analyses (Goldberg et al., 2017). Taken together, these findings suggest that few have adopted the recommendations for methodological improvement voiced repeatedly in the literature. As a result of these limitations, it may be that the mindfulness-based therapy trials with statistically significant results overstate the reality (Coronado-Montoya et al., 2016; Davidson & Kaszniak, 2015).

Mindfulness therapeutic programs have moved from the margins to the mainstream of clinical practice and continue to grow in popularity. Today, they are even being used outside the basic applications considered above. Among the many studies available, there are now some examining the reported positive effects of mindfulness in a wide range of clinical settings. These include pain relief, eating disorders, weight loss, stress-reduction, performance anxiety, relationship problems, symptoms of depression, post-traumatic stress disorder, obsessive–compulsive disorder and suicidal tendencies. Schools are starting to explore the possibility of offering mindfulness training to students. Even the military is taking a growing interest in the practice. Increasingly, mindfulness training is being combined with other interventions such as cognitive–behavioural therapy, counselling and psychotherapy, as well as other kinds of meditative practice like loving-kindness (Wilson, 2014).

Dimidjan and Segal have examined the idea of a clinical science of mindfulness-based interventions (MBI), considering the possibility that science and the practice of MBI might be at a crossroads. MBIs have grown enormously in prominence and popularity, with the establishment of many research and clinical centres dedicated to their study and delivery. There have also been many new academic journals, magazines and books on the subject.

Dimidian and Zindel, however, suggest that the time might be right for a pause in the movement to reflect on the durability and health impact of MBIs. They suggest evaluating them in the broader framework of clinical psychological science along the lines of the stage model recently proposed by the National Institutes of Health (NIH) (Onken, Carroll, Shoham, Cuthbert, & Riddle, 2014). The authors first propose using the NIH stage model as a map for organising the MBI evidence base. The reports in the NIH database addressing a specific 'target problem or population' are grouped in a 'Basic Stage 0', which is comprised of 'Stage I:Intervention generation/refinement' and 'Stage II: Efficacy in research clinic'. 'Stage II' includes 'Waitlist or treatment-as-usual control', and 'Active control'. There is also 'Stage III: efficacy in community clinic', 'Stage IV: Effectiveness', and 'Stage V: Implementation and dissemination'. The results obtained using this system suggest that only a small proportion of the trials in the database include active controls and an adequate evaluation of effectiveness, implementation and dissemination.

The authors therefore offer a series of recommendations, such as: attend to the basics, do not conflate promise with efficacy, engage with the thorny question of clinician training, get specific about the effects of MBI and beware of developing orphan innovation. The general conclusion of the investigation is that the field is moving in the direction outlined in the recommendations. More studies are therefore starting to incorporate active control conditions that can better determine efficacy. Dissemination and implementation, as well as studies of effectiveness, are more common. Studies of this kind may now start to avoid the limitations of repeated studies that have simply led to the accumulation of more and more of the same kind of observations without addressing the gaps in the existing research (Dimidjian & Segal, 2015).

Bright and curious pioneers first developed the idea of using meditation and similar practices to treat existential suffering and the various mental and bodily conditions afflicting humankind. After many years of refinement, this has even led to them being included in a range of different medical interventions.

Much work has gone into this field. In fact, there is now so much literature available on the matter that it is not possible to examine it all in detail here. Although the claims that mindfulness interventions can treat a huge range of human problems show the limitations of the research into this area, great progress has been made. It should also not be forgotten that significant limitations are inevitable when attempting to assess the efficacy of therapeutic interventions. These difficulties are ingrained into the process of defining a disease in order to recruit patients onto clinical trials connected with it. There are also always difficulties when setting criteria for evaluating the outcomes of treatments. These difficulties arise with clinical investigations into treatments for somatic diseases, but they are much harder to deal with in the field of psychiatry and psychotherapy. One key issue is the nature and definition of mental disease, as well as the corresponding problem of defining the appropriate outcome of a therapeutic intervention. Even more difficult is the problem of organising an adequate placebo control group for a pscychotherapeutic intervention.

It would now be wise to examine some practical examples. The next chapter will therefore focus on how MBI were developed in the UK and USA, and the challenges researchers faced when trying to design studies to assess their efficacy.

## References


Aflalo, A., & Price, A. (2005). *The failed assassination of psychoanalysis*. London: Karnac.

Baer, R. A. (2006). Mindfulness training as a clinical intervention: A conceptual and empirical review. *Clinical Psychology: Science and Practice, 10*(2), 125–143. https://doi.org/10.1093/clipsy.bpg015.

Bishop, S. (2002). What do we really know about mindfulness-based stress reduction? *Psychosomatic Medicine, 64*(1), 71–83. https://doi.org/10.1097/00006842-200201000-00010.

Bogart, G. (1991). The use of meditation in psychotherapy: A review of the literature. *American Journal of Psychotherapy, 45*(3), 383–412. https://doi.org/10.1176/appi.psychotherapy.1991.45.3.383.

Buchholz, L. (2015). Exploring the promise of mindfulness as medicine. *JAMA, 314*(13), 1327. https://doi.org/10.1001/jama.2015.7023.

Coronado-Montoya, S., Levis, A., Kwakkenbos, L., Steele, R., Turner, E., & Thombs, B. (2016). Reporting of positive results in randomized controlled trials of mindfulness-based mental health interventions. *PLoS One, 11*(4), e0153220. https://doi.org/10.1371/journal.pone.0153220.

Creswell, J. D. (2017). Mindfulness interventions. *Annual Review of Psychology, 68*(1), 491–516.

Davidson, R., & Kaszniak, A. (2015). Conceptual and methodological issues in research on mindfulness and meditation. *American Psychologist, 70*(7), 581–592. https://doi.org/10.1037/a0039512.

Dimidjian, S., & Segal, Z. (2015). Prospects for a clinical science of mindfulness-based intervention. *American Psychologist, 70*(7), 593–620. https://doi.org/10.1037/a0039589.

Frances, A. (2014). *Saving normal.* New York: William Morrow.
Giraldi, T. (2017). *Unhappiness, sadness and 'depression'.* Cham: Springer.
Goldberg, S., Tucker, R., Greene, P., Simpson, T., Kearney, D., & Davidson, R. (2017). Is mindfulness research methodology improving over time? A systematic review. *PLoS One, 12*(10), e0187298. https://doi.org/10.1371/journal.pone.0187298.
Gotink, R., Chu, P., Busschbach, J., Benson, H., Fricchione, G., & Hunink, M. (2015). Standardised mindfulness-based interventions in healthcare: An overview of systematic reviews and meta-analyses of RCTs. *PLoS One, 10*(4), e0124344. https://doi.org/10.1371/journal.pone.0124344.
Goyal, M., Singh, S., Sibinga, E., Gould, N., Rowland-Seymour, A., Sharma, R., et al. (2014). Meditation programs for psychological stress and well-being. *JAMA Internal Medicine, 174*(3), 357. https://doi.org/10.1001/jamainternmed.2013.13018.
Hall, E. (2006). *Guided imagery.* London: Sage.
Harrington, A., & Dunne, J. D. (2015). When mindfulness is therapy: Ethical qualms, historical perspectives. *American Psychologist, 70*(7), 621–631.
Hickey, W. (2010). Meditation as medicine: A critique. *Crosscurrents, 60*(2), 168–184. https://doi.org/10.1111/j.1939-3881.2010.00118.x.
Holmes, T. H., & Rahe, R. H. (1967). The social readjustment rating scale. *Journal of Psychosomatic Research, 11*(2), 213–218.
Horwitz, A., & Wakefield, J. (2012). *The loss of sadness.* Oxford: Oxford University Press.
Howick, J. (2011). *The philosophy of evidence-based medicine.* Chichester, West Sussex, UK: Wiley-Blackwell, BMJ Books.
Justman, S. (2010). From medicine to psychotherapy: The placebo effect. *History of the Human Sciences, 24*(1), 95–107. https://doi.org/10.1177/0952695110386655.
Kabat-Zinn, J. (2003). Mindfulness-based interventions in context: Past, present, and future. *Clinical Psychology: Science and Practice, 10*(2), 144–156. https://doi.org/10.1093/clipsy/bpg016.
Kabat-Zinn, J., Wheeler, E., Light, T., Skillings, A., Scharf, M., Cropley, T., et al. (1998). Influence of a mindfulness meditation-based stress reduction intervention on rates of skin clearing in patients with moderate to severe psoriasis undergoing photo therapy (UVB) and photochemotherapy (PUVA). *Psychosomatic Medicine, 60*(5), 625–632. https://doi.org/10.1097/00006842-199809000-00020.
Le Fanu, J. (2014). *The rise and fall of modern medicine.* London: Abacus.

Lieberman, J. A., & Ogas, O. (2015). *Shrinks: The untold story of psychiatry*. New York: Little, Brown.

Ludwig, D. (2008). Mindfulness in medicine. *JAMA, 300*(11), 1350. https://doi.org/10.1001/jama.300.11.1350.

Magid, B. (2002). *Ordinary mind: Exploring the common grounds of zen and psychoanalysis*. Boston: Wisdom Publications.

McLean, J. (2010). *Psychological eustress: An exploratory regulated process*. Saarbrücken: VDM Verlag Dr. Müller.

Moncayo, R. (2012). *The signifier pointing at the moon*. London: Karnac.

Ohayashi, H., & Yamada, S. (2012). *Psychological distress*. New York: Nova Science.

Onken, L. S., Carroll, K. M., Shoham, V., Cuthbert, B. N., & Riddle, M. (2014). Reenvisioning clinical science: Unifying the discipline to improve the public health. *Clinical Psychological Science, 2*, 22–34. https://doi.org/10.1177/2167702613497932.

Ospina, M. B. et al. (2007, June). *Evidence report/technology assessment number 155 meditation practices for health: State of the research*. AHRQ Publication No. 07-E010. Retrieved from https://archive.ahrq.gov/downloads/pub/evidence/pdf/meditation/medit.pdf. Accessed 16 April 2019.

Paykel, E. (1969). Life events and depression. *Archives of General Psychiatry, 21*(6), 753. https://doi.org/10.1001/archpsyc.1969.01740240113014.

Paykel, E. S., Prusoff, B. A., & Uhlenhuth, E. H. (1971). Scaling of life events. *Archives of General Psychiatry, 25*(4), 340–347.

Prioleau, L., Murdock, M., & Brody, N. (1983). An analysis of psychotherapy versus placebo studies. *Behavioral and Brain Sciences, 6*(2), 275–310. https://doi.org/10.1017/S0140525X00015867.

Rägo, L., & Santoso, B. (2008). Drug regulation: History, present and future. In C. Boxtel, I. Edwards, & B. Santoso (Eds.), *Drug benefits and risks: International textbook of clinical pharmacology*. Amsterdam: IOS Press.

Sapolsky, R. (2004). *Why zebras don't get ulcers*. New York: Henry Holt.

Selye, H. (1956). *The stress of life*. New York: McGraw-Hill.

Shorter, E. (2005). *A historical dictionary of psychiatry*. New York: Oxford University Press.

Shorter, E. (2015). *What psychiatry left out of the DSM-5*. New York: Routledge.

Wampold, B. E., Frost, N. D., & Yulish, N. E. (2016). Placebo effects in psychotherapy: A flawed concept and a contorted history. *Psychology of Consciousness: Theory, Research, and Practice, 3*(2), 108–120. https://doi.org/10.1037/cns0000045.

Whitaker, R. (2010). *Anatomy of an epidemic*. New York: Broadway.
Wilson, J. (2014). *Mindful America: The mutual transformation of Buddhism meditation and American culture.* Oxford, USA: Oxford University Press.
World Federation for Mental Health. (2012). *Depression: A global crisis world mental health day.* https://www.who.int/mental_health/management/depression/wfmh_paper_depression_wmhd_2012.pdf.

# 6

# The Marketing of Mindfulness in Great Britain and the United States

Kabat-Zinn is one of the key figures in the establishment of the mindfulness movement in the West. He endowed it with many of the key features that it still retains to this day. To examine how mindfulness came to its current form in the West, it may be useful to consider some of the other early leading lights of the mindfulness movement in the USA.

This is not easy to summarise in a limited space, since it involves engaging with a rich, complex and turbulent world—a world of radical changes connected with the counter-culture movement on the west coast of the USA in the 1960s. Two particularly popular subjects across the counter-culture were altered states of consciousness and experiments with psychedelic and hallucinogenic drugs (Grunenberg & Harris, 2007). Buddhism, with its Eastern associations and consciousness-altering practices, could hardly avoid getting caught up in this movement. The Theravada Hinayana and the Vietnamese Zen traditions attracted most attention in the West, and it was the doctrines and practices of these Buddhist traditions that provided the initial inspiration for mindfulness. If you are interested in following the history of the people and institutions involved in this in detail, you will find rich a rich and vivid



T. Giraldi, *Psychotherapy, Mindfulness and Buddhist Meditation*,
https://doi.org/10.1007/978-3-030-29003-0_6

description in *How the Swans Came to the Lake: A Narrative History of Buddhism in America*, published in 1999 by Rick Fields. Jeff Wilson's 2014 book *Mindful America* also covers more recent developments in Buddhism and mindfulness in great detail (Wilson, 2014).

One early pioneer in the USA was Chogyam Trungpa, one of the best-known Buddhist teachers in America in the seventies (Mukpo & Gimian, 2008). As well as his work, he was also famous for his charisma, which helped to spark the counter-culture's interest in Eastern spirituality. Unfortunately, an element of this was certain excesses such as drunkenness, womanising and his regular requests for royalties. In 1975, he went on to found an organisation called the Naropa Institute, which attracted many noted intellectuals of the time, including Allen Ginsberg and John Cage. Jack Cornfeld, Joseph Goldstein and Sharon Salzberg were also followers of Chogyam Trungpa, and founded the Insight Meditation Society (IMS). In 1988, Kornfeld also founded the Spirit Rock Meditation Centre.

These initiatives were mainly inspired by Therevada Buddhism and its more modernised approach. They were also made possible thanks to the availability of Asian teachers with authentic Buddhist training. It is worth mentioning that the Spirit Rock Meditation Centre was also open to the teachings of other traditions, and soon began to assimilate Western psychology into the study and practice of Buddhist mindfulness. This was stimulated by Kornfeld, who had a Ph.D. in psychology and later brought in other teachers from the worlds of psychology and psychotherapy ("Chögyam Trungpa—Shambhala", 2019; MacLean, 2016; Minds, 2019; Wilson, 2014).

Thich Nhat Hanh is someone else who played a vital part in the rooting of Buddhism and Buddhist meditation in Western culture. Thich Nhat Hanh was born and raised in Vietnam, where as a young monk he was fully trained and authorised to teach Vietnamese Zen. Thich Nhat Hanh later became very familiar with Western society and culture when he came to live in the USA. In 1961, he was appointed as a teacher of religion at Princeton University. From there, he went on to become a lecturer in Buddhism at Columbia University.

Thich Nhat Hanh was deeply concerned by the Vietnam war, and gained a great fame as a peace activist supporting non-violent peace efforts. At the end of the war, he was exiled from his native country, Vietnam, and established himself in the West permanently. From there, he travelled widely and began to teach Buddhism and meditation all around the world, particularly emphasising the social engagement aspects of mindfulness.

Thich Nhat Hanh belongs to the Thien Vietnamese lineage, which retains most of the characteristics of Japanese Zen, but is also influenced by the Therevada tradition ("Thich Nhat Hanh", 2019). This is relevant because, throughout his teachings on mindfulness, Thich Nhat Hanh has always emphasises the contents of the *Satipatthana Sutta*, one of the core texts of Theravada Buddhism as well as a guiding influence on *vipassana* meditation practices (Nyanaponika, 1996). According to Thich Nhat Hanh, the *Five Mindfulness Trainings* are among the best concrete ways to practise mindfulness. For him, this is because as they are non-sectarian, they can be universal—truly compassionate and understanding. According to Thich Nhat Hanh, all spiritual traditions have their equivalent to the *Five Mindfulness Trainings*. The first of these is to protect life, to decrease violence in oneself, in the family and in society. The second is to practise social justice, generosity, not stealing and not exploiting other living beings. The third is practising responsible sexual behaviour to protect individuals, couples, families and children. The fourth is deep listening and loving speech to restore communication and reconcile with people. The fifth is mindful consumption, to stop oneself from bringing toxins and poisons into the mind and body (Hạnh, 2009).

Thich Nhat Hanh's teachings proved to be remarkably attractive to many Westerners, and this audience came to form one of the most extensive modern movements inspired by Buddhism and mindfulness. In 1966 Thich Nhat Hanh created the *Order of Interbeing*, the forerunner of the *Plum Village Monastery*, which was founded in the south of France in 1982. When the first Plum Village was founded, members of the movement were beginning to use terms such as 'engaged buddhism', 'interbeing' and 'mindfulness', terms that were destined to become extremely popular and widespread and help recruit many more to the movement. Some were even inspired by Thich Nhat Hanh's teachings to take up a monastic life and join the Plum Villages either as lay devotees or monks and nuns.

From the original Plum Village, the movement sprouted many more, until today there are now 589 monks and nuns, 9 monasteries and 1271 practising communities around the world. Thich Nhat Hanh's followers of were inspired not only by his direct teachings but also by his extensive collection of writings ("Thich Nhat Hanh, 2019"; "Thich Nhat Hanh—Buddhism—Oxford Bibliographies—Obo", 2019). Life in the Plum Villages is also effectively portrayed in a fascinating and profound 2017 documentary featuring Thich Nhat Hanh and his initiatives ("Walk with Me [2017]—IMDb", 2019). It is therefore not surprising that Thich Nhat Hanh has gained great popularity—such popularity that he is now one of the most important figures in Western Buddhism, along with that other remarkable personality, Tenzin Gyatso, the 14th Dalai Lama.

It was against this background that Kabat-Zinn first encountered Buddhism and meditation, moving from a family of intellectuals and academics into his own academic career. In 1971, he completed a Ph.D. in molecular biology at the *Massachusetts Institute of Technology* (MIT), where he studied under Salvador Luria, a Nobel Laureate in medicine. Kabat-Zinn was first introduced to meditation by Philip Kapleau, a Zen missionary who came to speak at MIT while Kabat-Zinn was a student. From there, he went on to study meditation with other Buddhist teachers such as Thich Nhat Hanh and Seungsahn Haengwon. Seungsahn was one of the first Korean Zen masters to settle in the United States. He was well-known for his charismatic style and direct explanations of Zen, which translated well to Western audiences (Ford, 2006).

Kabat-Zinn was also actively involved in the *IMS*, and eventually taught there. It was here that he first developed the initiatives that would go on to form the basis of mindfulness as we know it today.

In the USA, there were also a number of other people, initiatives and institutions that made major contributions to the rise of mindfulness. One of these was Richard J. Davidson, a neuroscientist specialising in the brain substrates of emotion and of affective disorders, including depression and anxiety. In his studies, he applied modern neuroscience techniques such as quantitative electrophysiology, positron emission tomography and functional magnetic resonance (f-MRI)imaging. He used them to study the neural bases of emotion and emotional styles, as well as methods to human flourishing, including meditation and other contemplative practices (Minds, 2019).

In his autobiography, Davidson mentions that he was the founder and director of the *Center for Healthy Minds* at the University of Wisconsin Madison, and suggests that he is best-known for his ground-breaking studies of emotion and the brain. A friend and confidante of the Dalai Lama, he was also appointed as an expert for the *World Economic Forum*, where he served on the *Global Council on Mental Health*. Then, in 2006, he was named by Time Magazine as one of "The 100 Most Influential People in the World". Among his many publications, he also co-wrote *Altered Traits: Science Reveals How Meditation Changes Your Mind, Brain, and Body* (Goleman & Davidson, 2017) with author and science journalist Daniel Goleman.

Davidson's initiatives were particularly prominent and successful because he often worked on them with other well-known personalities in the field. Francisco Javier Varela García (1946–2001), for example, was a Chilean biologist, philosopher, and neuroscientist who, together with his teacher Humberto Maturana, is known for introducing the concept of 'autopoiesis' to biology. Varela encountered Tibetan Buddhism in the 1970s, initially studying with the meditation master Chögyam Trungpa Rinpoche. In 1987, Varela, along with R. Adam Engle, founded the *Mind and Life Institute*, which is now sponsoring a series of dialogues between scientists and the Dalai Lama about the relationship between science and Buddhism. They will no doubt make vital contributions to the development of mindfulness (Francisco J. Varela: 1946–2001, 2019).

Another important figure in the movement is R. Adam Engle, an American social entrepreneur who co-founded the *Mind and Life Institute* in 1990. In later years, he also became chief executive of the Institute and helped to establish contemplative science as a new field of research (Begley, 2009). Engle was also one of the organisers of the *Mind and Life Dialogues*, which were the forerunners of others run by the *Mind and Life Institute*. Apparently, his inspiration for the dialogues was hearing that the 14th Dalai Lama, Tenzin Gyatso, had an interest in modern science. The Dalai Lama then accepted Engle's invitation to a series of dialogues with various modern scientists. Around the same time, Varela also participated on a conference on consciousness with the Dalai Lama. Like Engle, he was a Buddhist devotee interested in further exploring the relationship between science and Buddhism (Wallace, 2007).

Tenzin Gyatso, the 14th Dalai Lama, is an extraordinary figure. During the 1959 Tibetan uprising, he fled to India, where he still lives as a refugee. By 1989, he had received the Nobel Peace Prize. He has travelled the world and spoken about the welfare of Tibetans, the environment, economics, women's rights, non-violence, interfaith dialogue, physics, astronomy, Buddhism and science, cognitive neuroscience, reproductive health, sexuality, as well as many topics to do with Mahayana and Vajrayana Buddhist teachings. Since his childhood in Lhasa, Tibet, The Dalai Lama has had a lifelong interest in science and technology. This began with his fascination with repairing, disassembling and reassembling mechanical objects like clocks, watches, telescopes, film projectors, clockwork soldiers and motor cars.

As a child, looking at the moon through his telescope, the young Tenzin Gyatso was shocked to observe that it was not a heavenly body emitting its own light as Tibetan cosmologists had taught him, but a crater-pocked lump of rock. He has said that if he had not been raised as a monk, he would probably have become an engineer. On his first trip to the West in 1973, he asked to visit Cambridge University's astrophysics department in the UK. There, he sought out renowned scientists such as Sir Karl Popper, David Bohm and Carl Friedrich von Weizsäcker, who taught him the basics of science. The Dalai Lama believes that there is important common ground between science and Buddhism in that both seek to challenge dogma with empirical evidence (Dalai Lama: Brief Biography, 2019; Dalai Lama: Investigating the Mind, 2019).

Engle organised the original *Mind and Life Dialogue* in October 1987, at the Dalai Lama's residence in Dharamshala. It was a week-long event in which six scientists, including Varela, as well as two interpreters and the Dalai Lama himself, spent five hours each day sharing their views and discussing the sciences of the mind. At the end, Engle asked the Dalai Lama if he wanted to do it again. The answer was "yes," and the series of dialogues was born. The second dialogue was a two-day event in October 1989, and at the third dialogue, held in Dharamsala in 1990, it was decided that the *Mind and Life Institute* should be incorporated as a non-profit organization in the USA. Engle was elected Chair and CEO, a post he held for 22 years until his retirement in 2012. In that time, he guided its development into "a worldwide and influential organization bringing together the highest standards of modern science and contemplative practice".

By 1998 *Mind & Life* had hosted seven dialogues between numerous world-renowned scientists, philosophers and the Dalai Lama on cognitive neuroscience and physics. In 2005, *Mind & Life* held its second public dialogue in Washington, DC, entitled *The Science and Clinical Applications of Meditation.* By 2013, there had been 27 dialogues with the Dalai Lama, as well as 11 books on the first 13 dialogues, plus a range of DVDs, videos and other books (Engle, 2008; Fields, 1992; "Mind & Life Dialogues—Mind & Life Institute", 2019; Wallace, 2007).

There are also interesting contributions in this area from Daniel Goleman, an author and science journalist. As well as a number of books on emotional intelligence, Goleman has also written about meditation (Goleman, 1977, 2015) and the Dalai Lama's vision for the future. He has also co-authored a book with Richard Davidson about the science of meditation, *Altered Traits: Science Reveals How Meditation Changes Your Mind, Brain, and Body* (Goleman & Davidson, 2017).

The initiatives to find common ground between Buddhism, meditation and science were not always met with enthusiasm and acceptance—even when the Dalai Lama was involved. In fact, the Dalai Lama was at the centre of a scientific row over his lecture at the annual meeting of the *Society for Neuroscience* in November 2005 in Washington, DC (Adam, 2019). The Dalai Lama was originally invited at the behest of Richard Davidson, based on the growing interest in how Buddhist meditation could affect the brain. This idea was supported by Matthieu Ricard, a Buddhist monk at the Shechenm monastery in Nepal, who had earned a Ph.D. in molecular biology from the Pasteur Institute in Paris. Numerous researchers, however, claimed the studies that had been used to support the invitation were invalid, and threatened to boycott the *Society's* meeting. They objected that it was not appropriate to have a prominent religious leader speak at a scientific event about a claim for which the scientific evidence is weak and controversial (Cyranoski, 2005; Knutson, 2019; Newberg, 2011).

Some controversies aside, however, the Dalai Lama's popularity and international renown as an enlightened thinker have helped enormously in opening up Eastern knowledge, traditions and wisdom to the West. As a result, Western neuroscience soon had access to experienced Buddhist monks who had been practising Tibetan meditation for many years, which led to many new research projects (Goleman & Davidson, 2017). In the US, people also began to take an interest in other Buddhist traditions, and to the differences between their traditional practices. Surprisingly, Zen Buddhism was hardly considered at all, despite the extraordinary interest in it after the Second World War and during the cultural revolution of the 1960s.

These early initiatives were destined to undergo various changes and transformations over the years. One new approach was to extend them neurosciences to the fields of meditation and mindfulness. Many powerful scientific techniques were soon developed and applied to this rapidly evolving scientific discipline. Many researchers, for example, began to investigate the effects of applying f-MRI as well as proton emission tomography (PET and SPECT) when applied to meditators (Newberg, D'Aquili, & Rause, 2008; Young et al., 2018). Other similar studies were based on progress in the field of molecular biology, which led to the mapping of the human genome and the study of the genetic polymorphisms responsible for individual constitutive differences (Buric, Farias, Jong, Mee, & Brazil, 2017; Hamer, 2005; Saatcioglu, 2013). The results of this research soon began to appear in books and scientific journals. New disciplines were even founded, addressing the problems that arose when new technologies were applied to biomedicine. One pertinent example of these new disciplines is 'neurotheology', an attempt to update the evidence about how science can be applied to spirituality (Newberg, 2011, 2018). Another is 'neurophilosophy', which addresses the limits of the applications of neuroscience to biomedicine (Churchland, 2014; Van Regenmortel & Hull, 2002).

These new fields were largely pioneered in the USA, where the 'science of meditation' became an important new field that was closely connected to the attempts to bring mindfulness into the realm of science. Research in this field aims to clearly define and explain the mechanism of how meditation affects the mind, brain and body, and to provide objective evidence for the effectiveness of mindfulness interventions in psychology and medicine. Through the work of Daniel Goleman and the Dalai Lama, the *Mind and Life Dialogues*, and the *Mind and Life Institute* became highly successful examples of work in this field. The results of these were published in books such as *The Science of Meditation: How to Change Your Brain, Mind and Body* (Goleman & Davidson, 2017) and *Altered Traits: Science Reveals How Meditation Changes Your Mind, Brain, and Body*, by Davidson and Goleman.

As a result of the sheer abundance of literature on the matter, it became possible to conduct a review of the science of mindfulness meditation, which was published in the authoritative journal *Nature Review Neuroscience* in 2015. The review begins with a description of the difficulties and challenges in meditation research. It then examines the changes in brain structure that were observed using imaging techniques in people who had just practised mindfulness—as well as the effects on attention, emotional regulation and self-awareness. The review ends by considering the questions still open for the future. Overall, it seems to follow a clear scientific structure, although it gives little consideration to the neurological effects of mindfulness as compared to various different meditative traditions. The abstract of the review, although unavoidably limited in length, is not particularly encouraging in terms of firm conclusions:

> Research over the past two decades broadly supports the claim that mindfulness meditation — practiced widely for the reduction of stress and promotion of health exerts beneficial effects on physical and mental health, and cognitive performance. Recent neuroimaging studies have begun to uncover the brain areas and networks that mediate these positive effects. However, the underlying neural mechanisms remain unclear, and it is apparent that more methodologically rigorous studies are required if we are to gain a full understanding of the neuronal and molecular bases of the changes in the brain that accompany mindfulness meditation. (Tang, Hölzel, & Posner, 2015)

It will is hardly surprising that respected researchers have criticised these approaches and findings. Their criticisms of the incorporation of meditation and mindfulness into neuroscience are summarised in two eloquently titled books: *Genes, Cells, and Brains: The Promethean Promises of the New Biology* and *Neuromania: On the Limits of Brain Science*. According to the sociologist Hillary Rose and the neurobiologist Steven Rose, brain scans and the decoding of the human genome can tell us who we really are. What they point out is that humans have roughly as many protein-encoding genes as a fruit fly, and that fMRI scanning is still such an inexact art that a team of satirical neuroscientists have demonstrated significant "brain activity" in a dead salmon. They express their concerns that the economic, political and social determinants of science are overlooked. The entrepreneurialisation of science is now a primary objective for many, and the policies governing science and technology actually impede rather than promote their progress (Rose & Rose, 2014).

An interesting book by Legrenzi and Umiltà examines the origins of psychology in the second half of the nineteenth century, when it starts to take precedence over philosophy as a means of studying the mind. The book argues that today, something similar is happening to psychology as it begins to be superseded by a range of new 'neuro-' prefixed disciplines. As fragments of knowledge that have been isolated from psychology and neuropsychology for decades are re-packaged as novelty new disciplines, many people are overlooking neuropsychology when it is, in fact, perfectly capable of covering most aspects of the mind's relationship with the brain. The authors conclude that if neuroscientific results were interpreted more appropriately, it would be possible to avoid the false representation of the role of biology in the mind and mind-body sciences (Legrenzi, Umiltà, & Anderson, 2014).

These concerns are not just expressed in these books: they are shared by more and more of the communities of researchers involved in the field. Technology has made it quick and affordable for scientists to examine the genome on a very large scale. Today, many so-called 'genome-wide association studies' (GWAS) have been performed. These studies have, however, attracted much criticism because their results show that it is possible to identify patterns of large numbers of genetic variants even in people with severe mental diseases, which means that they can only account for a tiny part of the risk of contracting the mental diseases in question. The 'In Focus News' recently published in *Nature* questions how far it is possible for GWAS to find useful disease links until we understand how exactly the networks of genetic variants we have discovered actually work (Callaway, 2017).

Similar concerns have been raised about the widespread use of MRI. A recent review suggests that data from MRI research is highly sensitive to common artefacts and that its findings are often inconclusive. The review suggests experts should be cautious about accepting these findings, as they may be deeply flawed and could run the risk of misinforming practitioners and patients (Weinberger & Radulescu, 2016).

These same concerns are raised about the various studies that attempt to find connections between severe mental diseases and the data produced by genomic analysis and brain imaging techniques. It is reasonable to suppose these concerns would be even more serious when the same investigative approaches are used to study more subtle and nuanced subjects such as meditation and higher mental states.

These criticisms are comparable to the charge that it is mechanically reductive to take a practice like meditation, which emerged from a spiritual ideology, transform it into a clinical intervention and reduce it to the restrictions of the world of neuroscience and biological psychiatry (Chuengsatiansup, 2003; Schreurs, 2002).

As well as its many other applications, such as *Mindfulness-Based Stress Reduction*, Kabat-Zinn also explored ways to integrate mindfulness into modern psychotherapeutic practices. This, in fact, proved to be extremely productive, and was destined to become extremely widespread.

The beginnings of psychotherapy, the 'talking cure', can be traced back to the development of psychoanalysis, which has received extensive—and deserved—cultural attention. The process of psychoanalysis being accepted by the medical community turned out to be complex and controversial.

Psychoanalysis was a radical new approach to caring for subjects suffering from mental conditions, which were seen as being 'neurotic' in origin. Neuroses were seen as functional in origin, and caused by patients' reactions to life events. A new approach to mental suffering was thus developed, based on medicine, psychology and psychiatry. It was a field in which certain mental conditions could be identified and new interventions to treat them could be developed. And, because these conditions were based on patients' reactions to life events, they came to be known as 'psychodynamic'.

Psychoanalysts rejected the idea that their theories and analytic practices could be seen as psychotherapeutic. They also rejected the empirical, objective and scientific evaluation of their procedures and results (Grünbaum, 1979; Milton & Frabricius, 2004). Despite serious criticism of the lack of scientific grounding for it (Masson, 1989), the lack of effective medical interventions in psychiatry led to the integration of psychoanalytic procedures into the field (Milton & Frabricius, 2004). Psychoanalytic practices were dominant in psychiatry—especially in the USA—until the late 1950s and early 60s, when new families of effective psychotropic drugs were discovered. These were capable of alleviating the symptoms of even the most serious mental disorders. These discoveries of were destined to cause rapid changes in the psychiatric profession and in the treatment of psychiatric patients (Healy, 2009; Le Fanu, 2014).

These extraordinary changes unavoidably affected psychoanalysis, was soon superseded and increasingly excluded from the world of mental health. Earlier approaches were abandoned and largely replaced by the new diagnostic criteria of biological psychiatry (Paris, 2017).

This drastic shift was soon followed by another that would help to drive the rapid decline of psychodynamic approaches and the rise of biological psychiatry: the development of the neurosciences. These changes were strongly helped along by developments in neuroimaging and molecular biology. Soon, many of the functions of psychoanalysis and the 'talking cure' were replaced by new psychotherapies grounded in the principles and discoveries of neuroscience (Beck, 1997, 2005).

Cognitive and cognitive-behavioural psychotherapies were accepted into psychiatry, and tests grounded in evidence-based medicine showed how effective they could be (Aflalo & Price, 2015). The rise of behavioural and cognitive-behavioural psychotherapy, along with biological psychiatry and neuroscience, pushed the world of mental health even further from psychodynamics and spirituality (Schreurs, 2002).

Concerns about mechanical reductionism were therefore left not only unaddressed, but heightened (Schaffner, 2013; Thompson, 2010).

This all led to a number of very different developments. As we have seen, mindfulness was largely accepted into modern, scientifically grounded medicine. According to evidence-based medicine, there had to be a disease that could be diagnosed using accepted diagnostic criteria. Then an intervention could be carried out, and the results evaluated using randomised controlled clinical trials. This was what happened with mindfulness. There are, however, major unresolved problems with the process of choosing the criteria for the initial diagnosis, as well as the subsequent evaluation of the results of the intervention. The criteria that allowed the integration of mindfulness into the toolbox of psychiatric and medical interventions came almost exclusively from biological psychiatry and the Diagnostic Statistical Manual of the American Psychiatric Association.

Psychotherapies were developed in a similar way to mindfulness in order to be incorporated into scientific medicine. In the years after the Second World War, psychoanalysis, on the other hand, experienced a sharp decline because of a number of factors. Medicine was becoming more firmly grounded in scientific principles and objective evaluation based on facts that were completely outside the realm of psychoanalysis. Another factor was time. While analysis could be an extremely lengthy process, psychotropic drugs produced much faster effective results. Finally, in this time, new psychotherapeutic approaches were also being developed: behavioural and cognitive behavioural therapies (CBTs) based on cognitive and neuro-sciences, which quickly became extremely popular and widespread. These practices also had the advantage of being firmly rooted in evidence-based medicine and its procedures. So quickly and enthusiastically were these practices accepted, in fact, that in the public eye the term CBT became almost a synonym for psychotherapy (Beck, 1997, 2005, 2011).

Interestingly, psychotherapy and mindfulness, then two completely unrelated practices, went through a very similar process. Cognitive-based psychotherapies lost their connection to the world of talk therapies and psychodynamics and were accepted into biological psychiatry and medicine. Mindfulness also lost its connection to traditional

Buddhist meditation and was transformed into a modern medical procedure. There was also the unexpected merging of the two practices into a new combined treatment: 'mindfulness-based cognitive therapy' (MBCT). This was largely based on the experience of applying CBT on a large scale outside conventional psychiatric care, in the UK NHS's Improving Access to Psychotherapy (IAPT) programme.

One of the major figures behind these developments was Richard Layard, a labour economist at the London School of Economics and Political Science (LSE). Initially, Layard's focus was unemployment and inequality, but this led him to the study of the economics of happiness, which also came to include mental health issues. His interest in this field, together with the 2006 publication of the LSE's *Depression Report* (The Depression Report: A New Deal for Depression and Anxiety Disorders, 2006), helped raise awareness and interest in unhappiness and mental suffering in the UK. Because of these studies, policymakers in the UK came to reconsider the treatment of less severe and more frequent cases of anxiety and depression (Layard, 2011). Richard Layard's work at the LSE was not centred only on the negative consequences of mood disorders for sufferers, but also on its economic costs. Layard was able to show that the investment needed for a specific new intervention could be offset by the reduction in medical and social care costs for people suffering from less severe anxiety and depression.

It is understandable that an economist examining mental health should examine not only personal factors, but also economic ones. What is remarkable is that in the course of his studies, Layard turned his attention not only to happiness, but also its opposite, unhappiness, and broadened the scope of his study to mental health interventions and psychotherapy (Layard, 2011). Here, Layard's collaboration with David M. Clark was also extremely important. Clark, a clinical psychologist of the University of Oxford, is an expert in CBT, a form of psychological intervention that has been proved to be effective for alleviating the symptoms of several mental conditions, including anxiety and depression (Layard & Clark, 2015). Layard and Clark began discussing the injustice of mentally ill people not usually being treated adequately despite the availability of effective treatments. Together they lobbied the British government until eventually, in 2006, it launched its landmark programme IAPT. Until that point, according to an editorial in the journal *Nature*, interventions in this area had been scandalously under-supported ("Therapy Deficit", 2012). This initiative, however, had a number of distinctive features. Combining their expertise and influence, Richard Layard and David Clark drove a major change in health policy in the UK, securing government backing for the training of many thousands of professionals in the science and practice of a range of evidence-based psychological therapies.

The IAPT programme was a response to the rapid and continuing spread of anxiety and particularly depression, which is so common as to be defined as an epidemic by the World Health Organisation (World Federation for Mental Health, 2012). Layard and Clark's contributions in this field coincided with the UK's development of the National Institute for Health and Care Excellence's (NICE) guidelines for recognising and managing depression.

NICE is the UK public health organisation that provides guidelines for the National Health Service (NHS), and is internationally recognised for its high scientific standards and independence (Sniderman, 2009). NICE's panels of experts carefully reviewed the extensive evidence available on the treatment of depression. The available literature, combined with the guidelines for managing depression, gave clear directions. First, depression had to be diagnosed, and the prevailing and generally accepted criteria for this come from the American Psychiatric Association's *Diagnostic Statistical Manual of Mental Disorders* (DSM). Using these, a distinction can be made between general 'depression' and 'major depressive disorder' (MDD). According to the guidelines, when MDD is diagnosed, the next step should be the prescription of one of the available antidepressant drugs.

This process was to come in for strong and growing criticism. The problem was that the DSM's criteria allowed changes of mood naturally caused by healthy responses to life events to be classed as clinical depression. Natural, healthy states of being thus came to be medicalised, and in the absence of a clear mental disease, inappropriate antidepressant drugs were prescribed (Frances, 2014).

These problems were exacerbated Irving Kirsch's evidence about the effectiveness of antidepressant drugs. Kirsch gained access to the original results of the Food and Drug Administration's clinical trials for the authorisation of 'selective serotonin reuptake inhibitor' (SSRI) antidepressants. Reviewing the data, Kirsch found that when MDD cases were measured on a psychometric scale, the antidepressants only had a statistically significant effect on the most severe cases. For milder cases, the effects of the SSRIs were identical to ineffective placebos (Kirsch, 2009).

NICE therefore developed guidelines for a 'stepped care protocol', where the first intervention for all known and suspected cases of depression was assessment, support, psychoeducation, active monitoring and referral for further assessment and treatment. When the depressive symptoms persisted, psychotherapy had to be included in the treatment plan, then antidepressants could be used if psychological interventions had little or no effect ("NICE Guidance. Depression in Adults: Recognition and Management", 2019). At first, the psychotherapy used was CBT—largely because of Layard's work with Clark's team at the University of Oxford. The decision to use CBT was supported by the extensive evidence-based literature on its clinical effectiveness (Layard & Clark, 2015).

The IAPT programme was developed, following the NICE guidelines, to provide evidence-based treatments for people with anxiety and depression. A large amount of investment went into organising community care facilities outside the psychiatric structures—and into training staff to provide the specific interventions called for by the stepped care programme (AIPT, NHS England, 2019). Although initially CBT was the main psychotherapy used in IAPT, it was not the only psychotherapy used. Several IAPT centres in the UK also applied a number of other psychotherapeutic strategies ("Psychological Therapies: Annual Report on the Use of IAPT Services 2015 to 2016", 2019).

The IAPT's stepped care intervention programme made it possible to avoid using antidepressants for milder cases of depression that were responsive to psychological support and psychotherapy. At the same time, after Kabat-Zinn's initial work, several other groups also focused their attention on applying cognitive and neuro-science to mindfulness. Ultimately, this would lead to the integration of mindfulness into cognitive psychotherapy.

Among the many groups that sprang up in the field of mindfulness, a there were a number at established universities applying the principles of scientific research to meditation. In the US, two prominent examples are the Meditation Awareness Research Center at the UCLA ("UCLA's Mindful Awareness Research Center (MARC)—Los Angeles, CA", 2019), and Clifford Saron's Meditation Research Team at UC Davis ("The Saron Lab", 2019). In Europe, there is also the *Resource Project* led by Tania Singer at the Max Plank Institute (The ReSourceProject, 2019).

Mindfulness is also extensively practised and researched in the UK, where there are active programmes at, among other institutions, Bangor University ("Welcome to the Centre for Mindfulness Research and Practice", 2019) and the University of Exeter (CEDAR Clinical Education Development and Research, 2019). Another remarkably active organisation is the Oxford Mindfulness Centre at Oxford University ("Oxford Mindfulness Centre", 2019).

The Oxford Mindfulness Centre, part of the Department of Psychiatry at the University of Oxford, has been at the forefront of mindfulness research and training since 2008. The centre works to advance the understanding of evidence-based mindfulness through research, publications, training and advocacy. It is also engaged in academic research and initiatives to promote mindfulness in the wider community, as well as professional training, lectures and charitable initiatives to make MBCT accessible to all ("Oxford Mindfulness Centre—About Us", 2019).

Outstanding research and other initiatives have emerged from this centre. This research was also essential for the development of MBCT. It provided the evidence that allowed MBCT to become the NICE-approved treatment of choice for preventing recurrent depression. This intense research work also led to an impressive number of articles in major scientific and medical journals.

The group there, led by Mark Williams and Willem Kuyken, worked hard to assess the potential clinical applications of cognitive psychotherapy and mindfulness using the protocols of evidence-based medicine ("Publications—Oxford Mindfulness Centre", 2019). This work, jointly developed with Zindel Segal as well as John Teasdale, focused on the specific mindfulness interventions first developed for Jon Kabat-Zinn's

Mindfulness-Based Stress Reduction (MBSR) programme. This made a major contribution to the establishment of MBCT (Mindfulness Based Cognitive Therapy, 2019).

A number of other key individuals contributed to the development of MBCT. One was John Teasdale, a leading researcher at Oxford University, and later the Cognition and Brain Sciences Unit at Cambridge. His work focused on the cognition behind depression, as well as possible cognitive therapeutic treatments for it—including mindfulness. Another key contributor to the establishment of MBCT was Zindel V. Segal, professor of psychology at the University of Toronto and also a cognitive psychologist and depression specialist.

Williams, Teasdale and Segal wrote extensively about the use of MBCT for depression. Their book, *Mindfulness-Based Cognitive Therapy for Depression*, sparked much interest and became an extremely common reference point in the field. Interestingly, it includes audio downloads for guided meditation. Since its first publication, it has been updated and reprinted as *Mindfulness-Based Cognitive Therapy for Depression. Second Edition: A New Approach to Preventing Relapse* (Williams & Segal, 2012; Zindel, Segal, & Mark, 2018).

The same authors published another work with Kabat-Zinn himself, called *The Mindful Way Through Depression: Freeing Yourself from Chronic Unhappiness*. This work also includes a CD of guided meditation practices (Williams & Teasdale, 2007). Williams published another separate work too, called *Mindfulness: A Practical Guide to Finding Peace in a Frantic World*. This work, too, includes a CD for guided meditation (Williams & Penman, 2014).

It is worth noting that the IAPT programme is the one and only example of an psychotherapeutic and psychological intervention offered on such a large, national scale. Since it was begun, the results of the stepped care model have been regularly monitored and reported. From the beginning, these were positive and encouraging, although some mental health professionals have voiced concerns and criticisms (Fonagy & Clark, 2015; "The Challenge of the Layard Initiative. The Psychologist", 2019).

This survey of the history of psychotherapy has been necessarily limited, spanning from Freud's early model of psychoanalysis and his 'talking cure' to Beck's CBT and its subsequent combination with mindfulness. It does not attempt to track the many related developments between Freud's psychoanalysis and the rise of modern cognitive approaches. Now, then, it would seem appropriate to examine some of the many important developments in clinical psychology between Freud and the present day.

Freud's psychoanalysis was soon followed by a number of new ideas about psychological functions. Two key pioneers of psychodynamic therapy (which includes many forms of therapy based on Freud's essential principles) were Alfred Adler and Carl Jung. There was a crucial change of direction in the 1920s, when behaviourism became the dominant approach and remained unchallenged until the 1950s. Behaviourism began with Joseph Wolpe, Hans Eysenck and B. F. Skinner, and used techniques based on the theories of operant conditioning, classical conditioning and social learning. The approach denied or ignored internal mental activity, however, and as a result came in for much criticism and was eventually sidelined.

There were two main but very different responses to behaviourism: cognitivism on the one hand and existential and humanistic psychotherapies on the other. During the 1950s, Albert Ellis developed the first form of CBT, Rational Emotive Behavior Therapy (REBT). Then, some years later, Aaron T. Beck went on to develop Cognitive Behaviour Therapy (CBT). Unlike the insight-based approach of psychodynamic therapies or the newer, relational approach of humanistic therapies, the aim of both REBT and CBT was to change a person's beliefs. Because it is focused on symptom relief, collaborative empiricism and the modification of core beliefs, this approach has been widely adopted as a primary treatment for many disorders. CBT, which is largely grounded in the cognitive sciences, was destined to be even more closely involved in the application of neuroscience to clinical psychology.

Unlike the cognitive-based psychotherapies, the humanist movement focused on promoting positive, holistic changes through the development of a supportive, genuine, and empathic therapeutic relationship. One of its core origins was the person-centred psychotherapy of Carl Rogers. Since the 1970s, it has also been accompanied by a range of developments in the field of 'transpersonal psychology', which focuses on the spiritual and transcendent aspects of the human experience. These years also saw the creation of a completely different intervention, 'systems therapy', which focuses on family and group dynamics (Heiden & Hersen, 1995; Norcross, 2011).

CBT became extremely popular, and inspired many efforts to develop further cognitive-based practices, which are collectively known as the 'third wave of cognitive behaviour therapies'. These include MBCT, which has been examined in some detail above. They also include a number of other mindfulness-based approaches, such as Dialectical Behaviour Therapy (DBT) and Acceptance Behaviour Therapy (ACT) (Leahy, 2006; Öst, 2008).

DBT is a modified form of CBT developed in the late 1980s by Marsha M. Linehan, a psychology researcher at the University of Washington, to treat people with a host of mental problems. DBT was shown to be effective for the treatment of numerous mental conditions, such as depression, drug and alcohol problems, post-traumatic stress disorder, and eating disorders. DBT combines standard cognitive behavioural techniques with mindful awareness largely derived from Buddhist meditative practice (Koerner & Linehan, 2012). The founder of DBT is Marha Linehan, and her life trajectory is particularly interesting for several reasons. She had the direct personal experience of being diagnosed with schizophrenia at the Institute of Living in Hartford, Connecticut, where she was an inpatient. She was subjected to electroconvulsive therapy, seclusion, as well as treatment with psychotropic drugs. She is believed to have developed DBT as a result of her own mental illness. It is noteworthy that Linehan had a first-hand involvement with Buddhism and Buddhist meditation, because she received spiritual training from Gerald May and Tilden Edwards. She is also an associate Zen teacher at both the Sanbo Kyodan School in Germany—under Willigis Jaeger Roshi—and the Diamond Sangha in the USA (Carey, 2019; Follette, Hayes, & Linehan, 2011; "Linehan Biography", 2019).

The idea of this history of the major developments in clinical psychology was to show some of the most important steps along the road to bringing Buddhist meditation, a religious approach to relieving the sufferings of life, into the world of clinical psychology and psychosocial intervention. It is important to consider in all this that in all Buddhist traditions, access to meditative training and other services in temples was essentially free. Devotees using such services were simply encouraged to contribute to the daily running of temples. The teaching and services offered by Buddhist masters and clergymen were essentially altruistic and could not be affected by business deals with laypeople. One reason for this is that in a person's progress along the Middle Way towards Awakening, they must stop just before reaching it to help others work towards the same goal. This comes from the ideal of the Bodhisattva in Mahayana traditions.

In Western society, however, clinical psychologists are not volunteers and charge fees for their professional services. In fact, some go so far as to call their patients 'clients', discussing the fees they will charge them in relation to their therapeutic aims and methods. The 'talking cure', along with other early psychotherapies, was mainly confined to the world of private practice, as was the training of professionals in these fields. Fees were therefore paid individually, and these would often add up to substantial amounts—particularly in cases where there were analytic sessions several times a week for many years. This picture changed with the rise of official certification and clinical psychologist and psychotherapist training in universities. As evidence of the efficacy of certain psychotherapeutic interventions began to emerge, health services in some countries even began to cover the costs of them for patients. Two worlds thus came to coexist (with some partial overlaps): traditional private psychotherapy and publicly funded psychotherapy.

When health interventions based on mindfulness became common, it was inevitable that there would be similar questions about funding and commercial interests. After all, funding was needed for the training of teachers and instructors, and there were also many patients willing to pay for mindfulness.

The amount of resources set in motion for mindfulness grew proportionally as its popularity grew, and now the field has an impressive amount of funding. There is now, for example, mindfulness-based cognitive therapy in the publicly-funded, national-scale IAPT programme in the UK.

Privately-funded mindfulness-based interventions are also becoming more and more popular across many affluent Western countries.

Mindfulness has become a generic term that can mean anything, and as Rosenbaum and Magid note in their book *What's Wrong with Mindfulness (and What Isn't)*, many people now believe its uses range from "how to cope with cancer to how to learn to play the harmonica". Some of its other perceived uses are: stress-reduction, meditation, focusing and paying attention, remaining alert, controlling thoughts and feelings, training the brain, treating physical illnesses, psychotherapy, being kind and compassionate, focusing on the present moment and attaining personal happiness (Rosenbaum & Magid, 2016).

All these perceived benefits raise the concern that mindfulness might be at risk of being turned into a free market commodity. *The Guardian* newspaper warned about the problem of a lack of regulation in an article called "Mindfulness: Secular, Religious, Both or Neither?" about a Buddhist Society conference in the UK. It warned that as the secular mindfulness movement continues to grow at a rapid pace, it could become a problem that there are so few regulations covering the training of mindfulness and meditation teachers. Madeleine Bunting, an adviser on mindfulness to the Mindfulness All-Party Parliamentary Group (MAPPG) in the UK cautioned: "Anyone can pop up and say they're a mindfulness teacher, so there is a lot of anxiety within the mindfulness community" ("Buddhist Society Conference in UK Examines the Commoditization of Mindfulness. Buddhistdoor", 2019; Sherwood, 2019).

The concern about the rise of a mass-market approach to mindfulness led to the creation of a landmark British initiative, "The Mindful Initiative". After an 18-month inquiry into mindfulness based on evidence from leading scientists, practitioners, and policymakers, the MAPPG concluded that secular meditation courses should be made available to 580,000 people in Britain who experience recurrent depression. It also advised that the state should train 1200 new meditation teachers, and that more mindfulness should be taught in British schools, as it has been shown to improve student behaviour and enhance academic performance. The MAPPG has also recommended that prisons and probation services test mindfulness programmes to reduce recidivism ("Mindful Nation UK. The Mindfulness All-Party Parliamentary Group", 2019).

The *Mindful Nation UK* report was then published in 2015. It is the first policy document of its kind, and proposes addressing mental health concerns in education, healthcare, the workplace and the criminal justice system using mindfulness-based interventions. The recommendations in this report are evidence-based, and urge policymakers both to invest resources in further pilot studies and also to increase public access to qualified teacher trainers.

In the UK, the MAPPG was a British parliamentary initiative. In the USA, Tim Ryan, a five-term member of congress on the House Armed Services Committee, wrote *A Mindful Nation: How a Simple Practice Can Help Us Reduce Stress, Improve Performance, and Recapture the American Spirit*. The enthusiastically written book shows the positive effects of mindfulness, especially the stimulation of attention and kindness in children, as well as improving health more generally. Two chapters are devoted to "how mindfulness can help us to rediscover our values and reshape our economy and can help us help ourselves and our country". Another chapter is on "how mindfulness can improve performance and build resiliency for our military and first responders" (Ryan, 2013). Ryan is evidently highly enthusiastic about mindfulness, and one possible clue to his interest in using mindfulness in the armed forces is his former role on the Armed Services Committee (Ryan eventually avers that mindfulness could be used for "helping people to serve their country").

The idea of using mindfulness on soldiers is not original. In fact, mindfulness has already been used professionally in the United States armed forced. 'Mindfulness-Based Mind Fitness Training' (MMFT) is a registered trademark for an intervention developed specifically for US soldiers. It was created by Elisabeth Stanley, a former US Army officer who also trained as a Buddhist nun in South East Asia. In the words of Stanley, "MMFT blends mindfulness skills training with information and skills that promote stress resilience and concrete applications for the operational environment". The result is a "mental armor" which both increases warriors' operational effectiveness and enhances their capacity to bounce back from stressful experience ("Mindfulness-Based Mind Fitness Training (MMFT): A Review", 2019; Stanley & Jha, 2009).

Mindfulness now has a remarkable number of different applications and forms, and the variety is possibly even broader in the USA, where mindfulness has become almost a full-blown industry. *SAGE Business Researcher* summarised the state of affairs in a report called "The Meditation Industry. Will success turn it into "McMindfulness"?" The report noted that four in ten adults in the United States say they meditate at least weekly, and major companies including Google, Apple, General Mills, Goldman Sachs and Aetna have adopted meditation programmes for their employees. The industry has attracted $260 million in investments since 2012. Health insurance giant Aetna reported that employees' annual productivity rose by about $3000 each after they participated in a mindfulness training programme. Headspace, the largest of nearly 1000 mindfulness apps, raised $36.7 million in funding in 2017, and offers in-flight meditation channels on eight airlines. It has even released plans for public, phone booth-sized relaxation "pods." Experts say the industry's growth raises concerns about the need for an accreditation system for the founders of new for-profit mindfulness initiatives ("The Meditation Industry—SAGE Business Researcher", 2019).

An article in the Huffington Post notes that what is termed "the burgeoning 'mindfulness revolution,'" is now estimated to be a $4 billion industry, leading to the increasing professionalisation of mindfulness training. The traditional roles of both teachers and students are now being transformed, with students and patients now increasingly being treated as consumers. As mindfulness teaching is professionalised, too, market logic has been introduced into it, with its demands for competition, marketing and entrepreneurialism. Competence and teacher standards are also a problem, as a professional mindfulness teacher who is also a Buddhist teacher in a Western sangha, admits:

> Inevitably, the emergence of the secular mindfulness movement means that mindfulness and meditation teaching are being professionalised. That affects Buddhists like myself who are earning a living in this way, and it is useful for all of us to recall that mindfulness is best taught as an expression of one's practice; when it is an aspect of one's profession it is unavoidably mixed with drives such as anxiety about money, ambition and the desire for status.

Expensive initiatives for professional certification are a new market, and branding for these is beginning to develop. Perhaps the best example of this is Kabat-Zinn's original *Center for Mindfulness* and *Mindfulness Stress Reduction* programme, which made the training of practitioners profitable and transformed patient-clients into consumers ("The Branding of Mindfulness", 2019).

In 2017, Marketdata Enterprises, Inc., released a new 62-page report called: *The US Meditation Market.* To uncover vital information about this little-researched but rapidly growing market, it examines meditation centres, retreats, books, smartphone apps, websites, online courses, employer programmes, DVDs and CDs. The report's key findings are that the value of the meditation market in the US was an estimated $959 million in 2015, growing to $1.08 billion in 2016 and $1.21 billion in 2017. Marketdata forecasts 11.4 per cent average yearly growth, building the sector to $2.08 billion by 2022. Approximately 9.3 million US adults have practised meditation in the last 12 months. A typical meditation user is a middle-aged female, highly educated (college or higher education degree), non-hispanic white, residing in a Western state of the US. There are an estimated 2450 meditation studios or centres in the US, mostly non-profit organisations: they generate $659 million in revenues and work closely with yoga studios. The average meditation centre grosses about $269,000, but non-profits are smaller, at $165,000. Marketdata's business research reveals that 369 of the US meditation centres are operated by three organisations: Kadampa Centers, Transcendental Meditation, and Shambhala Centers. Meditation books, CDs, DVDs and magazines make up a $112 million segment of the market. There are at least 1000 mediation smartphone apps now on the market, which, together with websites and online courses, generate over $100 million per year ($1.2 Billion U.S. Meditation Market, 2019).

The applications of mindfulness have the potential to generate commercial revenue, and developers may sometimes have to register a trademark to protect their rights. It is worth recalling here that MMFT, intervention for US soldiers developed by Elisabeth Stanley, is regularly registered as a trademark (Stanley & Jha, 2009).

Considering the revenue generated by mindfulness programmes—as well as the projected increase in turnover—it would not be surprising if more refined marketing techniques are developed to promote them in future. It is quite remarkable that the applications of mindfulness have multiplied so much that it is now even used as a tool to investigate the behaviour of consumers, and the resulting data is used to refine the operating tools used in marketing (Ndubisi, 2014).

There are a number of contrasting facets to the integration of mindfulness into Western culture. Buddhism's selfless and altruistic principles have largely faded and been replaced by a market- and consumer-oriented mentality. In time, there will be a sort of natural selection among the different approaches to mindfulness. Some will rise and some are destined to decline and disappear. This selection process, which cannot be easily predicted, will be determined by science, psychology, medicine, markets and consumer choice.

Of the many strands of mindfulness development, one vital one is medicine and psychotherapy. Here something peculiar happened, because mindfulness-based interventions are probably the only procedures in this field that did not develop from the worlds of biology, medicine or psychiatry. Nevertheless, they have been accepted and warmly received into current evidence-based medical science. This is unique, and did not happen with any other so-called alternative or complementary forms of medicine, which, although extremely popular and enthusiastically promoted by many practitioners and patients, are still highly debated.

It is now worth examining in more detail the evidence that justifies the use of mindfulness-based treatments in medicine. The medical problem that is probably best addressed with mindfulness is depression. Mindfulness-based cognitive therapy seems to have been used with some effect to treat cases of depression. In some cases, it is even claimed that it has been more effective than traditional treatments such as antidepressant drugs. These results have sparked even more interest because depression, according to the World Health Organization (WHO), is rapidly spreading around the world. In fact, by 2020 it is predicted it will become the second-biggest cause of world disability, and by 2030 it is expected to become the biggest contributor to disease burden.

The next chapter will therefore examine the best available evidence for the effectiveness of mindfulness-based interventions, as well as the rigor and overall validity of the research used to gather it.

## References

$1.2 Billion U.S. Meditation Market to Grow Strongly, Following Path of Yoga Studios. (2019). Retrieved from https://www.webwire.com/ViewPressRel.asp?aId=214152. Accessed 28 April 2019.

Adam, D. (2019). *Plan for Dalai Lama lecture angers neuroscientists*. Retrieved from https://www.theguardian.com/world/2005/jul/27/research.highereducation. Accessed 28 April 2019.

Aflalo, A., & Price, A. (2015). *The failed assassination of psychoanalysis*. London: Karnac.

AIPT, NHS England. (2019). *Adult improving access to psychological therapies programme*. Retrieved from https://www.england.nhs.uk/mental-health/adults/iapt/. Accessed 28 April 2019.

Beck, A. T. (1997). The past and future of cognitive therapy. *The Journal of Psychotherapy Practice and Research, 6*(4), 276–284.

Beck, A. (2005). The current state of cognitive therapy. *Archives of General Psychiatry, 62*(9), 953. https://doi.org/10.1001/archpsyc.62.9.953.

Beck, J. S. (2011). *Cognitive therapy*. New York: Guilford Press.

Begley, S. (2009). *The plastic mind*. London: Constable.

Knutson, B. (2019). Retrieved from http://stanford.edu/group/spanlab/Press/bk1105press3.html. Accessed 19 April 2019.

Buddhist Society Conference in UK Examines the Commoditization of Mindfulness | Buddhistdoor. (2019). Retrieved from https://www.buddhistdoor.net/news/buddhist-society-conference-in-uk-examines-the-commoditization-of-mindfulness. Accessed 28 April 2019.

Buric, I., Farias, M., Jong, J., Mee, C., & Brazil, I. (2017). What is the molecular signature of mind–body interventions? A systematic review of gene expression changes induced by meditation and related practices. *Frontiers in Immunology, 8*. https://doi.org/10.3389/fimmu.2017.00670.

Callaway, E. (2017). Genome studies attract criticism: Geneticists question ability of genome-wide association studies to find useful disease links. *Nature, 546*, 463.

Carey, B. (2019). *Expert on mental illness reveals her own struggle*. Retrieved from https://www.nytimes.com/2011/06/23/health/23lives.html. Accessed 28 April 2019.

CEDAR Clinical Education Development and Research. Mindfulness at the University of Exeter. (2019). Retrieved from http://cedar.exeter.ac.uk/mindfulness/. Accessed 19 April 2019.

Chögyam Trungpa—Shambhala. (2019). Retrieved from https://shambhala.org/teachers/chogyam-trungpa/. Accessed 19 April 2019.

Chuengsatiansup, K. (2003). Spirituality and health: An initial proposal to incorporate spiritual health in health impact assessment. *Environmental Impact Assessment Review, 23*(1), 3–15. https://doi.org/10.1016/s0195-9255(02)00037-9.

Churchland, P. (2014). *Brain-wise*. Cambridge, MA: MIT.

Cyranoski, D. (2005). Neuroscientists see red over Dalai Lama. *Nature, 436*(7050), 452. https://doi.org/10.1038/436452b.

Dalai Lama: Brief Biography. The 14th Dalai Lama. (2019). Retrieved from https://www.dalailama.com/the-dalai-lama/biography-and-daily-life/brief-biography. Accessed 28 April 2019.

Dalai Lama: Investigating the Mind. (2019). Retrieved from https://web.archive.org/web/20150219190156/, http:/investigatingthemind.org/hhdl.science.html. Accessed 28 April 2019.

Engle, R. A. (2008). About the mind and life institute. In A. Harrington & D. L. Bstan-'dzin-rgya-mtsho (Eds.), *The Dalai Lama at MIT*. Cambridge: Harvard University Press.

Fields, R. (1992). *How the swans came to the lake*. Boston: Shambhala.

Follette, V., Hayes, S., & Linehan, M. (2011). *Mindfulness and acceptance*. New York: Guilford Press.

Fonagy, P., & Clark, D. (2015). Update on the improving access to psychological therapies programme in England: Commentary on … children and young people's improving access to psychological therapies. *BJPsych Bulletin, 39*(5), 248–251. https://doi.org/10.1192/pb.bp.115.052282.

Ford, J. (2006). *Zen master who?* Boston: Wisdom Publications.

Frances, A. (2014). *Saving normal*. New York: William Morrow.

Francisco J. Varela: 1946–2001. (2019). Retrieved from http://www.enolagaia.com/Varela.htm. Accessed 28 April 2019.

Goleman, D. (1977). *The varieties of the meditative experience*. New York: Irvington.

Goleman, D. (2015). *A force for good: The Dalai Lama's vision for our world*. New York: Bantam Books.

Goleman, D., & Davidson, R. (2017). *The science of meditation*. New York: Penguin Random House.

Grünbaum, A. (1979). Is Freudian psychoanalytic theory pseudo-scientific by Karl Popper's criterion of demarcation? *American Philosophical Quarterly, 16*(2), 131–141.

Grunenberg, C., & Harris, J. (2007). *Summer of love*. Liverpool: Liverpool University Press.

Hamer, D. (2005). *The God gene: How faith is hardwired into our genes*. New York, NY: Anchor Books.

Healy, D. (2009). *Creation of psychopharmacology*. Cambridge: Harvard University Press.

Heiden, L. A., & Hersen, M. (1995). *Introduction to clinical psychology*. Boston, MA: Springer.

Kirsch, I. (2009). *Emperor's new drugs*. Boulder: Basic Books.

Koerner, K., & Linehan, M. (2012). *Doing dialectical behavior therapy*. New York: Guilford Press.

Layard, R. (2011). *Happiness*. New York: Penguin Books.

Layard, R., & Clark, D. (2015). *Thrive*. London: Penguin Books.

Le Fanu, J. (2014). *The rise & fall of modern medicine*. London: Abacus.

Leahy, R. (2006). *Contemporary cognitive therapy*. New York: Guilford Press.

Legrenzi, P., Umiltà, C., & Anderson, F. (2014). *Neuromania*. Oxford: Oxford University Press.

Linehan Biography. (2019). Retrieved from https://blogs.uw.edu/linehan/biography/. Accessed 19 April 2019.

MacLean, G. (2016). *From lion's jaws* [Place of publication not identified]. Mountain.

Masson, J. (1989). *Against therapy*. London: Collins.

Milton, J. A., & Frabricius, J. (2004). *A short introduction to psychoanalysis*. London: Sage.

Mind & Life Dialogues—Mind & Life Institute. (2019). Retrieved from https://www.mindandlife.org/mind-and-life-dialogues/. Accessed 28 April 2019.

Mindful Nation UK. The Mindfulness All-Party Parliamentary Group. (2019). Retrieved from https://www.themindfulnessinitiative.org.uk/images/reports/Mindfulness-APPG-Report_Mindful-Nation-UK_Oct2015.pdf. Accessed 28 April 2019.

Mindfulness Based Cognitive Therapy. (2019). Retrieved from http://mbct.com/. Accessed 19 April 2019.

Mindfulness-Based Mind Fitness Training (MMFT): A Review. (2019). Retrieved from http://ronniestanglermd.com/mindfulness-based-mind-fitness-training-mmft-a-review/. Accessed 19 April 2019.

Minds, C. (2019). *Founder of center for healthy minds, Richard J. Davidson—Center for healthy minds*. Retrieved from https://centerhealthyminds.org/about/founder-richard-davidson. Accessed 19 April 2019.

Mukpo, D., & Gimian, C. (2008). *Dragon thunder*. Boston, MA: Shambhala.

Ndubisi, N. O. (2014). Consumer mindfulness and marketing implications. *Psychology & Marketing, 31*(4), 237–250. https://doi.org/10.1002/mar.20691.

Newberg, A. (2011). *Principles of neurotheology*. Farnham: Ashgate.

Newberg, A. (2018). *Neurotheology*. New York: Columbia University Press.

Newberg, A., D'Aquili, E., & Rause, V. (2008). *Why God won't go away*. New York: Ballantine Books.

Hạnh, N. (2009). *Happiness*. Berkeley: Parallax press.

NICE Guidance. Depression in Adults: Recognition and Management. (2019). Retrieved from https://www.nice.org.uk/guidance/cg90/. Accessed 28 April 2019.

Norcross, J. (2011). *History of psychotherapy*. Washington: American Psychological Association.

Nyanaponika. (1996). *The heart of Buddhist meditation*. Kandy, Sri Lanka: Buddhist Publication Society.

Öst, L. (2008). Efficacy of the third wave of behavioral therapies: A systematic review and meta-analysis. *Behaviour Research and Therapy, 46*(3), 296–321. https://doi.org/10.1016/j.brat.2007.12.005.

Oxford Mindfulness Centre. (2019). Retrieved from http://oxfordmindfulness.org/about-us/about/. Accessed 19 April 2019.

Oxford Mindfulness Centre—About Us. (2019). Retrieved from http://oxfordmindfulness.org/. Accessed 19 April 2019.

Paris, J. (2017). Is psychoanalysis still relevant to psychiatry? *The Canadian Journal of Psychiatry, 62*(5), 308–312. https://doi.org/10.1177/0706743717692306.

Psychological Therapies: Annual Report on the Use of IAPT Services 2015 to 2016. (2019). Retrieved from https://www.gov.uk/government/statistics/psychological-therapies-annual-report-on-the-use-of-iapt-services-2015-to-2016. Accessed 28 April 2019.

Publications—Oxford Mindfulness Centre. (2019). Retrieved from http://oxfordmindfulness.org/about-us/research/publications/. Accessed 19 April 2019.

Rose, H., & Rose, S. (2014). *Genes, cells, and brains: The promethean promises of the new biology*. London: Verso.

Rosenbaum, R., & Magid, B. (2016). *What's wrong with mindfulness (and what isn't)*. Somerville, MA: Wisdom Publications.

Ryan, T. (2013). *A mindful nation: How a simple practice can help us reduce stress, improve performance, and recapture the American spirit*. Carlsbad, CA: Hay House.

Saatcioglu, F. (2013). Regulation of gene expression by yoga, meditation and related practices: A review of recent studies. *Asian Journal of Psychiatry, 6*(1), 74–77. https://doi.org/10.1016/j.ajp.2012.10.002.

Schaffner, K. (2013). Reduction and reductionism in psychiatry. *Oxford Handbooks Online*. https://doi.org/10.1093/oxfordhb/9780199579563.013.0059.

Schreurs, A. (2002). *Psychotherapy and spirituality*. London: Jessica Kingsley.

Sherwood, H. (2019). *Mindfulness at risk of being 'turned into a free market commodity'*. Retrieved from https://www.theguardian.com/lifeandstyle/2015/oct/28/mindfulness-free-market-commodity-risk. Accessed 28 April 2019.

Sniderman, A. (2009). Why guideline-making requires reform. *JAMA, 301*(4), 429. https://doi.org/10.1001/jama.2009.15.

Stanley, E., & Jha, A. (2009). Mind fitness: Improving operational effectiveness and building warrior resilience. *JFQ—Joint Force Quarterly, 55*, 144–151.

Tang, Y., Hölzel, B., & Posner, M. (2015). The neuroscience of mindfulness meditation. *Nature Reviews Neuroscience, 16*(4), 213–225. https://doi.org/10.1038/nrn3916.

The Branding of Mindfulness. (2019). Retrieved from https://www.huffpost.com/entry/the-branding-of-mindfulness_b_5a35a283e4b02bd1c8c60750?guccounter=1&guce_referrer_us=aHR0cH%E2%80%A6. Accessed 28 April 2019.

The Challenge of the Layard Initiative. The Psychologist. (2019). Retrieved from https://thepsychologist.bps.org.uk/volume-22/edition-5/challenge-layard-initiative. Accessed 19 April 2019.

The Depression Report: A New Deal for Depression and Anxiety Disorders. (2006). *The centre for economic performance's mental health policy group*. London School of Economics and Political Sciences. http://cep.lse.ac.uk/textonly/research/mentalhealth/DEPRESSION_REPORT_LAYARD2.pdf.

The Meditation Industry—SAGE Business Researcher. (2019). Retrieved from http://businessresearcher.sagepub.com/sbr-1946-105603-2878495/20180129/the-meditation-industry. Accessed 28 April 2019.

The ReSource Project. (2019). Retrieved from https://www.resource-project.org/en/. Accessed 28 April 2019.

The Saron Lab. (2019). Retrieved from http://saronlab.ucdavis.edu/. Accessed 28 April 2019. Accessed 19 April 2019.

Therapy Deficit. (2012). *Nature, 489*(7417), 473–474. https://doi.org/10.1038/489473b.

Thich Nhat Hanh. (2019). Retrieved from https://plumvillage.org/about/thich-nhat-hanh/biography/. Accessed 28 April 2019.

Thich Nhat Hanh—Buddhism—Oxford Bibliographies—Obo. (2019). Retrieved from http://www.oxfordbibliographies.com/view/document/obo-9780195393521/obo-9780195393521-0138.xml#obo-9780195393521-0138-bibItem-0004. Accessed 28 April 2019.

Thompson, E. (2010). *Mind in life*. Cambridge, MA: The Belknap Press of Harvard University Press.

UCLA's Mindful Awareness Research Center (MARC)—Los Angeles, CA. (2019). Retrieved from https://www.uclahealth.org/marc/body.cfm?id=16&iirf_redirect=1. Accessed 28 April 2019.

Van Regenmortel, M., & Hull, D. (2002). *Promises and limits of reductionism in the biomedical sciences*. Chichester: Wiley.

Walk with Me (2017)—IMDb. (2019). Retrieved from https://www.imdb.com/title/tt2331100/. Accessed 28 April 2019.

Wallace, B. (2007). *Buddhism & science* (pp. 417–421). New York: Columbia University Press.

Weinberger, D., & Radulescu, E. (2016). Finding the elusive psychiatric "lesion" with 21st-century neuroanatomy: A note of caution. *American Journal of Psychiatry, 173*(1), 27–33. https://doi.org/10.1176/appi.ajp.2015.15060753.

Welcome to the Centre for Mindfulness Research and Practice. (2019). Retrieved from https://www.bangor.ac.uk/mindfulness. Accessed 28 April 2019.

Williams, J., & Penman, D. (2014). *Mindfulness*. London: Piatkus.

Williams, J., & Segal, Z. (2012). *Mindfulness-based cognitive therapy for depression* (2nd ed.). New York: Guilford Press.

Williams, M., & Teasdale, J. (2007). *The mindful way through depression: Freeing yourself from chronic unhappiness (includes guided meditation practices CD)*. New York: Guilford Press.

Wilson, J. (2014) *Mindful America: The mutual transformation of Buddhism meditation and American culture.* Oxford: Oxford University Press.

World Federation for Mental Health. (2012). *Depression: A global crisis world mental health day.* https://www.who.int/mental_health/management/depression/wfmh_paper_depression_wmhd_2012.pdf. Accessed 28 April 2019.

Young, K., van der Velden, A., Craske, M., Pallesen, K., Fjorback, L., Roepstorff, A., & Parsons, C. (2018). The impact of mindfulness-based interventions on brain activity: A systematic review of functional magnetic resonance imaging studies. *Neuroscience & Biobehavioral Reviews, 84,* 424–433. https://doi.org/10.1016/j.neubiorev.2017.08.003.

Zindel, V., Segal, Z., & Mark, J. G. (2018). *Williams mindfulness-based cognitive therapy for depression, second edition: A new approach to preventing relapse.* New York: Guilford Press.

# 7
# Methodological Flaws and the Evidence of Efficacy

Mindfulness as initially proposed by Kabat-Zinn has been irrefutably successful. It became most widespread and popular when it lost the forms and traditions originally associated with meditation and found a new place in Western culture. The difficulty and exoticism of the practices were replaced by procedures that could be easily learned and taught by teachers and instructors—and could even be translated into the realms of psychology and medicine.

Mindfulness was destined be accepted into the world of medicine, and the reasons for this deserve to be examined in detail. In the years before the development of mindfulness, mind-body medicine had been established as a new discipline. It became extremely popular and, in fact, still retains many of its grounding principles today, except they are now supported by new scientific advances (Harrington, 2008). Ancient as well as more recent practices such as meditation, imagery and yoga, together with hypnosis and autogenic training, were subjected to scientific study and analysed for possible clinical uses (Bird & Pinch, 2002; Brann, Owens, & Williamson, 2012; Wolsko, Eisenberg, Davis, & Phillips, 2004). However, despite widespread interest in the studies and the possible clinical uses of these interventions, they were still not



T. Giraldi, *Psychotherapy, Mindfulness and Buddhist Meditation*,
https://doi.org/10.1007/978-3-030-29003-0_7

generally accepted into modern scientific medicine in the same way that mindfulness was.

Soon, by contrast, mindfulness became a therapeutic intervention prescribed for a whole host of medical conditions. In the years that followed the development of mindfulness, there were many advances in clinical medicine—especially through the application of evidence-based trials of safety and clinical effectiveness. Many traditional medical remedies were shown to be ineffective and abandoned, and new treatments were introduced only after clinical trials of their effectiveness.

Mindfulness was established against this backdrop, and as such Kabat-Zinn and others had to focus their efforts on getting mindfulness-based treatment accepted using evidence-based trials.

There is an accepted gold standard of practice in clinical trials. Its protocols are designed to provide clear evidence of the effectiveness of treatments. This standard is the randomised controlled clinical trial (RCT). Because the principles of this procedure are evidently relevant for mindfulness-based treatments, it is worth briefly recalling them here. Clinical trials are designed to answer the question of whether a specific treatment is effective for a specific disease, in a way that is clearly reproducible. The protocols of a trial are crucial for its success.

The first step in a clinical trial is identifying the disease to be treated and defining it as precisely as possible. A group of subjects suffering from this precise condition can then be found. This step guarantees that a pathological condition is present, and that its severity has been determined. If this step is not carried out correctly, researchers could wrongly believe they have found effective treatments when the results are actually caused by misdiagnosis or the patients having a less severe form of the condition.

The next step is to divide the patients into groups, one of which will receive the treatment, while one or more of the others will be control groups for comparison. The selection process for these must be completely based on chance, a process called 'randomisation'. This basically avoids any possible bias that might affect the results.

Once the subjects have had the treatment, the next step is objectively evaluating the results. One crucial part of this is the statistical analysis of the results. This shows the magnitude of the effects, and that the probability that they were caused by chance is negligible.

One key feature of the protocols is the so-called 'blind' procedure: it essentially ensures that each patient does not know whether they are receiving the real treatment or if they are part of the control group. The treatment-giver should also be similarly 'blinded'. There should also be a second or 'double' blinding, in that the person who is evaluating the outcome should not know the identities of the patients in the different groups. This removes bias from the judgement of the outcomes (Howick, 2011).

The nature of the control groups is another key concern. It has been established that using ineffective interventions provokes a not-in-substantial therapeutic response. This is called the 'placebo effect'. Evidence-based clinical trials therefore require additional experimental groups, treated with a double-blind procedure identical to the other treated groups, but without the specific active ingredient being tested (Shapiro, 2000; Shorter, 2011). This is easy to do with medicines, where the same medication can be prepared without the active ingredient. It is more difficult—and perhaps impossible—with psychotherapies and meditation.

After considering the methodology, we can begin to analyse the evidence collected for the effectiveness of mindfulness. The starting point for this must be identifying the diseases that have been treated with mindfulness. There is little doubt that the majority of the evidence gathered in the decades since the introduction of mindfulness interventions concerns depression (Gotink et al., 2015; Hofmann, Sawyer, Witt, & Oh, 2010; Sorbero et al., 2015; Strauss, Cavanagh, Oliver, & Pettman, 2014). The many investigations made make it possible to use another powerful analytical technique, meta-analysis. This technique essentially involves the joint evaluation of the data from several reports that share the same research aims (even if the protocols used are not entirely the same).

The first studies examined the Mindfulness-Based Stress Reduction programme, but were followed by analysis of interventions that combined mindfulness with cognitive psychotherapy, as well as Mindfulness-Based Cognitive Therapy (MBCT). The basis of these studies was the evaluation of the effectiveness of mindfulness applications compared to existing treatments for depression. These were predominantly antidepressant drugs, many of which were ineffective and had negative side effects.

Depression treatments were chosen for these studies because the condition has become alarmingly common around the world. Therefore, before considering the studies of mindfulness-based treatments for depression, it may be useful to better understand the problem of depression.

It is generally accepted that the first term for a condition roughly corresponding to "depression" is "melancholy", which dates back to Hippocrates and the dawn of medicine in the Hellenic world (fifth to fourth century BC). "Melancholy" refers to the basic foundation of Hippocratic medicine: the theory that the human body was made up of four "humours". Melancholy was a condition that caused prolonged fear and discouragement it was broadly associated with the dry cold of autumn and the earth. The theoretical framework was that the human body is made up of four humours: blood, yellow bile, black bile and phlegm. Each of the humours was believed to have particular qualities (warm and moist, warm and dry, cold and dry, cold and moist). It was thought that the prevalence of a particular humour gave rise to certain personality types or "temperaments": sanguine (blood), choleric (yellow bile), melancholic (black bile) and phlegmatic (phlegm). Balanced humours (eucrasia) resulted in good health, whereas unbalanced humours (discrasia) led to disease (Cabras, Lippi, & Lovari, 2005). Melancholy was attributed to an excess of black bile (*melaina chole*), from which it takes its name. And since then, terms such as 'black mood' and 'melancholia'—with its linguistic variants 'melanconia' and 'malinconia'—have become common descriptions for a depressed state.

Humourist theory led to a number of treatments based on the idea of correcting unbalanced humours in a patient's body. The most common therapeutic procedures were bloodletting (which was still extensively performed until the end of nineteenth century), vomit-inducing medication (emetics such as ipecac and emetic tartar), laxatives (cathartics such as cascara and senna), and cupping together with the application of irritants and blistering agents. Demonic possession, which was seen as a disease in itself, was the only exception to these treatments because it was thought that it would not respond to medical intervention: sufferers were instead left in the hands of religious authorities and exorcists (Belofsky, 2013; Greenstone, 2010; Grube, 1954; Lawlor, 2012; Neuburger, 1944). The administration of laxatives and emetics came from the idea of 'catharsis', or purification by releasing the moods or toxic substances causing the suffering. The term was then extended to symbolic and psychological catharsis (Mattern, 2011).

When considering the history of depression, it should be noted that for many centuries, very little attention was paid to the mental illnesses and mood disorders of people from more disadvantaged classes, who found themselves facing physical hardships such as wars and terrible epidemics. With the dawn of the Enlightenment, however, physical conditions began to improve for many, and more attention was paid to mental suffering. In English society at the end of the seventeenth century, the term melancholia became much more associated with the milder conditions that we usually see as connected to the Victorian period, such as hypochondria, hysteria, spleen, vapours, the English malady and the nervous breakdown (Shorter, 2013). This paved the way for the distinction between serious depressive disorders and milder but more widespread personal suffering. This latter category is associated with emotional and existential distress. It is a cultural, anthropological and medical construct that has changed continuously through the years (Shorter, 2013). This is largely because the socially and medically accepted ways of describing the personal suffering caused by familial and social hardship have changed drastically over the years (Shorter, 1994).

When tracing the history of depression from ancient Greece and Rome to the modern day, there are a few key points we must consider. Between the eighteenth and nineteenth centuries, a number of different frameworks were developed across England, Germany and France. This was largely because of the contradiction between the somatic and functional theories of mental suffering. The first saw mental illness as a disease of the body, akin to many illnesses that were treated with internal medicine. Mental illness was believed to be caused by a range of anatomical, functional and pathological factors that could be traced back to the nascent neurology of Willis and his followers.

There were also alternative theories that traced mental disorders to a functional discomfort or disturbance. In the hands of Sigmund Freud and Emil Kraepelin, this notion would later develop into the fields of psychology and psychoanalytics on the one hand, and psychiatry on the other. When psychiatry was firmly established in the medical world, it had to create a system that would allow it to effectively define and diagnose mental illnesses. Psychiatry found its system in the work of Kraepelin: his nosographic classification. Kraepelin's system laid the foundations for essential psychiatric diagnostic tools like the American Psychiatric Association's *Diagnostic and Statistical Manual of Mental Disorders* (DSM) which has had a profound impact on mental health.

Returning to the present day, the pervasiveness of depression in contemporary society is examined in the 2012 World Health Organisation (WHO) publication *Depression: A Global Crisis*. It was published for the organisation's 2012 World Mental Health Day, which was dedicated to depression. This work has become a sort of mantra, and has been almost compulsorily cited in most reports published since. Its contents are indeed alarming. The chapter 'Depression: A Global Public Health Concern' shows how depression is now making a major contribution to the global illness burden. The WHO calculated that the total number of depression sufferers was approximately 350 million. A study carried out in 17 different countries also found that an average of one in 20 people had reported an episode of depression in the previous year. The WHO's publication also shows how depressive disorders often begin at a young age, then re-emerge after the initial outbreak, reducing the sufferer's ability to function. Reports suggest depression is becoming the principle cause of disability: by 2030 it is set to become the main contributor to the global illness burden (WHO, 2012).

The WHO's evaluation of the spread of depression is based on diagnostic criteria that are predominantly for major depressive disorder (MDD), as defined in the American Psychiatric Association (APA) DSM-III and DSM-IV Diagnostic Statistical Manuals.

Depression has also sometimes been diagnosed using the ICD-10 categorisation (ICD-10, 2010). The International Classification of Diseases (ICD) was compiled by the World Health Organization (WHO) and published for the first time in 1948: it reached its tenth edition in 1992. The various editions of the ICD, which, unlike the DSM, cover all illnesses rather than just those of a psychiatric nature, have been embraced as useful classification and communication tools.

Other published studies agree with the WHO publication that depression is now a major contributor to the global burden of disease (GBD). In 2010, a study comparing all diseases found that depressive disorders were the second largest cause of years lived with disability (YLD), and the main cause for the reduction of disability adjusted life years (DALY) (Ferrari et al., 2013).

A study from 2010 also found that depressive disorders were particularly prevalent in Europe, where a third of the population of the European Union suffer from mental disorders each year. Depression, together with neurological problems, appear to be the leading cause of disease in Europe. Only a third of cases receive some form of medical treatment, showing that there are considerable unmet medical needs (Wittchen et al., 2011).

More generally, studies about the epidemiology of depression agree that its prevalence varies significantly across different regions and cultures around the world (Kessler & Bromet, 2013), not to mention across genders (Culberston, 1997) and more and less globalised areas (Bhugra, 2003; Bhugra & Mastrogianni, 2004). The USA has a particularly high incidence of depression. A psychiatric interview based on the DSM-III showed that almost 50 per cent of respondents reported at least one mental disorder over the course of their lives. In fact, 30 per cent reported one in the previous year alone, with the most common problem being a major depressive episode. Affective and anxiety disorders were most prevalent among women, and only a minority of people who took part in the study had received any kind of treatment (Kessler, 1994).

All these studies refer to *depression*, and depression is almost invariably defined as MDD, the 'major depressive disorder' of the DSM. There is then the question of how exactly depression is defined and diagnosed, as well as what type of condition it is. The WHO publication offers further insight on this. For the WHO:

> Depression is a significant contributor to the global burden of disease and affects people in all communities across the world. Today, depression is estimated to affect 350 million people. The World Mental Health Survey conducted in 17 countries found that on average about 1 in 20 people reported having an episode of depression in the previous year. Depressive disorders often start at a young age; they reduce people's functioning and often are recurring. For these reasons, depression is the leading cause of disability worldwide in terms of total years lost due to disability. The demand for curbing depression and other mental health conditions is on the rise globally. A recent World Health Assembly called on the World Health Organization and its member states to take action in this direction. (WHO, 2012)
>
> What is depression? Depression is a common mental disorder that presents with depressed mood, loss of interest or pleasure, decreased energy, feelings of guilt or low self-worth, disturbed sleep or appetite, and poor concentration. Moreover, depression often comes with symptoms of anxiety. These problems can become chronic or recurrent and lead to substantial impairments in an individual's ability to take care of his or her everyday responsibilities. At its worst, depression can lead to suicide. Almost 1 million lives are lost yearly due to suicide, which translates to 3000 suicide deaths every day. For every person who completes a suicide, 20 or more may attempt to end his or her life (WHO, 2012). There are multiple variations of depression that a person can suffer from, with the most general distinction being depression in people who have or do not have a history of manic episodes.

The diagnostic criteria for depression are not explicitly mentioned, but from the definition in the text, and from the papers cited in the references, it is clear that depression is defined as MDD, the *major depressive disorder* of the American Psychiatric Association's Diagnostic Statistical Manual.

The next chapter of the WHO's publication is particularly important here, because it contrasts so strikingly with the rest of the work. The title is 'Depression as a Consequence of the Economic Crisis'. It says:

> Normal sadness and depression. Under adverse conditions like the death of a relative, personal humiliation (especially in certain cultures),

> disappointment, loss of social status, even financial loss, a psychological response is expected and is, of course normal. Under these circumstances, it is lack of response that would be abnormal, as is the case with the absence of response (apathy) often encountered in patients with schizophrenia and some patients with personality disorders. It is, therefore, important to differentiate between sadness and depression, i.e. between an "adaptive" and a "dysfunctional" response to an adverse life event, even though this distinction is sometimes difficult. Both sadness and depression are expected during periods of economic crisis. In the former case, active labor market programs, family support, solidarity and psychological support are needed. In the latter case, in addition to the above, treatment for depression is also required.

This part of the document is particularly important because it addresses the problem ignored by the various editions of the DSM: the distinction between sadness as a normal feeling or emotion (for example, when adapting to difficult life events) and the sadness that accompanies endogenous depression, which is a dysfunctional state that cannot be traced to external events (Maj, 2008). This subject was addressed by Horwitz in his book *The Loss of Sadness, How Psychiatry Transformed Normal Sorrow into a Depressive Disorder* (Horwitz, Wakefield, & Spitzer, 2007). Interestingly, the introduction to this book was written by Robert Spitzer, the architect of the early editions of the DSM. In it he discusses the importance of distinguishing between normal sadness and the morbid mood change of endogenous depression. The WHO note that sadness and unhappiness both appear more frequently in times of crisis, and that to address them more action must be taken in the labour market, and more solidarity and psychological support must be provided.

There is, therefore, an important distinction between a mood change that may be a healthy reaction to a life event and a morbid mental disorder that is not a reaction to external factors. Understandably, many have criticised the DSM for failing to distinguish between these two forms. The DSM also does not use objective criteria and tools, and this has led to many diagnostic variations. Shorter, an established psychiatric researcher, points out that psychiatry has seen many inferior diagnostic methods and prescriptions (fads) over the years, and analyses why this has happened in psychiatry more than in other fields (Shorter, 2013). His concerns are clear when he discusses the difficulty of psychiatric diagnosis and the unfulfilled promise that pharmacology and neuroscience could help bring psychiatry and depression into the world of scientific medicine. It may now, therefore, be useful to consider the problems highlighted by Krishan and Nestler's review of the neurobiology of depression, published in *Nature* in 2008.

Krishan and Nestler's introduction refers to a number of common questions about the DSM's diagnostic criteria and the prevalence of mental disorders. They note that despite the huge impact of depression, we still only have a rudimentary understanding of its pathophysiology compared to other serious multifactorial diseases such as diabetes. They also admit that the diagnosis of depression is subjective, and based the presence of a number of symptoms over a certain period of time, which often occur alongside stress and anxiety. They note, too, that it is based on subjective-qualitative diagnosis using standardised questionnaires.

The treatments available for depression are listed and include: antidepressants, anticonvulsant therapy, psychotherapy and deep brain stimulation. They note that "exercise (physical) promotes recovery". In terms of pathogenesis, numerous conflicting features, followed by a question mark, are outlined: hyper- or hypo-cortisolism (abnormal activity of the hypothalamic-pituitary-adrenal axis), alterations in neurotrophin signalling and abnormal hippocampal neurogenesis, deficits in brain reward processing and abnormal cognitive styles (negative thinking). The authors conclude that: "enormous gaps in the knowledge of depression and its treatment persist, and that researchers and clinicians must embrace the polysyndromic nature of depression and use a multidisciplinary approach to explore the neurobiological bases for the many subtypes of depression" (Krishnan & Nestler, 2008).

The DSM was first published by the APA in 1952, and described 106 diagnostic categories in 130 pages. From there, the number of pages and categories would increase dramatically. The second edition, published in 1960, listed 182 categories over 134 pages. After a number of relevant innovations, the 1980 DSM-III increased this number to 265 categories, listed over 494 pages. This then increased to 292 categories over 567 pages in the revised 1987 edition, DSM-III-R. In 1994, the DSM-IV listed 297 diagnostic categories over 886 pages. After a number of minor tweaks, this turned into the revised 2000 DSM-IV-TR. Then, after a 13-year interval, the DSM-5 was finally released, but not without significant difficulties and criticisms (DSM-I, 1952; DSM-II, 1968; DSM-III, 1980; DSM-IV, 1994; DSM-IV-TR, 2000; DSM-5, 2013).

The DSM came about because of the drive to create a "universal" diagnostic tool that listed and defined symptoms or groups of symptoms (syndromes). The aim was to enable commonly accepted diagnoses for mental illness, which had been discussed before, but still remained elusive. Surprisingly, from the first edition of the DSM, the APA actually sidestepped the problem of how to define mental illnesses themselves. In the title and text of the DSM they are referred to as "disorders (disturbances, discomfort or mental disorders)", avoiding the term "illness" altogether. There were, of course, many limitations to this approach, not least the decision to consider only the presence of signs and symptoms in the diagnosis, along with the wide abandonment of references to psychology, psychodynamics and external factors that may have caused or contributed to the mental suffering of the patient. The APA also chose not to consider internal and external factors, and their interactions.

The numerous revisions to later editions, as well as the startling increase in both pages and diagnostic categories, show that the authors remained concerned that the DSM, despite countless modifications, might still be inadequate (Fischer, 2012). Despite these criticisms and limitations, however, the DSM has experienced enormous success. Each of the DSM's diagnostic categories effectively identified and defined a specific new *illness* (thus over 300 *new illnesses* were identified in the DSM-IV alone). Allen Frances's introduction to the 2013 DSM-5 offers an in-depth analysis of how the DSM has encouraged more and more mental disorder diagnoses. In fact, one of the original authors of the DSM, grew so concerned by the scale of the phenomenon that he addressed it (Frances, 2013a), also in his book: *Saving Normal: An Insider's Revolt Against Out-of-Control Psychiatric Diagnosis, DSM-5, Big Pharma, and the Medicalization of Ordinary Life* (Frances, 2013b).

When the DSM-II was published in 1968, it defined "neurotic depression" using psychodynamic interpretations of internal conflict or the loss of loved ones based on Freudian-Meyerian theories. There was a radical shift away from this when the DSM-III was published in 1980 (Wilson, 1993), with a move away from psychodynamic and psychoanalytical diagnostic criteria. As a result, diagnostic criteria came to be based on statistical analysis of the frequency of symptoms. This was an important move because it was part of an effort to overcome many of the contradictions remaining in psychiatry at that time (Kendler, Muñoz, & Murphy, 2010). Depression came to be seen as a unified disease, and all non-manic forms of it were put in a single category, despite the evidence for the difference between "neurotic depression" and "unipolar psychotic depression" (which is not associated with mania). According to the DSM-III, anyone who met these criteria should be diagnosed as depressed. No clear distinction was made between reactive and endogenous depression, however, because there were no criteria for differentiating normal sadness from a morbid depressive state.

The DSM-III had a major impact on American psychiatry and, indirectly, on psychiatry right across the world. It defined a new entity, "major depressive disorder" (MDD), a unipolar disorder distinct from other depressive conditions, which, the DSM-III claimed, could be easily diagnosed with its criteria. Some psychiatrists criticised the DSM-III's approach, however, because of its emphasis on symptoms rather than aetiology. They also criticized its failure to account for other concomitant external factors. There was still no differentiation between sadness as a normal emotion and morbid sadness; this allowed the medicalization of people experiencing non-pathological moments of difficulty (Horwitz et al., 2007). All the references to the neurotic and psychotic aspects of depression were also removed, as were the links to psychodynamics and psychoanalysis.

In 2000, the DSM-IV-TR was published, and there were no radical differences with its predecessor. MDD was still categorised as a unipolar mood disorder, which could manifest itself in "major depressive episodes", and was distinct from "dysthymia", a less intense depressive disorder. It also kept the category of MDD "sub-threshold cases", which was introduced by the DSM-III. Mourning could still be diagnosed as

MDD when the symptoms lasted for longer than two months (Fischer, 2012; Sanders, 2011).

In hospitals and outpatient facilities today, general practitioners and specialists arrange extensive and sophisticated clinical and laboratory tests for their patients, using the most advanced equipment and methodology. Psychiatrists, on the other hand, try to diagnose their depressed patients by tracing their symptoms in the updated and enlarged version of the DSM-IVR, the DSM-5—often turning to the MDD diagnostic category. Today, the term "depression", if not accompanied by further details, is almost universally associated with the DSM's "major depressive disorder". The word "major" in this definition, if nothing else, suggests a threatening degree of severity. The WHO World Mental Health Day publication, on the other hand, defines depression as "a disorder that can be reliably diagnosed and treated in primary care" (WHO, 2012). It will probably be useful now, therefore, to examine in detail how depression is diagnosed in the DSM.

Mood disorders are divided into "depressive disorders" (unipolar depression) and "bipolar disorders", together with "depression induced by substances". The "depressive disorders" are "major depressive disorder", "dysthymia" and "depressive disorder not otherwise specified" (which is divided into "adjustment disorder with depressed mood" and "adjustment disorder with mixed anxiety and depressed mood"). There are also further possible sub-categories, depending on the severity of cases, the presence of psychotic or melancholic symptoms and postpartum presentations.

Next, the diagnostic procedure for "major depressive disorder". The first criterion of the DSM is that: "five (or more) of the following symptoms have been present during the same 2-week period and represent a change from previous functioning; at least one of the symptoms is either (1) depressed mood or (2) loss of interest or pleasure."

Depressive disorders, therefore, cannot be diagnosed unless the patient has at least a "depressed mood" or a "loss of interest or pleasure". It is surprising, therefore, that nowhere in all its 900 pages does the DSM-IV-TR or DSM-V specifically define the term "depressed mood". The term is colloquially recognisable, and it appears regularly in psychiatric terminology and literature, but the DSM does not offer a specific definition. There is, however, a definition in Hamilton's paper about the psychometric scale for depression, the Hamilton Depression Rating Scale (HDRS) (Hamilton, 1960). The HDRS questionnaire's first question describes a "depressed mood" as a "feeling of sadness, hopelessness, helplessness and worthlessness". The problem with the Hamilton scale, however, is that it should only be used after depression has been diagnosed, so neither the scale's definition of a "depressed mood" nor any of its other contents should be used as diagnostic criteria. The DSM also fails to include a precise definition of "loss of interest or pleasure". This means that the diagnosis of depression is based on the subjective judgement of the examiner, in the absence of clear objective criteria for a "depressed mood" and "loss of pleasure or interest".

The descriptions of the other symptoms are also quite surprising because of the stark contrasts you find in them:

1. *Depressed mood for most of the day, nearly every day, as indicated by either subjective report (feels sad or empty) or observation made by others (appears tearful). Note: in children and adolescents, can be irritable mood*
2. *Markedly diminished interest or pleasure in all, or almost all, activities most of the day, nearly every day (as indicated by either subjective account or observation made by others)*
3. *Significant weight loss when not dieting or weight gain (e.g., a change of more than 5 percent of body weight in a month), or decrease or increase in appetite nearly every day. Note: in children, consider failure to make expected weight gains)*
4. *Insomnia or hypersomnia nearly every day*
5. *Psychomotor agitation or retardation nearly every day (observable by others, not merely subjective feelings of restlessness or being slowed down)*
6. *Fatigue or loss of energy nearly every day*
7. *Feelings of worthlessness or excessive or inappropriate guilt (which may be delusional) nearly every day (not merely self-reproach or guilt about being sick)*
8. *Diminished ability to think or concentrate, or indecisiveness, nearly every day (either by subjective account or as observed by others)*

9. *Recurrent thoughts of death (not just fear of dying), recurrent suicidal ideation without a specific plan, or a suicide attempt or a specific plan for committing suicide.*

Thus, only if the "depressed mood and loss of pleasure or interest" last longer than two months should the subject be diagnosed with major depressive disorder. The DSM-5, however, did attenuate the diagnosis in bereavement-related cases.

A further important point is the possibility of extending the diagnosis to children and adolescents. In this case, the "depressed mood" symptom is replaced by "irritable mood", which the DSM does not go on to define more clearly. Depression in children and adolescents is a delicate and complex matter, and it is a phenomenon that is growing at such a rapid rate that some guidelines deal with it in detail. The issue of postpartum depression, however, receives little attention in the DSM, despite the severity of the problem. This is demonstrated by the University of Toronto's extensive literature review, which was carried out for the Canadian health system (Stewart, Robertson, Dennis, Grace, & Wallington, 2003), as well as the guidelines that have been adopted by various countries (Haran, van Driel, Mitchell, & Brodribb, 2014).

What is so surprising about the DSM's description of depression symptoms is that it seems to be based on a mix of psychiatric and layman's terms. It also makes no reference to objective scientific sources, instead using terms that can be interpreted arbitrarily, such as "nearly", "largely", "excessive" and "inappropriate".

So far, we have examined the current definition and diagnosis of depression—the ones used in most studies, including those involving mindfulness-based interventions. Now, after defining and diagnosing the disorder, the next important step is assessing its severity. This is important for an appropriate clinical judgement of the patient, and for deciding on the best therapeutic intervention. It is also important for evaluating the effectiveness of the therapy used.

The severity of depression is assessed using psychometric scales and questionnaires to be answered by either a clinical examiner or the patient. The most widely used scale for depression is the Hamilton Rating Scale for Depression (HRSD), originally published in 1960

(Hamilton, 1960), and amended numerous times since then—generally in response to a range of criticisms.

There are also, however, a range of other psychometric questionnaires for assessing depression, such as clinical interview schedules, the Menninger Health-Illness Scale and patient self-rating scales like those created by Zung and Beck (FDA, 1997). The results gained from assessments depend entirely on the psychometric scale used.

Extensive use of the Hamilton Scale has shown that it is especially effective for reflecting the mood disorder symptoms described in the various editions of the DSM. It has also been found to be very effective for measuring the changes caused by interventions—particularly first-generation antidepressant drugs. The Beck Depression Inventory is also believed to be very effective for highlighting cognitive changes. This is hardly surprising as the scale was designed to identify mood disorder patients who could be treated with cognitive-behavioural psychotherapy, and to judge the effectiveness of the treatment (Healy, 1997; Leucht et al., 2013).

The Hamilton Rating Scale for Depression (HAM-D) was originally made up of 17 items (Hamilton, 1960), but this was extended to 21 in later versions (Hamilton, 1967). There are now many other versions with a range of different entries and amendments. The items in the HAM-D are graded according to severity, some on a three-point scale (0-2) and others on a five-point scale (0-4), to give an overall score at the end. When psychiatrists have initially diagnosed depression using the DSM diagnostic criteria, they then conduct a clinical interview using the Hamilton Scale to outline the severity of the disorder and the change caused by treatment. The scale's 17 items are:

1. *Depressed mood (Feelings of sadness, hopelessness, helplessness, worthlessness)*
2. *Guilt*
3. *Suicide*
4. *Initial insomnia*
5. *Middle insomnia*
6. *Delayed insomnia*
7. *Work and interests*

8. *Retardation (ideation, speech, lack of concentration, motor disturbance)*
9. *Agitation*
10. *Anxiety (psychic symptoms)*
11. *Anxiety (most common somatic symptoms: dry mouth, flatulence, belching, indigestion, diarrhoea, abdominal cramps, palpitations, headaches, hyperventilation, sighing, frequent urination, excessive sweating)*
12. *Gastro-intestinal symptoms*
13. *General somatic symptoms (heavy limbs, back or head, headache or backache, muscular aching, loss of energy and easily tired)*
14. *Loss of libido*
15. *Hypochondriasis*
16. *Loss of weight*
17. *Loss of insight*

Despite the widespread use of the Hamilton Scale and the DSM's major depressive disorder diagnosis, there are still no official or scientific criteria to determine the severity of depression. As it stands, a score of between seven and 10 is deemed to reflect the absence of depression, while up to 17 is indicates mild depression, 18–24, moderate depression, and over 24, severe depression. According to the American Psychiatric Association (APA), however, the severity of depression is mild if the score is between eight and 13, moderate between 14 and 18, severe between 19 and 22, and very severe if over 22 (Rush, First, & Blacker, 2000).

Almost all the clinical trials for the treatment of depression are still based on the gold standard of double-blind, randomised, placebo-controlled protocols. Researchers then judge how effective treatments have been based on how much patients' Hamilton Scale scores drop (or other similar psychometric scales). Now, then, it may be useful to examine the methods used in the clinical trials of mindfulness-based interventions.

Because of the large number of studies on depression treatments—and the growing number on mindfulness-based treatments—it is now possible to conduct systematic reviews and meta-analysis. Some of the studies available address general issues, such as psychological stress and wellbeing (Gotink et al., 2015; Goyal et al., 2014; Grossman, Niemann, Schmidt, & Walach, 2004), whereas others specifically consider psychiatric disorders (Goldberg et al., 2018). There are many studies focusing on depression, and this is not surprising given the concern about the seeming epidemic of mood disorders. In some instances, studies also examine anxiety, which frequently accompanies depressive symptoms (Hofmann et al., 2010; Piet & Hougaard, 2011; Strauss et al., 2014). Some studies look specifically at certain young or old age groups (Geiger et al., 2015; Zoogman, Goldberg, Hoyt, & Miller, 2014).The mindfulness-based interventions examined have developed over the years from Mindfulness-Based Stress Reduction (MBSR) to Mindfulness-Based Cognitive Therapy (MBCT), which combines MBSR with elements from cognitive therapy to treat depression.

Now, to examine the available meta-analyses in detail. Meta-analysis essentially allows us to evaluate the combined information from several studies—even when the protocols used are not exactly the same. Providing the studies are based on RCTs, and that they do not use drastically different criteria to select their patients, it should be possible examine the results obtained from a much larger cohort of subjects, giving the results greater statistical force and significance. Two key points to consider when preparing meta-analysis, however, are the criteria for selecting subjects, and the tools used for diagnosing and enrolling them. It is also important to consider the criteria for assessing the outcomes of interventions, as well as the nature of the control groups the studies use.

One useful thing to consider here is a comprehensive report published in 2014 called *Mindfulness-Based Interventions for People Diagnosed with a Current Episode of an Anxiety or Depressive Disorder: A Meta-Analysis of Randomised Controlled Trials*. It is a meta-analysis of randomised controlled trials (RCTs) of mindfulness-based interventions (MBIs). All the subjects considered met the diagnostic criteria for a experiencing an episode of depressive or anxiety disorder.

The titles and abstracts of the available reports were found on: MEDLINE, Web of Science, Scopus, ProQuest and PsycINFO. They were from the first available year on each database until 4 July 2013. The search terms used were: mindfulness, MBCT or MBSR combined with anxiety, depression, OCD, obsessive compulsive disorder, post-traumatic stress disorder, PTSD, agoraphobia, panic disorder, acute stress disorder, acute stress reaction or phobia. These terms were combined with random or RCT. Three leading clinical trial registers were also searched to find unpublished but complete trials.

The reports then had to meet a number of inclusion criteria:

1. Designs were Randomized Control Trials;
2. Participants aged 18 years or over;
3. Mindfulness was a core part of the MBI, with mindfulness practice in each therapy session and daily practice encouraged between sessions;
4. Studies included a psychometrically reliable and valid outcome measure of depression or anxiety; and
5. Data was presented for participants who met full diagnostic criteria for a current episode of a DSM-IV (or later version) or ICD-10 anxiety or depressive disorder.

Hypochondriasis (health anxiety) was also included, given the central role that anxiety plays in the disorder.

The exclusion criteria were:

1. Participants had marked cognitive impairment (e.g. learning disability or brain injury);
2. Participants were currently engaged in substance misuse;
3. MBI was not delivered in a group format;
4. MBI was not delivered in-person (e.g. self-help);
5. Studies not in the English language.

The next phase of the analysis was finding studies that fitted these criteria. Of the 1571 initially identified, 12 met the inclusion and exclusion criteria. The studies measured the primary outcomes of interventions using a range of widely employed psychometric scales: *Anxiety Disorders Interview Schedule for DSM-IV-Lifetime version, Beck Depression Inventories, Composite International Diagnostic Interview, Patient Health Questionnaire-9 for depression, Hamilton Rating Scale for Depression, Five Facet Mindfulness Questionnaire, Kentucky Inventory of Mindfulness, Liebowitz Social Anxiety Scale-Self-Report, LSAS-avoidance subscale, LSAS-fear subscale, Mindfulness Attention and Awareness Scale,*

*Mini Mood and Anxiety Symptom Questionnaire, Penn State Worry Questionnaire, Short Health Anxiety Inventory, Mini International Neuropsychiatric Interview, Structured Clinical Interview for DSM–IV–TR Axis I disorders, Spielberger State Trait Anxiety Inventory, Southampton Mindfulness Questionnaire, Yale Brown Obsessive Compulsive Scale.*

These scales are evidently extremely varied, but in each case, interventions are deemed to have had a positive outcome if there is a score reduction. The studies also used a range of different active control conditions: group psychoeducation, treatment as usual (TASU), wait list and aerobic exercise.

As the authors note, their study is the first meta-analysis of mindfulness intervention RCTs where all the studies consider only participants who have been diagnosed with a current episode of depressive or anxiety disorder. The mindfulness-based interventions that were found to a positive impact were Mindfulness Stress Reduction (MBSR), Mindfulness-Based Cognitive Therapy (MBCT) and Personalised-Based Cognitive Therapy (PBCT). The meta-analysis did not, however, include a comparison of the specific effects of each intervention—particularly PBCT. These treatments were found to have a significant impact on the symptoms of depressive disorder, but not anxiety. The authors therefore cautiously concluded that "mindfulness based interventions *might* be considered as an intervention for this population" (Strauss et al., 2014).[1]

Another meta-analytic review on the effect of mindfulness-based therapy on anxiety and depression was published in 2010 by a different group of researchers. It analysed studies if they included: a mindfulness-based intervention, a clinical sample (i.e., participants had a diagnosable psychological or physical/medical disorder), adult samples (ages 18–65) and a measure of anxiety and/or mood symptoms both pre- and post-intervention. The meta-analysis also left out studies that included mindfulness programmes coupled with Acceptance and Commitment Therapy (ACT) or Dialectic Behaviour Therapy (DBT). Of the 116 reports initially identified, 12 met the inclusion and exclusion criteria and were included in the analysis.

[1] Italics added by the author.

The studies judged the effects of interventions using a range of different psychometric scales: *Beck Anxiety Inventory, Beck Scale for Suicidal Ideation, Center for Epidemiologic Studies Depression Scale, Dysfunctional Attitudes Scale, Depression Anxiety Stress Scales, Fear of Negative Evaluation Scale, Hospital Anxiety and Depression Scale, Hamilton Depression Rating Scale, Inventory of Pain Regulation, Interpersonal Sensitivity Measure, Liebowitz Social Anxiety Scale, Medical Symptom Checklist, Profile of Mood States, Penn State Worry Questionnaire, Rumination Scale, Response Style Questionnaire, Hopkins Symptom Checklist- Revised, Self Consciousness Scale, Self-Focused Attention Scale, Social Interaction Scale, Symptoms of Stress Inventory, Social Phobia and Anxiety Inventory, Social Phobic Belief Scale, Social Phobia Scale, State-Trait Anxiety Inventory.*

As in the previous meta-analysis, there is a remarkable variety of psychometric scales in the various different studies used.

To compare the different studies—particularly their control groups—the meta-analysis created an index of their relative quality. The researchers evaluated the quality of each study using these criteria: (1) the study was described as randomised; (2) participants were adequately randomised; (3) the study was described as double-blinded; (4) the method of double-blinding was appropriate; and (5) a description of drop-outs and withdrawals was provided. One point was assigned for each criterion met, giving the studies a maximum of five points.

The authors concluded that the results suggest mindfulness-based therapy is moderately effective for improving mood symptoms. In contrast to the previously mentioned study, the authors said they found the same results for anxiety. The interventions had a sizeable effect, and this effect was maintained in follow-up examinations. As cautiously stated in the paper, the results "*suggest* that mindfulness-based therapy is a promising intervention for treating anxiety and mood problems in clinical populations" (Hofmann et al., 2010).[2]

These two meta-analyses, both using carefully chosen studies of the effects of mindfulness-based interventions, thus seem to show that

---

[2]Italics added by the author.

mindfulness-based interventions can definitely be effective for treating depressive conditions.

A recent systematic review and meta-analysis of mindfulness-based interventions also came to a similar conclusion. It was performed to examine the efficacy of mindfulness-based interventions for patients with psychiatric symptoms for a range of specific disorders. Again, for comparison, the authors created an index of the subjects based on their level of treatment. The five categories were: no treatment, minimal treatment, non-specific active control, specific active control and evidence-based treatment. A total of 142 non-overlapping samples were found, including 12,005 participants.

To be included, studies had to be RCTs of mindfulness-based interventions for adult patients, and the patients had to have had been diagnosed using American Psychological Association directives. Further, each sample had to have either a formal diagnosis or elevated symptoms of a given disorder (i.e., above a given cut-off on a symptom inventory). The researchers included samples that were receiving treatment in a facility focused on a specific disorder (for example, substance abuse treatment). They excluded, however, samples with only elevated stress levels, as these were not considered to reflect a clinical condition. Interventions that combined mindfulness with other approaches (such as MBCT) were included, while therapies that emphasised the attitudinal aspects of mindfulness instead of the formal practice of mindfulness meditation were excluded (such as Acceptance and Commitment Therapy, ACT and Dialectical Behaviour Therapy, DBT). Other forms of meditation (such as mantra repetition) were also excluded. The researchers initially found a total of 9067 studies, but after the exclusion criteria were applied, this dropped to 171 studies, published between 2000 and 2016. They represented a total of 142 independent samples and 12,005 participants.

The researchers analysed the statistically significant differences between the studies' scores before and after interventions. After treatments, mindfulness-based interventions were found to be better than no treatment, minimal treatment, non-specific active controls and specific active controls. Mindfulness-based treatments were at the same level as evidence-based treatments. Follow-up examinations found that mindfulness-based interventions were superior to no treatment conditions. They did not differ from minimal treatment conditions and evidence-based treatments.

In terms of specific disorder subgroups, the results supported the use of mindfulness for treating depression. For pain and weight/eating, mindfulness performed on a par with other active therapies and was superior to no treatment controls. For schizophrenia, mindfulness outperformed no treatment control conditions. For anxiety, mindfulness outperformed no treatment control conditions and was equivalent to other active therapies, including EBTs. For smoking, mindfulness outperformed evidence-based treatments (EBT)s, while the effects on other additions varied.

Overall, mindfulness therapies were superior to no treatment, minimal treatment and psychological placebo control groups. Mindfulness-based interventions were on average also roughly at the same level as first-line, evidence-based therapies such as cognitive behavioural therapy and antidepressant medications. The authors conclude that their results suggest there is an empirical basis for mindfulness-based therapies for depression and other psychiatric conditions, with relatively little variation across disorders (Goldberg et al., 2018).

These show the results when research considers the many reliable and comparable reports on the effects of mindfulness. It may now be useful to look at some recent meta-analyses of mindfulness interventions with specific characteristics, such as using certain subject age groups, preventing *relapses* of depression rather than active mood disorders, and treating psychiatric problems or wellbeing. When the meta-analysis focused on these more specific areas, however, there were fewer studies, subjects, conditions and outcomes available to consider.

One particular study from 2014 claims to be the first published meta-analysis of the growing literature on youth-focused mindfulness. Its aim was to attempt to identify conditions that mindfulness could be particularly effective at treating in young people. The inclusion criteria were that studies had to be peer-reviewed journal articles published in English, their participants had to be under 18, and mindfulness had to be the chief element of the interventions analysed. Of the 1784 initially found, 20 were mindfulness studies using 16-21-year-olds. Most of the interventions were administered in schools. They were: Mindfulness-Based Stress Reduction, Mindfulness-Based Cognitive Therapy for Children and other interventions using elements of Mindfulness-Based Stress Reduction. Most of the studies used non-clinical samples, while four used clinical samples. The dependent variables included a variety of psychometrically determined outcomes, including measures of psychological symptoms (e.g., anxiety, depression), measures of general functioning (e.g., social skills, quality of life) and measures of mindfulness and attention.

Interventions were found to be helpful for young people; and did not result in iatrogenic harm. Overall, mindfulness treatments were found to be superior to the active control conditions used. Mindfulness was also found to have a much greater effect on psychological symptoms compared to the dependant variables mentioned above. Although the majority of studies on youth mindfulness interventions use healthy participants recruited from schools, the authors suggest it may be useful for future research to focus on targeting symptoms of psychopathology in young people in clinical settings (Zoogman et al., 2014).

As well as young people, there is also a critical review of the effects of mindfulness-based interventions on older adults. The literature for this was found on PsycINFO, Academic Search Complete and Medline. It was found using keywords such as gerontology, geriatric, elder, aging, older adults and mindfulness. The search yielded 285 articles, and of these, 15 met the inclusion criteria. The psychometric scales used in these studies are, again, very varied, although there is some overlap with the other critical reviews mentioned above: *Loneliness Scale, Short-Form General Health Survey, Geriatric Depression Scale-12R, Geriatric Depression Scale-Short From, Ruminative Responses Scale, Short Form, Hospital Anxiety and Depression Scale, 7-item Anxiety subscale, Sleep Problems Scale, Center for Epidemiologic Studies Depression Scale, Hamilton Rating Scale for Depression, Positive Affect Negative Affect Scale, Penn State Worry Questionnaire-Abbreviated, Mindful Attention Awareness Scale, Cognitive Affective Mindfulness Scale-Revised, McGill Pain Questionnaire-Short Form, Chronic Pain Acceptance Questionnaire, Roland & Morris Disability Questionnaire, 6-minute Walk Test, Saint George Respiratory Questionnaire, Visual Analogue Scale, Memorial*

*Symptom Assessment Scale, Five Facet Mindfulness Questionnaire, Perceived Stress Scale, Beck Depression Inventory-II, Harvard Trauma Questionnaire-Part IV. Inventory of Complicated Grief-Revised, Centrality of Events Scale, Depression Anxiety Stress Scales, Kentucky Inventory of Mindfulness Skills, Neuropathic Pain Scale, Neuopathy-Specific Quality of Life Tool, Pittsburgh Sleep Quality Index, Profile of Mood States- Short Form.*

Some of the psychometric scales were based on physical symptoms, and biological measures (IGF-1, IL-6, (Ig)M, IgG, systolic and diastolic blood pressure) were also considered. The results, in terms of both physical and emotional wellbeing, offer some support for the use of mindfulness-based interventions with older adults. The authors, however, said that their results were limited because of methodological flaws, and suggested that more older subjects should be included in future mindfulness-based empirical research (Geiger et al., 2015).

In 2014, the *Journal of the American Medical Association, Internal Medicine*, published a systematic review and meta-analysis of meditation programmes for psychological stress and wellbeing (Goyal et al., 2014). After explaining that many people meditate to reduce psychological stress and stress-related problems, the authors argue that people should be properly counselled about the practice, and that clinicians should know what the evidence says about the health benefits of meditation. The study therefore sets out to determine how effective meditation programmes are at improving stress-related conditions such as anxiety, depression, stress/distress, negative mood, mental health–related quality of life, lack of attention, substance use, poor eating habits, sleeplessness, pain, and weight disorders.

The subject groups examined are very varied and somewhat difficult to define. This may be because of the broader range of conditions considered. The authors found clinical trials with active controls for placebo effects on MEDLINE, PsycINFO, EMBASE, PsycArticles, Scopus, CINAHL, AMED, the Cochrane Library, as well as manual searches. Two independent reviewers screened citations, extracted data and graded the strength of evidence for the risk of bias, precision, directness and consistency. After reviewing a total of 18,753 citations, they found and analysed 47 trials including 3515 participants.

For studies to be included, they had to be examining adults with a clinical medical or psychiatric diagnosis. Stressors were also included, and all the studies had to be RCTs with an active control. The research defined an active control as being matched in time and attention to the real intervention. The idea of this is to make certain that all participants expect roughly the same benefits, and examples of this included: attention control, educational control or another therapy, such as progressive muscle relaxation.

Many interventions were excluded, showing just how many caring practices there are that involve less rigorous and clearly defined procedures. Programmes in which meditation was not the main part of the intervention included: dialectic behaviour therapy (DBT) and acceptance and commitment therapy (ACT). These were xcluded together with any of the movement-based meditation therapies, such as yoga (eg. Iyengar, Hatha, shavasana), tai chi, and qi gong (chi kung). Also excluded were aromatherapy, biofeedback, neurofeedback, hypnosis, autogenic training, psychotherapy, laughter therapy, therapeutic touch, eye movement desensitization reprocessing, relaxation therapy, spiritual therapy, breathing exercises, pranayama exercises, as well as any intervention that is given remotely or only by video or audio without a physically present practitioner.

The study concludes that there is some evidence that 8-week and 3–6 month mindfulness meditation programmes improve anxiety and depression, There is also evidence of reduced pain, as well as a small amount of evidence of improved stress/distress and mental health–related quality of life. There was no or insufficient evidence, however, that they have any effect on positive mood, attention, substance use, eating habits, sleep and weight. There was also no evidence that meditation programmes are better than any active treatment such as drugs, exercise and other behavioural therapies. The authors stressed that there was no evidence from the meta-analysis that meditation programmes cause harm, although few trials focused specifically on this question.

The results of the critical review and meta-analyses are very valuable because they use a much larger and statistically analysed sample to provide evidence for the efficacy of mindfulness for treating certain conditions. Many of the mindfulness studies they consider are focused on the problem of depression, and it may now be worth examining in detail one of the most thorough of the studies evaluating the effectiveness of mindfulness interventions and mindfulness-based cognitive therapy for treating depression.

This study is called *Effectiveness and cost-effectiveness of mindfulness-based cognitive therapy compared with maintenance antidepressant treatment in the prevention of depressive relapse or recurrence (PREVENT): a randomised controlled trial.* It was carried out by a large group of researchers from several of the leading British academic institutions for the study of mindfulness. Willem Kuyken is the lead author, and the report was published 2015 in the journal *The Lancet*.

One of the key reasons the study was made was the high risk of repeated depressive relapse or recurrence among patients with a history of recurrent depression. The current recommendation for these patients is that they should be treated with antidepressant drugs for at least two years. MBCT has been shown to be more effective than usual care at reducing the risk of relapse or recurrence. It had not yet been compared with maintenance antidepressant treatment in a definitive trial, however.

The PREVENT study was therefore set up as a single-blind, parallel, group randomised controlled trial. The researchers gathered adult patients with three or more previous major depressive episodes, who were also on maintenance antidepressants, from primary care general practices across the UK. The aim of the study was to test whether MBCT with support to taper or discontinue antidepressant treatment (MBCT-TS) was better than maintenance antidepressants. The primary finding was that it is more effective at preventing depressive relapses and recurrence over a 24-month period. It also found that produced more depression-free days, and was more effective against residual depressive symptoms, psychiatric and medical comorbidity. It also had better results in terms quality of life and cost-effectiveness. The participants were randomly assigned to either MBCT-TS or maintenance antidepressants, and were grouped according to their centre and symptomatic status. The study's participants were aware of which treatments were allocated, but the research assessors were masked to this.

The inclusion criteria were that participants had to be recruited from general practices in urban and rural settings in four parts of the UK.

They also had to have been diagnosed with recurrent major depressive disorder in full or partial remission, based on the Diagnostic and Statistical Manual of Mental Disorders-IV (DSM-IV). They also had to have suffered three or more previous major depressive episodes, be 18 years old or above, and they had to be on a therapeutic dose of maintenance antidepressant drugs in line with British National Formulary (BNF) and NICE guidance. The exclusion criteria were that they must not be experiencing a current major depressive episode, have comorbid diagnoses of current substance misuse, organic brain damage or either current or past psychosis, including bipolar disorder, persistent antisocial behaviour and persistent self-injury needing clinical management or therap. They also could not be having formal concurrent psychotherapy.

Great care was taken with the organisation of the MBCT intervention, and this was explained in extensive detail in the method section of the report. The report describes its MBCT as a manualised, group-based skills training programme designed to help patients learn skills that will prevent the recurrence of depression. Their MBCT also involves participants being instructed about mindfulness practices and cognitive-behavioural skills both in their sessions and in homework assignments. The programme they used consisted of eight 2.25-hour group sessions, normally over consecutive weeks. There were also four refresher sessions offered roughly every three months for the following year. The competency of each therapist was carefully evaluated before they could run any of the trial groups. An experienced MBCT therapist independent of the trial also rated at least two videotapes for every potential therapist using the *Mindfulness-Based Interventions Teacher Assessment Criteria* and *MBCT Adherence Scale* (MBCT-AS). Then patients in the MBCT-TS group also received support with tapering or discontinuing their maintenance antidepressants—both from the MBCT-TS therapist and their general practitioners.

Participants were randomly allocated to receive either maintenance antidepressant treatment or an eight-week MBCT class that included support to taper or discontinue their maintenance antidepressant medication (MBCT-TS). They were randomly assigned to the two groups, and stratified according to their symptoms using the GRID-Hamilton

Rating Scale for Depression. Less than eight was classified as asymptomatic and equal or over eight was classified as partially symptomatic. The trial administrator told the participants which group they had been assigned to in a letter, while the assessors were blinded to the different groups throughout the trial and during the follow-up period.

The participants were assessed before randomisation, one month after the eight-week MBCT-TS programme (or the equivalent in the maintenance antidepressant group), and at nine, 12, 18, and 24 months after the randomisation. Primarily, the researchers measured the time until relapse or the recurrence of depression. For this, a recurrence was defined as an episode meeting the DSM-IV criteria for a major depressive episode. The secondary measures were the number of depression-free days, residual depressive symptoms, psychiatric and medical comorbidity, quality of life and cost-effectiveness. The primary analysis was based on the principle of intention to treat.

The researchers found participants by searching computerised general practitioner databases to find patients who were being prescribed a therapeutic dose of antidepressants; interested patients could also self-refer.

The details of the enrolment process are quite interesting. The initial search found 28,597 possible patients. Of these, 8989 were excluded by their general practitioners, 19,608 were invited to participate to the trial, 1881 declined further contact, 14,756 did not respond and 872 could not contact back. 89 people also self-referred. 2188 patients were then assessed for eligibility, and of these a further 8989 were excluded by general practitioners. Ultimately, 424 were selected and randomised.

212 patients were assigned to MBCT-TS, and of those, 176 completed four or more sessions, 30 started treatment but did fewer than four sessions, while six did not start the treatment. 212 were also assigned to maintenance antidepressant medication, and of those, 162 remained on the antidepressants. In both groups several patients withdrew, were lost at follow-up or even died. In the end, in both groups, remarkably, there were 183 people who completed the 24-month follow-up. Five adverse events were reported, including two deaths, in each of the MBCT-TS and maintenance antidepressants groups. These adverse events were not attributed to the interventions or the trial.

In the maintenance antidepressant medication group, 76 per cent of the patients stayed on the therapeutic dose; in the MBCT with support to taper or discontinue antidepressants, three per cent of patients did not initiate MBCT treatment. The overall mean number of sessions attended was six, and 83 per cent completed four or more MBCT sessions. Of the patients who attended four or more MBCT-TS sessions, 13 per cent did not reduce their dosage, 17 per cent reduced their dosage and 71 per cent stopped taking their antidepressants.

In the summary of the study, the authors said: "We found no evidence that MBCT-TS is superior to maintenance antidepressant treatment for the prevention of depressive relapse in individuals at risk for depressive relapse or recurrence. Both treatments were associated with enduring positive outcomes in terms of relapse or recurrence, residual depressive symptoms, and quality of life." The original aim of the study was to see whether MBCT with support to taper or discontinue antidepressant treatment (MBCT-TS) was superior to maintenance antidepressants for preventing depressive relapses and recurrences over a 24-month period. The summary of the study, however, seems to work hard to minimise its importance, suggesting that mindfulness-based intervention is just as effective as standard antidepressants for preventing depressive relapses.

It must be remembered that the concepts of 'superiority' and 'inferiority' applied here derive from the vocabulary of trial protocols designed using the principles of evidence-based medicine. The evidence suggests, however, that although mindfulness-based interventions may not be *more* effective, they are no *less* effective than the standard antidepressant drug treatments. This is important—especially given the fact that many antidepressant drugs cause significant adverse side effects that mindfulness does not.

There was no evidence that MBCT-TS led to a statistically significant reduction in the hazard of relapse or recurrence compared with maintenance antidepressant treatment. In one specific group, however, there was a significant difference. MBCT-TS reduced the risk of relapse or recurrence for participants who had reported severe childhood abuse. This reduction was higher than with antidepressant drugs.

For many, these results may seem cause for optimism, bit this is to ignore the matter of statistical significance. The risk of recurrence or relapse to depression is smaller for the mindfulness group compared with the drug treated group during the follow-up period. Between five and 15 months, the number at risk drops by approximately 10 per cent. This may be more definitive with a larger sample, translating to a large proportion of the total population suffering from mood disorders.

A critical analysis of this study would probably raise other concerns. This makes the need for the using the most accurate procedures during clinical trials even more evident. Using the most rigorous protocols would produce results that were beyond criticism. Let us for the moment, however, move on to the procedures that were used for selecting and enrolling the subjects in this trial. The 28,597 people who were initially found were all being treated for a depressive condition by the UK NHS. To try to gather statistically significant results from a homogenous group, this number was reduced to 414. In terms of judging inferiority and superiority, the study partially achieved its aim. There are, however, still unanswered questions about why the other 28,183 depression sufferers were excluded from the sample. If they were indeed significantly different from the sample considered, what were their distinctive qualities, and how would the results have changed if they had been included.

Nor are the need for statistically significant results and the highly restricted sample the only concerns. For its inclusion criteria, the study used the Diagnostic and Statistical Manual of Mental Disorders-IV (DSM-IV). The criteria for defining a relapse or recurrence were similar to the DSM-IV's major depressive episode criteria. The study then measured the severity of depression with psychometric scales such as the GRID-HAMD22 and the self-reported Beck Depression Inventory (BDI).

Much effort was clearly put into using the most rigorous protocols. The researchers also worked hard to adhere to accepted, manual-based standards for delivering cognitive psychotherapy and mindfulness-based interventions. Surprisingly, however, their succinct description of MBCT does not once mention meditation, although it does refer to three published sources that describe the practice in more detail

(Crane et al., 2013; Segal, Teasdale, Williams, & Gemar, 2002; Segal, Williams, & Teasdale, 2013).

Before the trial, cognitive psychotherapy, mindfulness-based stress reduction and various forms of meditation had been already used on subjects with mood disorders, with positive and encouraging results. It is evident that the PREVENT trial was aimed at evaluating just MBCT. When examining a complex procedure, however, it may be necessary determine whether the whole intervention (in this case MBCT) is responsible for the observed effects, or whether they are caused by individual components (CBT, MBSTR or just meditation).

This becomes relevant when considering the COBRA trial, which was carried out in 2016 in the UK by a number of groups that were involved in the PREVENT study. The main aim of the COBRA trial was to compare Cognitive Behavioural Therapy for Depression with a simpler intervention, Behavioural Activation (Richards et al., 2016). The authors rightly mention that most widely used and best-evidenced form of therapy is cognitive behavioural therapy (CBT), which is complex, costly and requires highly skilled and trained therapists. The study was therefore designed to test whether a simpler depression therapy, behavioural activation (BA), might be as effective and cheaper.

The trial's protocols were largely similar to PREVENT's. The COBRA trial was a randomised, controlled, non-inferiority trial, which used adults aged 18 or over who met the *Diagnostic and Statistical Manual of Mental Disorders IV* criteria for a major depressive disorder. The patients were also taken from primary care and psychological therapy services from across the UK. They then tested for depression symptoms after 12 months using the PHQ-9 psychometric scale questionnaire.

The authors found that BA, a psychological treatment simpler than CBT, delivered by junior mental health workers with less intensive and costly training, has no lesser effect than CBT. They found that effective psychological therapy for depression can be delivered without the need for costly and highly trained professionals. Although the aims of the PREVENT and COBRA trials were not identical, the latter's results suggest the need to determine whether the results obtained with MBCT are specifically caused by this intervention or its individual components.

There are several issues with these trials that are still unresolved. First, the inclusion criteria are based only on a single diagnostic tool, the DSM. The outcome criteria are also based solely on scores from psychometric scale questionnaires. Another issue is the fact that the trials use single-blinding, which only partially avoids potential biases when evaluating interventions, since the subjects and therapists are aware of which intervention has been given. This is because of the recognised difficulty and perhaps even impossibility of devising and delivering placebo interventions that would allow double-blinding, as well as providing useful comparison placebo groups. Exploring these issues would strengthen the results that have been obtained so far, as well as clarifying how much the effect of mindfulness-based interventions is down to mindfulness itself, and how much is caused by the other procedures involved.

The meta-analyses previously examined are somewhat more robust because they can analyse all available literature on the subject of mindfulness applications. They are not without problems, however, which are similar to those that affect the individual reports they analyse. These problems arise from the fact that many meta-analyses use small samples of the many available reports. The meta-analyses considered above found a total of 33,250 studies, and chose no more than 300 reports—0.9 per cent of the original selection. This adds to the issues with individual trials that have already been listed.

It may now be useful to examine the results of the UK's IAPT programme. NICE took the first step in developing the IAPT by issuing clinical guidelines that strongly recommended psychological therapy. It is sufficient to note here that NICE has continuously researched ways of treating depression and anxiety and issued numerous guidelines over the years, which included psychological therapy, and ultimately led to the development of the IAPT programme.

One of the key researchers behind the programme, David Clark, has recently published an analysis of the results of IAPT. He reminds us that effective psychological therapies have been developed for depression and all the anxiety disorders, and that NICE recommends these treatments as first line interventions. Layard and Clark argued that making evidence-based psychological therapies more widely available would save money as well as reduce suffering. On the basis of their studies, the UK government funded two pilot projects which had positive and encouraging results. Starting in 2008, the Government developed a plan to Improve Access to Psychological Therapies (IAPT) throughout England by training a large number of therapists in psychological treatments. These would then be provided in new community services for depression and anxiety disorders. IAPT services used a new session-by-session outcome monitoring system, which took performed pre-treatment and post-treatment anxiety and depression tests on 98 per cent of all treated patients. From small beginnings, IAPT has grown to the point where it now treats over 560,000 people each year. Overall results reveal that around 50 per cent of patients recover and two-thirds show reliable improvement (Clark, 2018).

The NICE guidelines introduced a Stepped Care model of intervention for the therapeutic treatment of depression and anxiety. Step 1 occurs in Primary Care outside the IAPT service, and involves recognising cases of moderate to severe depression. The guidelines recommend assessment, referral, active monitoring and collaborative care. Step 2 consists of low intensity interventions, which for depression are Individual Guided Self-Help based on CBT, Computerized CBT, Behavioural Activation, and a Structured Group Physical Activity Programme. Step 3 is in high intensity IAPT services. It is for mild to moderate depression and delivers CBT or IPT, Behavioural Activation (BA), Couples Therapy, Counselling for Depression, and Brief Psychodynamic Therapy. Moderate to severe cases of depression received these as well as CBT or IPT medication (NICE's 2009, 2019a, 2019b).

Depression is identified using the patients health questionnaire scale PHQ-9 (Kroenke, Spitzer, & Williams, 2001), and the scoring obtained using this scale is used to assess the outcome of the intervention. A patient becomes a *case* if their score is nine or above on the PHQ-9 scale. The outcome is measured on a session-by-session basis. Patients are deemed to have recovered if their depression score is above the clinical cut-off point at the start of their treatment and falls below 9 by the end.

The IAPT programme is an extraordinary project. It is a unique example of a health service identifying and treating depressive conditions on a national scale. The initiative uses interventions that are structured along strict guidelines, and which integrate psychological support and psychotherapy as the first line of response, then add antidepressant medication for less responsive and more severe cases.

The data from the IAPT programme has been carefully collected and analysed, and it may now be useful to examine it in more detail. IAPT is still a work in progress, but by 2017, it had been established in all 209 of England's local health regions. Over 7000 new therapists have been trained, approximately 60 per cent of whom are high intensity therapists and 40 per cent of whom are Psychological Wellbeing Practitioners (PWPs). IAPT services see over 960,000 people a year, which is around 16 per cent of those with depression and anxiety disorders in the UK (McManus, Bebbington, Jenkins, & Brugha, 2016). Some people are only seen once to be assessed and given advice. They are then referred to other services for further intervention if necessary. Over 560,000 people (approximately 60% of the total) go on to a course of treatment involving two or more therapy sessions. 36 per cent only receive low-intensity interventions, 28 per cent receive high-intensity interventions, and 34 per cent receive both. This means that during the course of their treatment in IAPT's stepped care services, 70 per cent of patients receive at least one low-intensity intervention and 62 per cent receive at least one high-intensity intervention.

Everyone who has two or more treatment sessions before discharge is assessed after their interventions. 98.5 per cent of them have pre-treatment and post-treatment scores on both the depression and anxiety measures. The overall recovery rate among them is 51 per cent, while 66.3 per cent show some level of improvement. For depression cases the pre-post effect size on the PHQ-9 is 1.4. The effect size on the PHQ-9 scale is vital for identifying depressed patients—as well as for assessing their recovery after intervention. It may therefore now be useful to examine this psychometric tool in more detail (Kroenke et al., 2001).

PHQ-9 is a self-administered questionnaire, which has to be filled in by the patient. The possible answers are "Not at all", "Several Days", "More than half the days" and "Nearly every day" for the question: "Over the last 2 weeks, how often have you been bothered by any of the following problems?"

The problems are:

1. Little interest or pleasure in doing things
2. Feeling down, depressed, or hopeless
3. Trouble falling or staying asleep, or sleeping too much
4. Feeling tired or having little energy
5. Poor appetite or overeating
6. Feeling bad about yourself—or that you are a failure or have let yourself or your family down
7. Trouble concentrating on things, such as reading the newspaper or watching television
8. Moving or speaking so slowly that other people could have noticed? Or the opposite—being so fidgety or restless that you have been moving around a lot more than usual
9. Thoughts that you would be better off dead or of hurting yourself in some way.

A score is attributed to each answer: 0 for "Not at all", 1 for "Several Days", 2 for "More than half the days" and 3 for "Nearly every day". The PHQ-9 total score is the total from these. This is then used for diagnosis and determining whether a patient has recovered or not.

You can immediately see a number of parallels between the IAPT protocols, the DSM's diagnostic criteria for major depressive disorder and the HDRS used for assessing the effectiveness of antidepressant drugs. The IAPT uses the PHQ-9 psychometric scale to evaluate the effectiveness of its interventions. Its criteria overlap significantly with the DSM, the Hamilton and various other similar scales.

The concerns about the DSM's diagnostic criteria for depression have already been discussed in some detail, and many similar points can be raised about the PHQ-9. There is particular uncertainty about how it measures the magnitude of the reduction after treatment, and this has been widely debated in the context of antidepressant drugs. These concerns raise questions not only about their clinical use, but also about national regulatory agencies authorising their sale and prescription (Giraldi, 2017). In the case of the IAPT programme, for a patient to have technically recovered from their depressive disorder, their PHQ-9 scores must drop by two points for the same question or one for two separate questions. This assessment is broadly accepted despite its obvious limitations (Clark, 2018; The Improving Access to Psychological Therapies Manual Appendices and Helpful Resources, 2019).

General conclusions can be drawn about the 560,000-plus patients the IAPT programme currently treats. Around 50 per cent of patients treated in IAPT services recover and two-thirds show worthwhile benefits. These results have been analysed in detail and publicly reported each year from 2012/13 to 2017/18. It may be useful to look more closely at these results now (Psychological Therapies: Annual Report on the Use of IAPT Services England, 2019).

The core purpose of the IAPT project was to improve access to psychological support and psychotherapy. Antidepressant drugs were to be limited to cases that did not respond adequately to psychological intervention, thus avoiding the associated negative side effects where possible. The programme's report for 2014–15 includes a table showing the recovery rates for a range of different therapy types:

| | |
|---|---|
| Computerised Cognitive Behavioural Therapy (CCBT) | 58.4% |
| Interpersonal Psychotherapy (IPT) | 53.9% |
| Couples therapy | 52.0% |
| Guided self-help | 47.8% |
| Brief psychodynamic psychotherapy | 47.0% |
| Counselling | 45.2% |
| Other HI | 45.1% |
| Behaviour activation | 44.8% |
| Cognitive Behaviour Therapy (CBT) | 44.1% |
| Psychoeducational peer support | 43.0% |
| Not specified | 39.6% |
| Pure self-help | 38.5% |

This table does not seem to be intended as a thorough investigation of the individual benefits of the different interventions. The sizes of the different groups are different depending on whether the treatments were high- or low-intensity. However, considering the national scale of the IAPT, the results from all the groups are not negligible and deserve attention. Cognitive Behaviour Therapy (CBT) was the psychological intervention that was initially proposed for the IAPT project.

The recovery rate for CBT is 44.1 per cent, and is between the top score of 58.4 per cent (Computerized Cognitive Behavioural Therapy—CCBT) and the lowest score of 38.5 per cent (pure self-help). The other interventions based on cognitive, psychodynamic and other principles also came up with intermediate recovery rates (Psychological Therapies: Annual Report on the Use of IAPT Services England, 2019). There were slightly different results in the 2015–16 report (Psychological Therapies: Annual Report on the Use of IAPT Services England 2014/15, 2019). There were also similar results for anxiety treatments.

The yearly reports on the results of the IAPT do not refer to MBCT. However, the clinical guideline *Depression in adults: recognition and management CG90* published in 2009 by NICE states that people with depression and who are deemed to be at significant risk of relapse or who have residual symptoms should be offered either individual CBT or MBCT (Psychological Therapies: Annual Report on the Use of IAPT Services England, 2015–16, 2019). The IAPT has also laid out guidelines for a Mindfulness-based Cognitive Therapy National MBCT Training Curriculum to improve the quality of this type of therapy (NICE Depression in Adults: Recognition and Management, CG90, 2019; IAPT: Mindfulness-Based Cognitive Therapy National MBCT Training Curriculum, 2019).

This chapter has considered the available evidence about the many different interventions based on mindfulness. A very large number of reports have been published on this matter, focusing on a range of different conditions and mindfulness-based approaches.

Depression is now a global health concern, both because of its cultural prevalence and the fact that it now forms a major part of the world disease burden. According to available estimates and diagnostic criteria, depression has now become effectively an epidemic, with even more worrying implications for the future. At the same time, however, more and more attention has been focused on mindfulness as a treatment for depression, producing encouraging results—particularly, when combined with cognitive psychotherapy, in terms of preventing recurrences and relapses.

The quality of the reports published on the subject varies widely from simple observational studies to rigorous clinical trials. There have been, as we have seen in this chapter, very many studies of the effects of mindfulness-based interventions on depression. This allowed meta-analysis to come up with more meaningful results from a much larger cohort of subjects. The exclusion criteria for meta-analysis led to a much smaller selection of studies. In fact, the meta-analyses considered only approximately one per cent of all the available studies.

The UK's *Improving Access to Psychological Therapy* programme is a unique case where it was possible to assess the depression treatment of an extremely large number of subjects. UK researchers also made a major contribution to the integration of mindfulness into cognitive therapy, developing MBCT. This, in the end, was one of the key IAPT interventions. Because of the enormous scale of the intervention, its future results will be particularly significant.

There are still, however, problems with providing objective and definitive evidence for the effectiveness of mindfulness. These are to do with the quality of the protocols followed by many of the studies, as well as the intrinsic problems with a treatment that relies on meditation as its core component. This is to do with the coexistence and interrelation of cognitive-based psychotherapies and psychodynamic, humanist and interpersonal practices. Another important question is how Buddhist practices are being integrated into Western cultures, shorn of their religious origins and transformed into almost secular disciplines. It may in the next chapter, therefore, be interesting to trace and summarise the various evolutions of traditional meditation and how it is being integrated into the worlds of spiritual, health and personal development.

## References

Belofsky, N. (2013). *Strange medicine: A shocking history of real medical practices through the ages*. London: Perigee Book.

Bhugra, D. (2003). Migration and depression. *Acta Psychiatrica Scandinavica, 108*(s418), 67–72. https://doi.org/10.1034/j.1600-0447.108.s418.14.x.

Bhugra, D., & Mastrogianni, A. (2004). Globalisation and mental disorders. *British Journal of Psychiatry, 184*(1), 10–20. https://doi.org/10.1192/bjp.184.1.10.

Bird, J., & Pinch, C. (2002). *Autogenic therapy: Self-help for mind and body.* Dublin: Newleaf.
Brann, L., Owens, J., & Williamson, A. (2012). *The handbook of contemporary clinical hypnosis.* Chichester, UK: Wiley-Blackwell.
Cabras, P. L., Lippi, D., & Lovari, F. (2005). *Due millenni di melancholia.* Bologna: CLUEB.
Clark, D. (2018). Realizing the mass public benefit of evidence-based psychological therapies: The IAPT program. *Annual Review of Clinical Psychology, 14*(1), 159–183. https://doi.org/10.1146/annurev-clinpsy-050817-084833.
Crane, R., Eames, C., Kuyken, W., Hastings, R., Williams, J., Bartley, T., et al. (2013). Development and validation of the mindfulness-based interventions: Teaching assessment criteria (MBI: TAC). *Assessment, 20*(6), 681–688. https://doi.org/10.1177/1073191113490790.
Culberston, F. M. (1997). Depression and gender: An international review. *American Psychologist, 52*(1), 25–31.
DSM-I. (1952). *Diagnostic and statistical manual of mental disorders.* Washington, DC: American Psychiatric Association.
DSM-II. (1968). *Diagnostic and statistical manual of mental disorders* (2nd ed.). Washington, DC: American Psychiatric Association.
DSM-III. (1980). *Diagnostic and statistical manual of mental disorders* (3rd ed.). Washington, DC: American Psychiatric Association.
DSM-IV. (1994). *Diagnostic and statistical manual of mental disorders* (4th ed.). Washington, DC: American Psychiatric Association.
DSM-IV-TR. (2000). *Diagnostic and statistical manual of mental disorders* (4th ed. text revision). Washington, DC: American Psychiatric Association.
DSM-5. (2013). *Diagnostic and statistical manual of mental disorders* (5th ed.). Washington, DC: American Psychiatric Association.
FDA. (1997). *Guidance for industry. Guidance for the clinical evaluation of antidepressant drugs.* Center for Drug Evaluation and Research. U.S. Department of Health and Human Services, Food and Drug Administration. U.S. Food and Drug Administration: Protecting and promoting your health (2019). Retrieved from http://www.fda.gov/downloads/Drugs/GuidanceComplianceRegulatoryInformation/Guidances/ucm071299.pdf. Accessed 19 April 2019.
Ferrari, A., Charlson, F., Norman, R., Patten, S., Freedman, G., & Murray, C., et al. (2013). Burden of depressive disorders by country, sex, age, and year: Findings from the global burden of disease study 2010. *PLoS Medicine, 10*(11), e1001547. https://doi.org/10.1371/journal.pmed.1001547.

Frances, A. (2013a). The new crisis in confidence in psychiatric diagnosis. *Annals of Internal Medicine*. https://doi.org/10.7326/0003-4819-159-3-201308060-00655.

Frances, A. (2013b). *Saving normal: An insider's revolt against out-of control psychiatric diagnosis, DSM-5, Big pharma, and the medicalization of ordinary life*. New York: HarperCollins.

Geiger, P., Boggero, I., Brake, C., Caldera, C., Combs, H., Peters, J., & Baer, R. (2015). Mindfulness-based interventions for older adults: A review of the effects on physical and emotional well-being. *Mindfulness, 7*(2), 296–307. https://doi.org/10.1007/s12671-015-0444-1.

Giraldi, T. (2017). *Unhappiness, sadness and 'depression'*. Cham: Springer.

Goldberg, S., Tucker, R., Greene, P., Davidson, R., Wampold, B., Kearney, D., & Simpson, T. (2018). Mindfulness-based interventions for psychiatric disorders: A systematic review and meta-analysis. *Clinical Psychology Review, 59*, 52–60. https://doi.org/10.1016/j.cpr.2017.10.011.

Gotink, R., Chu, P., Busschbach, J., Benson, H., Fricchione, G., & Hunink, M. (2015). Standardised mindfulness-based interventions in healthcare: An overview of systematic reviews and meta-analyses of RCTs. *PLoS One, 10*(4), e0124344. https://doi.org/10.1371/journal.pone.0124344.

Goyal, M., Singh, S., Sibinga, E., Gould, N., Rowland-Seymour, A., & Sharma, R., et al. (2014). Meditation programs for psychological stress and well-being. *JAMA Internal Medicine, 174*(3), 357. https://doi.org/10.1001/jamainternmed.2013.13018.

Greenstone, G. (2010). The history of bloodletting. *BC Medical Journal, 52*(1), 12–14.

Grossman, P., Niemann, L., Schmidt, S., & Walach, H. (2004). Mindfulness-based stress reduction and health benefits. *Journal of Psychosomatic Research, 57*(1), 35–43. https://doi.org/10.1016/s0022-3999(03)00573-7.

Grube, G. (1954). Greek medicine and the Greek genius. *Phoenix, 8*(4), 123. https://doi.org/10.2307/1086122.

Hamilton, M. (1960). A rating scale for depression. *Journal of Neurological and Neurosurgical Psychiatry, 23*, 56–62.

Hamilton, M. (1967). Development of a rating scale for primary depressive illness. *British Journal of Social and Clinical Psychology, 6*(4), 278–296.

Haran, C., van Driel, M., Mitchell, B., & Brodribb, W. (2014). Clinical guidelines for postpartum women and infants in primary care—A systematic review. *BMC Pregnancy and Childbirth, 14*(1). https://doi.org/10.1186/1471-2393-14-51.

Harrington, A. (2008). *The cure within*. London: W. W. Norton.

Healy, D. (1997). *The antidepressant era*. Cambridge, MA: Harvard University Press.

Hofmann, S., Sawyer, A., Witt, A., & Oh, D. (2010). The effect of mindfulness-based therapy on anxiety and depression: A meta-analytic review. *Journal of Consulting and Clinical Psychology, 78*(2), 169–183. https://doi.org/10.1037/a0018555.

Horwitz, A. V., Wakefield, J. C., & Spitzer, R. L. (2007). *The loss of sadness: How psychiatry transformed normal sorrow into depressive disorder*. Oxford: Oxford University Press.

Howick, J. (2011). *The philosophy of evidence-based medicine*. Chichester, UK: Wiley-Blackwell and BMJ Books.

IAPT: Mindfulness-Based Cognitive Therapy National MBCT Training Curriculum Version 1.0 June 2017. (2019). Retrieved from https://www.hee.nhs.uk/sites/default/files/documents/MBCT%20in%20IAPT%20curriculum.pdf. Accessed 7 April 2019.

Kendler, K. S., Muñoz, R. A., & Murphy, G. (2010). The development of the feighner criteria: A historical perspective. *American Journal of Psychiatry, 167*(2), 134–142.

Kessler, R. (1994). Lifetime and 12-month prevalence of DSM-III-R psychiatric disorders in the United States. *Archives of General Psychiatry, 51*(1), 8. https://doi.org/10.1001/archpsyc.1994.03950010008002.

Kessler, R., & Bromet, E. (2013). The epidemiology of depression across cultures. *Annual Review of Public Health, 34*(1), 119–138. https://doi.org/10.1146/annurev-publhealth-031912-114409.

Krishnan, V., & Nestler, E. (2008). The molecular neurobiology of depression. *Nature, 455*(7215), 894–902. https://doi.org/10.1038/nature07455.

Kroenke, K., Spitzer, R., & Williams, J. (2001). The PHQ-9. *Journal of General Internal Medicine, 16*(9), 606–613. https://doi.org/10.1046/j.1525-1497.2001.016009606.x.

Lawlor, C. (2012). *From melancholia to prozac: A history of depression*. Oxford: Oxford University Press.

Leucht, S., Fennema, H., Engel, R., Kaspers-Janssen, M., Lepping, P., & Szegedi, A. (2013). What does the HAMD mean? *Journal of Affective Disorders, 148*(2–3), 243–248. https://doi.org/10.1016/j.jad.2012.12.001.

Maj, M. (2008). Depression, bereavement, and "understandable" intense sadness: Should the DSM-IV approach be revised? *American Journal of Psychiatry, 165*(11), 1373–1375. https://doi.org/10.1176/appi.ajp.2008.08071047.

Mattern, S. (2011). Galen and his patients. *The Lancet, 378*(9790), 478–479. https://doi.org/10.1016/s0140-6736(11)61240-3.

McManus, S., Bebbington, P., Jenkins, R., & Brugha, T. (2016). *Adult Psychiatric Morbitity Survey. 2014. Mental health and wellbeing in England.* Leeds, UK: NHS Digital.

National Institute for Health and Care Excellence (NICE). (2009). *Depression in adults: The treatment and management of depression in adults.* Retrieved from https://www.nice.org.uk/guidance/cg90. Accessed 12 April 2015.

Neuburger, M. (1944). An historical survey of the concept of nature from a medical viewpoint. *Isis, 35*(1), 16–28. https://doi.org/10.1086/358659.

NICE. (2019a). *Clinical guideline 91. Depression in adults with chronic physical health problem: treatment and management.* National Institute for Clinical Excellence; London, UK, 2009 (2019). Retrieved from https://www.nice.org.uk/guidance/cg91/evidence/full-guideline-243876061. Accessed 7 April 2019.

NICE. (2019b). *Clinical guideline 90. Depression in adults: Recognition and management.* Clinical guideline (2019). Retrieved from https://www.nice.org.uk/guidance/cg91/evidence/full-guideline-243876061. Accessed 7 April 2019.

NICE Depression in Adults: Recognition and Management, CG90. (2019). *Clinical guideline.* Retrieved from https://www.nice.org.uk/guidance/cg90. Accessed 7 April 2019.

Piet, J., & Hougaard, E. (2011). The effect of mindfulness-based cognitive therapy for prevention of relapse in recurrent major depressive disorder: A systematic review and meta-analysis. *Clinical Psychology Review, 31*(6), 1032–1040. https://doi.org/10.1016/j.cpr.2011.05.002.

Psychological Therapies: Annual Report on the Use of IAPT Services England. (2019). Retrieved from https://digital.nhs.uk/data-and-information/publications/statistical/psychological-therapies-annual-reports-on-the-use-of-iapt-services. Accessed 7 April 2019.

Psychological Therapies: Annual Report on the Use of IAPT Services England 2014/15. (2019). Retrieved from https://digital.nhs.uk/data-and-information/publications/statistical/psychological-therapies-annual-reports-on-the-use-of-iapt-services/annual-report-2014-15. Accessed 7 April 2019.

Psychological Therapies: Annual Report on the Use of IAPT Services England, 2015–16. (2019). Retrieved from https://files.digital.nhs.uk/pdf/1/0/psyc-ther-ann-rep-2015-16_v2.pdf. Accessed 7 April 2019.

Richards, D., Ekers, D., McMillan, D., Taylor, R., Byford, S., Warren, F., et al. (2016). Cost and outcome of behavioural activation versus cognitive behavioural therapy for depression (COBRA): A randomised, controlled, non-inferiority trial. *The Lancet, 388*(10047), 871–880. https://doi.org/10.1016/s0140-6736(16)31140-0.

Rush, A. J., First, M. B., & Blacker, D. (2000). *Handbook of psychiatric measures*. Washington, DC: American Psychiatric Press.

Sanders, J. (2011). A distinct language and a historic pendulum: The evolution of the diagnostic and statistical manual of mental disorders. *Archives of Psychiatric Nursing, 25*(6), 394–403. https://doi.org/10.1016/j.apnu.2010.10.002.

Segal, Z., Teasdale, J., Williams, J., & Gemar, M. (2002). The mindfulness-based cognitive therapy adherence scale: Inter-rater reliability, adherence to protocol and treatment distinctiveness. *Clinical Psychology & Psychotherapy, 9*(2), 131–138. https://doi.org/10.1002/cpp.320.

Segal, Z. V., Williams, J. M. G., & Teasdale, J. D. (2013). *Mindfulness-based cognitive therapy for depression*. New York: Guilford Press.

Shapiro, A. K. (2000). *The powerful placebo: From ancient priest to modern physician*. Baltimore, MD: Johns Hopkins University Press.

Shorter, E. (1994). *From the mind into the body*. New York: Free Press.

Shorter, E. (2011). A brief history of placebos and clinical trials in psychiatry. *The Canadian Journal of Psychiatry, 56*(4), 193–197. https://doi.org/10.1177/070674371105600402.

Shorter, E. (2013). *How everybody became depressed*. New York: OUP USA.

Sorbero, M., Ahluwalia, S., Reynolds, K., Lovejoy, S., Farris, C., Sloan, J., & Herman, P. (2015). *Meditation for depression: A systematic review of mindfulness-based cognitive therapy for major depressive disorder*. RAND Corporation. Retrieved from http://www.jstor.org/stable/10.7249/j.ctt19w7254. Accessed 7 April 2019.

Stewart, D. E., Robertson, E., Dennis, C-L., Grace, S. L., & Wallington, T. (2003). *Postpartum depression: Literature review of risk factors and interventions*.

Strauss, C., Cavanagh, K., Oliver, A., & Pettman, D. (2014). Mindfulness-based interventions for people diagnosed with a current episode of an anxiety or depressive disorder: A meta-analysis of randomised controlled trials. *PLoS One, 9*(4), e96110. https://doi.org/10.1371/journal.pone.0096110.

The ICD-10. (2010). *Classification of mental and behavioural disorders*. Retrieved from https://www.who.int/classifications/icd/en/bluebook.pdf. Accessed 8 April 2019.

The Improving Access to Psychological Therapies Manual Appendices and Helpful Resources. (2019). Retrieved from https://www.england.nhs.uk/wp-content/uploads/2018/06/iapt-manual-resources-v2.pdf. Accessed 7 April 2019.

WHO. (2012). *World Federation for Mental Health. Depression. A global crisis World Mental Health Day*. https://www.who.int/mental_health/management/depression/wfmh_paper_depression_wmhd_2012.pdf. Accessed 28 April 2019.

Wilson, M. (1993). DSM-III and the transformation of American psychiatry: A history. *American Journal of Psychiatry, 150*(3), 399–410.

Wittchen, H., Jacobi, F., Rehm, J., Gustavsson, A., Svensson, M., Jönsson, B., et al. (2011). The size and burden of mental disorders and other disorders of the brain in Europe 2010. *European Neuropsychopharmacology, 21*(9), 655–679. https://doi.org/10.1016/j.euroneuro.2011.07.018.

Wolsko, P., Eisenberg, D., Davis, R., & Phillips, R. (2004). Use of mind-body medical therapies. *Journal of General Internal Medicine, 19*(1), 43–50. https://doi.org/10.1111/j.1525-1497.2004.21019.x.

Zoogman, S., Goldberg, S., Hoyt, W., & Miller, L. (2014). Mindfulness interventions with youth: A meta-analysis. *Mindfulness, 6*(2), 290–302. https://doi.org/10.1007/s12671-013-0260-4.

# 8
# Epilogue

Mindfulness is a remarkable phenomenon that emerged from the cultural world of the USA in the late seventies. From Jon-Kabat Zinn's initial proposal at the University of Massachusetts Medical School, it grew enormously. And from the US, it quickly spread to other Western countries. Initially, mindfulness was used for helping people who were struggling to cope with difficult life events. It was for this reason that the Stress Reduction Clinic and the Centre for Mindfulness in Medicine, Health Care, and Society were created at the University of Massachusetts Medical School. Kabat-Zinn's stress-reduction programme, mindfulness-based stress reduction (MBSR), started life there. Later, it was adopted in medical centres, hospitals and health maintenance organisations, where it was used to help people cope with stress, anxiety, pain and illness.

Kabat-Zinn's secular technique, which combines meditation with Hatha yoga, has since spread worldwide. Its basic structure is still retained in almost all current mindfulness applications, which are now used in a wide range of fields beyond psychology, medicine and wellbeing.

During the course of its development, mindfulness absorbed many of the cultural and social characteristics of the places where it was used.



T. Giraldi, *Psychotherapy, Mindfulness and Buddhist Meditation*,
https://doi.org/10.1007/978-3-030-29003-0_8

In US, mindfulness was developed and popularised to a large extent because of the work of a number of individual institutions and pioneers. Mindfulness interventions then spread in the private economy in no small part because of marketing. The story was different in the UK, however, where the Mindful Initiative was set in motion by Parliament (The Mindful Initiative, 2018), which led to the release of the *Mindful UK Report* in 2015. It is the first policy document of its kind, proposing the use of mindfulness interventions to address mental health concerns in education, health, the workplace and the criminal justice system. The report's recommendations are evidence-based and informed by experienced practitioners, who have all had notable successes in their fields. They urge policymakers to invest resources in further pilot studies and also to increase public access to qualified teacher trainers (Mindful Nation UK, 2015).

It is clearly worth exploring the extraordinary popularity of mindfulness, and this has been attempted in the previous chapters. The extensive diffusion of mindfulness in itself demonstrates that many people—patients, teachers and practitioners—have had positive experiences with it. It may, therefore, be worthwhile now to examine the state of mindfulness today, and determine the particular characteristics and challenges that have emerged during the many years it has been practised. It is also worth considering the future of mindfulness: the new applications that are being developed and implemented.

Since the beginning of mindfulness in the West, its relationship with Buddhism has been both vital and complex. Kabat-Zinn based mindfulness on simple principles that were easy to understand and engage with. His familiarity with Buddhism allowed him to pick out one of its simplest core messages—a message that is universal to all Buddhist traditions from China, Tiber, Nepal and Ceylon to South East Asia and Japan. But in reality, although the message he chose was simple, it was supported by a hugely extensive and complex literature based on the sutras, the many sayings of the original Buddha, Siddhartha Gautama. These became the basic texts of Buddhism, and crystallised into the Teachings. It is not easy to imagine "what Buddha really taught" (Rāhula, 1974), however, and this is one of the major concerns of the modern "secular Buddhism" movement (Batchelor, 2011).

The Buddhist message that Kabat-Zinn adopted for his mindfulness programme is the *Four Noble Truths*:

- *Dukkha*, life unavoidably has suffering;
- *Dukkha* has an identifiable cause;
- That cause may be overcome;
- The *Noble Eight-fold Noble Path* is the *Middle Way* to follow to overcome *Dukkha* (Snelling, 1998).

One can easily see why people might be interested in Buddhism as a means of overcoming the pains of existence. However, the relationship between mindfulness today and the *Noble Eight-fold Noble Path* and its original Buddhist origins is less clear.

The steps of *The Noble Eightfold Path* are *Moral Virtue* (right speech, action and livelihood), *Meditation*[1] (right effort, mental presence[2] and concentration) and *Insight and Wisdom* (right view and resolve) (Snelling, 1998). As has already been discussed, "mindfulness" is the translation of the original *Pali* term "sati" (Van Dam et al., 2017). Sati is one of the components of meditation (*samadhi*), and *samadhi* and *sati* (right mental presence and meditation) are both parts of a complex framework that is deeply grounded in morality. The adjective "right", with its clear moral meaning, is repeated in all the descriptions of *Moral Virtue*, *Meditation* and *Insight and Wisdom* in the *Noble Eightfold Path* (Snelling, 1998).

We find here the essence of Kabat-Zinn's initial idea: he isolated *sati* from the *Noble Eight-fold Noble Path*, and stripped the moral requirement from the *right sati* of Buddhist teachings. His new programme was thus based solely on the practice of meditation, renamed "mindfulness" and stripped of the more complex nuances of *sati* such as *smrti* and *samadhi*. Kabat-Zinn essentially disregarded the deep moral values that

---

[1]"samadhi", the original Pali word commonly translated as "meditation".

[2]"sati", the original Pali word for the active watchful and constantly present mind, commonly translated as "mindfulness".

form an essential part of Buddhism (Harvey, 2013; Heine & Wright, 2008).

In developing mindfulness, Kabat-Zinn also overlooked another key aspect of Buddhism: the fact that most of even the most devoted Buddhist populations do not practise meditation. It is actually only practised by a small number of monks living in monasteries (Harvey, 2013; Heine & Wright, 2008). Different Buddhist Schools also practise very different forms of meditation. Masters guide meditation in ways that are specific to each traditional school, but in all cases, meditation is essentially a process of focusing one's attention inwards in silence. In mindfulness, however, instructors or therapists give extended guidance throughout meditation—usually via a CD or other recording.

When mindfulness was incorporated into cognitive psychotherapy, the procedures were still based on Kabat-Zinn's original eight-week MBSR programme. It is becoming increasingly difficult, however, to distinguish meditation from the forms of cognitive and behavioural therapy it has been melded with (Kuyken et al., 2015; Segal, Williams, Teasdale, & Kabat-Zinn, 2013).

It is no simple thing, however, to propose practising Buddhist meditation in Western culture, however. Robert Scharf raises concerns about the danger of oversimplification in his paper *Buddhist modernism and the rhetoric of meditative experience*. Scharf notes that meditation is a Buddhist monastic practice meant to foster specific religious or mystical experiences in the minds of practitioners. Historical and ethnographic studies also show that certain twentieth century Asian reform movements that urged a "return" to zazen or vipassana meditation, were profoundly influenced by religious developments in the West (Sharf, 1995).

It is therefore understandable that Kabat-Zinn was concerned about proposing a therapeutic intervention based on Buddhist principles to Western audiences in the late 70s. Buddhism is a unique ideology, and in spite of its basic philosophical and existential roots, it is considered one of the great religions. Kabat-Zinn's seminal idea, therefore—which later became almost a mantra—was to detach his practice from this complex religion; he therefore proposed "Buddhist meditation without the Buddhism" (Fisher, 2010). This was generally an effective way to avoid the risk of religious or cultural resistance to his programme.

However, it did not escape the attention of careful observers, such as the *American Center for Law & Justice* (ACLJ), a highly conservative, Christian-based social organisation, which recently posted an article called "The Deception of Buddhist-Based Mindfulness in Our Schools". The ACLJ expressed its concern about the diffusion of mindfulness in American schools, given that the practice is ultimately based on Buddhism. The ACLJ even started a petition to "stop forcing Buddhist meditation on kids in schools" (Stierhoff, 2019).

The use of Buddhist-based meditation for mindfulness raised questions about introducing an ancient tradition into modern Western society. These difficulties did not hold back enthusiastic practitioners and patients, however. There have been some widely reported positive results from mindfulness, and this has led to the practice being adopted by more and more people. Many are now seeking this new apparently effective intervention, and more and more instructors and practitioners are now happy to offer it.

If we try to put this picture in perspective, the obvious question arises: how effective has mindfulness been in the years since it was first developed? This is not easy to answer because of the many different applications of mindfulness now, ranging from improving performance in healthy subjects to treating the most serious mental conditions. Evaluating results also depends on the definition of the condition treated, as well as the criteria for assessing the effects of treatment. This is particularly difficult when the methodology used for evaluating mental conditions was developed for assessing somatic diseases.

To properly evaluate mindfulness interventions, therefore, we must first choose an appropriate application to assess. Depression is an appropriate mental disorder to address here, both because of its relevance and its great prevalence today. It is also appropriate because mindfulness and mindfulness-based applications have been found to be effective for treating it and particularly for preventing relapses.

The challenges to do with diagnosing depression have already been considered in the previous chapter. The most prominent of these is the fact that almost all the investigations into the effects of mindfulness-based applications are based on the Diagnostic Statistical Manual (DSM) criteria for major depressive disorder. In some instances, such as the UK's IAPT programme, other, similar psychometric scales like the Patient Health Questionnaire are used.

There have been many serious and well-substantiated criticisms of the DSM. The main objection is that it permits diagnosis based only on the presence of a collection of symptoms, and that this process cannot differentiate between healthy and morbid conditions. Over the years, the various editions of the manual have changed the criteria. A panel of experts has repeatedly voted to revise and elaborate on the diagnostic criteria for each disorder. The problem is, however, that this process is open to external cultural and political pressures. In several instances, this has led to radical changes to the different editions of the Manual.

There have been a number of books published criticising the DSM, and you can get some sense of their subject matter from their titles: *They Say You're Crazy: How the World's Most Powerful Psychiatrists Decide Who's Normal* (Caplan, 1996), *Making Us Crazy: DSM. The Psychiatric Bible and the Creation of Mental Disorders* (Kutchins & Kirk, 1999) and the *Book of Woe: The DSM and the Unmaking of Psychiatry* (Greenberg, 2013). Other examples are: *Saving Normal: An Insider's Revolt Against Out-of-Control Psychiatric Diagnosis, DSM-5, Big Pharma, and the Medicalization of Ordinary Life.* Its author, Allen Frances, previously chaired the DSM-IV Task Force, and was also part of the leadership group for the DSM-III and DSM-IIIR. He then, however, radically changed his views and began to publicly criticise the DSM (Frances, 2014).

Depression, which has been recognised by many cultures over the centuries, has been transformed into major depressive disorder, as defined by the DSM's diagnostic criteria. According to alarming publications by the WHO, there is now what appears to be a depression epidemic around the world (World Federation for Mental Health, 2012). It does not seem likely that this seeming epidemic will abate any time soon. In 2016, the Journal of the American Medical Association welcomed a recommendation from the US Preventive Services Task Force (USPSTF) that adults aged 18 or over should be screened for depression (Baucher, Fontanarosa, & Golug, 2016; Thase, 2016). It recommended using "commonly used depression screening instruments". These are specifically: "the Patient Health Questionnaire (PHQ) in various forms and the Hospital Anxiety and Depression Scales in adults, the Geriatric Depression Scale in older adults, and the Edinburgh Postnatal Depression Scale (EPDS) in postpartum and pregnant women. All positive screening results should lead to additional assessment that considers severity of depression and comorbid psychological problems (e.g., anxiety, panic attacks, or substance abuse), alternate diagnoses, and medical conditions" (Siu et al., 2016).

Not everybody is convinced by this initiative. Allen Frances wrote in the *New Scientist*: "Screen everyone for depression? Good intention, very bad idea. Routinely checking US adults for depression will create an army of pseudo-patients while the really sick are shamefully neglected" (Frances, 2016).

Presumably using these broad criteria would result in a large number of people being diagnosed with depression, which would include cases of "understandable sadness", which would not be deemed "clinical cases" by the WHO publication (Christodoulou, 2012) or Mario Maj (2011).

Studies of the effectiveness of depression interventions—including mindfulness—almost all use the DSM's diagnostic criteria. Because of the limitations of these criteria, it is impossible to determine how many of the trials' subjects are suffering from real clinical depressive conditions, and how many merely have minor, non-morbid mood changes. The criteria for evaluating the effects of the interventions are also a vital factor to consider.

Researchers assess the effectiveness of interventions based on statistically significant differences between subjects' pre- and post-treatment scores. These scores are calculated using the same psychometric scales originally used for selecting the patients. To be accepted, the score differences have to be reproducible, which means that if the trial is repeated a similar difference has to be found in 95 per cent of the re-runs. Statistical significance is a prerequisite, but it must be reproducible.

The significance of the intervention is actually indicated by the scale of the difference between the pre- and post-treatment measures. In other words, what really counts is how pronounced the specific effect being investigated is, and the clinical meaning of this.

This is a crucial, but perhaps underappreciated point in psychological and medical research. It is dealt with in Ziliak and McCloskey's excellent book, *The Cult of Statistical Significance: How the Standard Error Costs Us Jibs, Justice, and Lives* (Ziliak, 2008).

It is important to bear considerations like this in mind when looking at mindfulness interventions. In 1998, Irving Kirsch published a meta-analysis called *Listening to Prozac but Hearing Placebo: A Meta-Analysis of Antidepressant Medication* (Kirsch & Sapirstein, 1998). It caused considerable uproar. Kirsch based his meta-analysis on 19 published RCTs. Control group patients had a consistent response to placebos in all of the studies, and this correlated closely with the responses in the treatment groups. What Kirsch found was that in groups treated with antidepressants, the placebo effect accounted for 75 per cent of their response. That means that antidepressants accounted for only 25 per cent of observed effects (Kirsch & Sapirstein, 1998).

The main criticism of Kirsch's work was that it only used published studies, even though they were selected for their perfectly adequate qualitative standards. There was also, however, the problem that there were many unpublished results that Kirsch did not have access to because of industry confidentiality. To defend the meta-analysis, Kirsch had to include the unpublished data, for which he had to resort to the US Freedom of Information Act (FOIA), which grants access to confidential data if it is in the interest of US citizens. Kirsch gained access to data from clinical trials on six of the seven SSRI antidepressants approved by the *Food and Drug Administration* (FDA) between 1987 and 1992.

The stated purpose of Kirsch and his colleagues' work was to assess whether including the unpublished data would change the results of the meta-analysis, and whether the results depended on the severity of the mood disorder. When each group's Hamilton Depression Rating Scale (HRSD) score was related to the severity of their depression at the start of the study, the researchers found that the effect of the antidepressants was constant. The original analysis was correct that the effect on placebo-controlled groups was lower the higher the initial depression score was. There was only a significant difference between the effects of the drugs and the placebos in initially severe depression cases (subjects who had a score greater than 28 on the HDRS) (Kirsch et al., 2008).

As Kirsch noted: "Drug-placebo differences in antidepressant efficacy increase as a function of baseline severity, but are relatively small even for severely depressed patients. The relationship between initial severity and antidepressant efficacy is attributable to decreased responsiveness to placebo among very severely depressed patients, rather than to increased responsiveness to medication."

There was also a major contribution to this subject by Thomas Insel, when he was Director of the National Mental Health Institute (NMIH) of the US National Institutes of Health (NIH). Although there have been many studies, meta-analyses and critical reviews, there are still serious doubts about the effectiveness and safety of antidepressants. This led to a study called the Sequenced Treatment Alternatives to Relieve Depression (STAR*D), sponsored by the National Institute of Mental Health (NIMH) (2006). Launched in 2000, it was a six-year comprehensive evaluation of antidepressant medication, costing 35 million dollars. Its organisers described it as the largest practical trial to examine the treatment of major depressive disorder with pharmacotherapy and cognitive behavioural psychotherapy (Sinyor, Schaffee, & Levitt, 2010).

Patients enrolled had to have been diagnosed with a major depressive disorder according to the DSM criteria and have at least a 14-point score on the HRSD. These patients then received standard treatment with second-generation selective serotonin reuptake inhibitors (SSRI). If the treatment was ineffective, however, patients were put on randomised trials with other treatments. These included changing drugs (switching and increasing doses), augmentation therapy and the conjunction of more than one drug (combination therapy); one group was also treated with psychotherapy. The primary outcome measure was remission at the end of the treatment, which was assessed on the HRSD. The study did not use placebo-controlled groups, however, so in this sense it did not meet the RCT standard (Warden et al., 2007). The subjects enrolled on the study included institutionalised patients and outpatients from general medicine. The overall results, however, did not quite meet the expectations implied in the title *STAR*D. Revising conventional wisdom* (Rush et al., 2009). Essentially, for the initial steps of the study there was between 13 per cent and 37 per cent remission. Overall cognitive behavioural psychotherapy turned out to be more effective than pharmacotherapy (Rush et al., 2009).

Insel was one of those who seriously criticised the DSM-5. He publicly stated that: "patients with mental disorders deserve better". He added that the DSM's diagnostic categories are based on a cluster of symptoms, and that:

> In the rest of medicine, this would be equivalent to creating diagnostic systems based on the nature of chest pain or the quality of fever. Indeed, symptom-based diagnosis, once common in other areas of medicine, has been largely replaced in the past half century as we have understood that symptoms alone rarely indicate the best choice of treatment.

NIMH soon launched the Research Domain Criteria (RDoC) project to transform psychiatric diagnosis, research and treatment and create a new classification system incorporating genetics, cognitive sciences and modern brain-imaging techniques (Insel, 2013).

All this must be taken into account when considering Kabat-Zinn's studies attempting to have mindfulness accepted into mainstream medicine. With time, the number of mindfulness studies grew extraordinarily. They also improved in quality, and a large proportion of them are now carried out using the principles of evidence-based medicine and are randomised clinical trials. More and more studies are also now trying to use the principle of blinding the intervention for participants. The better-organised studies are now also ensuring that examiners are not aware of whether individual participants are part of the control group or receiving the real treatment. As we have seen, the placebo effect can be particularly important in depression treatment trials—particularly in less severe cases, where it may be completely responsible for perceived improvements after antidepressants have been administered.

It is likely that something similar may happen when studying mindfulness-based interventions. However, it is extremely difficult—and may even be impossible—to devise similar placebos for mindfulness. To create a placebo for drug trials, researchers have to produce an identical pharmaceutical product but without the active ingredient. The patients, staff and evaluators then have to be blinded to who has the placebo and who has the active treatment.

We have already seen how difficult it can be to devise placebo interventions in psychotherapy (Shapiro & Shapiro, 2000). But what exactly would be an appropriate psychotherapy placebo? Psychotherapy delivered by qualified psychotherapists, who do not "administer the active ingredient" to the placebo group? Or an unqualified psychotherapist doing their best to simulate a real one? The problem of placebos in psychotherapy is so important now that in 2005 the Journal of Clinical Psychology devoted a whole issue to the matter (Herbert & Gaudiano, 2005).

It is even more difficult to imagine effective placebos for mindfulness and mindfulness-based interventions. How exactly do you create a system where subjects participating in a trial do not know whether they are receiving "real" mindfulness or some sort of "sham" form?

It may be useful here to consider the challenges encountered when designing the STEP trial. STEP was a multi-centre randomised trial to assess the therapeutic effects of intercessory prayer in cardiac bypass patients. It was published in 2006 in the American Heart Journal. This study is useful for several reasons, and it was examined in detail in Richard Dawkins's book *The God Delusion*, where he does not shy away from a distinctly sarcastic tone (Dawkins, 2006). The STEP study was funded by the Templeton Foundation, to experimentally test the notion that praying for sick patients might improve their health. The trial was double-blinded: patients were randomly assigned to an experimental group (which received prayers) or a control group (which did not receive prayers). None of the assessors were allowed to know who had and had not been prayed for.

The team of researchers, under the leadership of Dr. Herbert Benson, the cardiologist at the Mind/Body Medical Institute near Boston, spent a total of $2.4 million on the trial. Dr. Benson and his team monitored 1802 patients at six hospitals, all of whom received coronary bypass surgery. The patients were divided into three groups. Group 1 received prayers and didn't know it. Group 2 (the control group) received no prayers and didn't know it. Group 3 received prayers and did know it. The comparison between Groups 1 and 2 was to test for the efficacy of intercessory prayer. Group 3 was designed to test for the possible psychosomatic effects of knowing that one is being prayed for. Prayers were delivered by the congregations of three churches: one in Minnesota, one in Massachusetts and one in Missouri—all distant from the three hospitals. The people praying were given only the first name and initial letter of the surname of each patient. It is good experimental practice to standardise as far as possible, and they were all told to include in their prayers the phrase “for a successful surgery with a quick, healthy recovery and no complications”.

The results of the trial, reported in the American Heart Journal, were clear-cut. There was no difference between patients who were prayed for and those who were not. There was a difference between those who knew they had been prayed for and those who did not know one way or the other. The difference, however, went in the wrong direction: patients who knew they had been prayed for suffered significantly more complications than those who did not. The authors concluded that intercessory prayer itself had no effect on patients recovering from coronary artery bypass grafts, but that receiving intercessory prayer was associated with a higher incidence of complications (Benson et al., 2006).

Although the study did not consider mindfulness interventions, it is useful for giving an idea of the difficulties researchers run into when trying to apply the rigorous methodology of double-blind controlled randomised trials to the worlds of psychology and spirituality.

There are other aspects of mindfulness-based interventions that are still not clearly defined and need further attention. One key issue that has come up repeatedly is that mindfulness, as defined by Kabat-Zinn, was a new concept derived from Buddhism, but detached from the principles that were supposed to accompany meditation. We could term it a secular approach, but in a recent interview, Kabat-Zinn objected to “his” mindfulness concept being termed secular.

It is clear from the extensive literature available, however, that the terms “mindfulness” and “meditation” are not clearly defined and are often used interchangeably. Given this lack of clarity, it may now be worth examining the meditative procedures involved in mindfulness today in more detail. Mindfulness-Based Cognitive Therapy (MBCT) is a good place to start.

The PREVENT study by Kuyken's team was an attempt to assess how effective MBCT is at preventing relapses of depression. This is one of the most serious therapeutic challenges today. The study used the best methodological procedures available to provide robust evidence of its efficacy (Kuyken et al., 2015). As we have already seen, of course, there are unavoidable challenges when trying to use randomised controlled clinical trials to investigate nuanced aspects of mental health. The term "meditation" also does not appear in the study, only appearing in the references when it cites a 1982 Kabat-Zinn paper on "mindfulness meditation" (Kabat-Zinn, 1982).

It defines MBCT as a manualised, group-based skills training programme designed to allow patients to learn skills to prevent the recurrence of depression. It also refers to the book *Mindfulness-based Cognitive Therapy for Depression* by Segal et al. A large proportion of this book focuses on meditation, which it presents as practically identical to MBSR as it was presented decades before. The meditation involved here is largely guided, using the *Series I and II meditation instruction* CDs recorded by Kabat-Zinn (Segal, Williams et al., 2013).

The procedures Kuyken's paper describes are (Crane et al., 2013; Segal, Teasdale, Williams, & Gemar, 2002):

> Participants learn mindfulness practices and cognitive-behavioural skills both in session and through homework assignments. [...]
>
> Before therapists progressed to running trial groups, an independent check on their competency was established. An experienced MBCT therapist independent of the trial rated at least two videotapes for every potential therapist using the Mindfulness-Based Interventions Teacher Assessment Criteria and MBCT Adherence Scale (MBCT-AS). She made an overall judgment as to whether the therapists were competent and adhered to the MBCT manual, and therapists only progressed once competency in all domains was clearly established....

There is evident concern that the procedures should be reproducible. The study refers repeatedly to manuals to test the competence of the therapists. Segal's book also refers to training guidelines for MBCT "instructors". Both Oxford and Exeter Universities offer postgraduate training leading to a master's degree in MBCT, while Bangor University offers a master's in mindfulness, focusing predominantly on MBSR and MBCT. These U.K. programmes are taught part-time over two to three years, and cover the experiential and didactic elements of MBCT—as well as its evidence base. In general, these courses require a minimum of a qualification in clinical practice and mental health training, including the use of structured, evidence-based therapeutic approaches to treating affective disorders such as CBT, interpersonal psychotherapy, and behavioural activation (Segal, Williams et al., 2013).

This issue has become so important that the UK NHS has even issued a Mindfulness-based Cognitive Therapy National MBCT Training Curriculum, which is used by a network of centres around the country.

The training curriculum is for training High Intensity IAPT workers in cognitive-behavioural therapy (CBT). They need to have either been practising for at least one year or be fully accredited CBT therapists. Their training therefore assumes that students will have basic CBT or other therapeutic skills, and that they will be experienced in working with people with anxiety disorders and depression (IAPT, 2017).

There is more of a variety of different mindfulness training options in the USA than the UK, where there was an effort to standardise training through the IAPT programme. In the USA, the University of Massachusetts Medical School, where the original MBSR programme was developed, offers several different levels of high-quality training ("Oasis Institute for Mindfulness-based Professional Education & Teacher Training", 2019).

The UK's IAPT programme was developed to allow the NHS to comprehensively address depressive mood disorders on a national scale. Psychological interventions and psychotherapies were included as an alternative to antidepressant drugs, and the psychotherapy that was most commonly used at the outset was CBT—chosen mainly because of the evidence for its effectiveness. In time, however, the IAPT also began to include other psychotherapeutic approaches, grounded in psycho-dynamical principles, as well as cognitive-based approaches.

When an effective intervention is transformed into a new and more complex approach, evidence must be provided to show its effectiveness.

It should also be proved that the new approach is more effective than the previous one—and that the changes are responsible for the difference. Much empirical evidence was therefore collected to show that CBT is effective for treating several mental conditions—particularly depression (Butler, Chaapman, Forman, & Beck, 2006). A similarly large amount of evidence is available for the effectiveness of MBSR at treating depression (Hofmann, Sawyer, Witt, & Oh, 2010). When CBT was combined with MBST, as happened with the development of MBCT, it had to be determined whether it was more effective than CBT (and MBSR).

The PREVENT trial showed that MBCT is not inferior to drug treatment for a number of different mood disorders (it is also more cost-effective). It does not, however, show whether it is superior to CBT. There are numerous studies now available on MBCT, using various types of active controls. Together, they provide some possible evidence for its superiority (Kocovski & MacKenzie, 2016). There have also been some studies comparing MBCT and CBT in particular circumstances, such as diabetic patients with depression (Tovote et al., 2017).

When Richards et al. judged that CBT is the best-evidenced therapy, they also noted that it is complex and costly. Their COBRA trials therefore also tested whether a simpler and cheaper therapy, Behavioural Activation (BA), could be as effective for adults with depression. They found that BA could be delivered by junior mental health workers with less intensive and costly training, with no lesser effect than CBT (Richards et al., 2016).

The IAPT has used numerous different psychotherapies, and the results of these have regularly been presented and evaluated. The 2014/15 recovery rates from depression are particularly interesting because they suggest the relative effectiveness of the various psychotherapies used. Although the data has not been evaluated for statistical significance, it is still extremely interesting. The reported recovery rates range from 44.1 per cent with CBT, and 58.4 per cent with Computerised Cognitive Behavioural Therapy (CCBT). Brief psychodynamic therapy fell between the extremes with 47.7 per cent. Even if the differences were not statistically significant, they appear to show that CCBT is more effective than CBT, and that a psycho-dynamic intervention can be at least as effective as cognitive-based psychotherapies (IAPT, 2015).

The results reported for CCBT have been studied in the REEACT trial, which assessed CCBT as a treatment for depression in primary care, using a pragmatic, multi-centre, randomised controlled trial. Treatment allocation was not blinded. The participants were adults with symptoms of depression who were randomised to receive a commercially produced CCBT programme (*Beating the Blues*) or a free CCBT programme (*MoodGYM*), as well as the usual GP-prescribed care. The results showed that CCBT did not substantially improve depression outcomes compared to usual GP care alone. Neither commercial nor free computerised CBT intervention was superior to usual GP care (Gilbody et al., 2015).

A systematic review of CCBT examined 16 studies: of these, 11 were RCTs and the remaining 5 were pilot or cohort studies. In the studies comparing CCBT with therapist-led CBT (TCBT), five showed that CCBT had similar outcomes to TCBT. One study of depressed inpatients found TCBT was significantly more effective than CCBT. Four studies found CCBT to be more effective than treatment as usual (TAU). Two studies found CCBT to be no more effective than TAU. Two studies compared CCBT with bibliotherapy, and of these, one found CCBT to be as effective and one found bibliotherapy to be significantly more effective on some outcome measures (Kaltenthaler, Parry, & Beverley, 2004).

These results suggest that more studies are needed to properly evaluate CCBT. When interventions are needed in remote rural areas, this form of treatment may be particularly useful. CCBT may also be more acceptable among rural communities than urban areas, where patients may be more likely to expect face-to-face contact with a practitioner (Vallury, Jones, & Oosterbroek, 2015). The fact that CBT and CCBT show similar levels of effectiveness in the IAPT yearly report suggests that more should be done to compare these treatments. More should also be done to compare CBT and brief psychodynamic therapy.

There have been a number of developments in cognitive-based psychotherapy, collectively known as the third wave of cognitive behavioural therapies. This group includes heterogeneous treatments, such as acceptance and commitment treatment, behavioural activation, the cognitive behavioural analysis system of psychotherapy, dialectical behavioural therapy, metacognitive therapy, MBCT and schema therapy. There have been several randomised controlled trials, longitudinal case series and pilot studies that suggest it is worth continuing to explore these (Kahl, Winter, & Schweiger, 2012).

There was a Cochrane Systematic Review comparing third-wave cognitive and behavioural therapies with other psychological therapies for depression. It included a total of three studies involving 144 eligible participants. Two of the studies compared an early version of acceptance and commitment therapy (ACT) with CBT, and one compared extended behavioural activation with CBT. Post-treatment results showed no evidence of any difference between third-wave CBT and other psychological therapies. Results after two months showed no evidence of any difference between third-wave CBT and other psychological therapies (Hunot et al., 2013).

There are now many different psychotherapies in general use—particularly for treating depression—and this number is only rising. Scholars are now increasingly asking whether some are more effective than others (Lilienfeld & Arkowitz, 2012).

According to a report called *Are All Psychotherapies Created Equal?* there are at least 500 different types of psychotherapy. The most frequently used approaches include behaviour therapy (altering unhealthy behaviours), CBT (altering maladaptive ways of thinking), psychodynamic therapy (resolving unconscious conflicts and adverse childhood experiences), interpersonal therapy (remedying unhealthy ways of interacting with others), and person-centred therapy (helping clients to find their own solutions to life problems). Concerns about the varying effects of different psychotherapies are not new. In 1936, Rosenzweig introduced the metaphor of the Dodo, after the bird in Lewis Carroll's *Alice in Wonderland*, who declared after a race: "everyone has won, and all must have prizes." The "Dodo Bird verdict" is now used to refer to the notion that all therapies have equivalent effects (Hunsley & Di Giulio, 2002).

In the years that followed, there were many investigations into the effectiveness of different approaches. These were particularly relevant to the diffusion throughout the medical world of behavioural and cognitive psychotherapies, which eroded the popularity of psychodynamic psychotherapies (Wampold & Imel, 2015). There are now many meta-analyses of the effectiveness of psychotherapies. Schedler's 2010 meta-analysis is particularly interesting because it compares psychodynamic therapies with other common therapies (Shedler, 2010). Here is his concise summary:

> Empirical evidence supports the efficacy of psychodynamic therapy. Effect sizes for psychodynamic therapy are as large as those reported for other therapies that have been actively promoted as "empirically supported" and "evidence based." In addition, patients who receive psychodynamic therapy maintain therapeutic gains and appear to continue to improve after treatment ends. Finally, non-psychodynamic therapies may be effective in part because the more skilled practitioners utilize techniques that have long been central to psychodynamic theory and practice. The perception that psychodynamic approaches lack empirical support does not accord with available scientific evidence and may reflect selective dissemination of research findings.

The results of the meta-analysis are clear and convincing. For psychodynamic psychotherapy, the standardised effect size was between 0.78 and 1.8. For CBT and related therapies, it was between 0.58 and 1.0. For other "general psychotherapies" between, it was between 0.73 and 0.85. Amazingly, the effects of antidepressant medication were between 0.17 and 0.31. Schedler's review considers the delicate and complex issues in these two very different fields. The meta-analysis shows quite convincingly that there is no clear difference in effectiveness between the psychotherapies examined—despite their very different theoretical and practical foundations. If there is any difference to note, it is that antidepressant medication seems to have a much more limited effect than the psychotherapies considered (Shedler, 2010).

Among the so called "third wave" developments of cognitive behavioural therapy, Dialectical Behaviour Therapy (DBT) and ACT deserve particular mention because they include some mindfulness principles (Thoma, Pilecki, & McKay, 2015). Based on a concept of suffering similar to that found in Buddhism, ACT uses strategies to cultivate acceptance and bring people closer to the present moment. It is a similar notion to mindfulness, which is less common in traditional CBT approaches. Similar to traditional meditative practices, ACT attempts to focus on decoupling experience (thoughts and emotions) from overt behaviour. Acceptance and mindfulness strategies are not the end goal of ACT, but rather a method of helping people live a more meaningful life and achieve values-based goals. ACT has been found to be helpful for treating a variety of disorders including depression, anxiety, and chronic pain.

DBT is a therapy that was originally developed in the late 1980s to treat borderline personality disorder. In contrast to most forms of CBT, DBT involves a more long-term treatment lasting up to several years, which includes individual therapy and groups for learning skills such as emotion regulation and mindfulness. DBT emphasises the principles of mindfulness and incorporates traditionally Eastern philosophical influences. It combines standard cognitive behavioural techniques for regulating emotions with mindful awareness, acceptance and distress tolerance—concepts and practices largely derived from Buddhist meditation.

Marsha Linehan is a Professor of Psychology and adjunct Professor of Psychiatry and Behavioral Sciences at the University of Washington. She is also Director of the Behavioral Research and Therapy Clinics, a consortium of research projects developing and testing new treatments for severely disordered, multi-diagnostic and suicidal patients. Linehan developed DBT while suffering from her own mental illness. Linehan had received spiritual guidance and training from Gerald May and Tilden Edwards, and became an associate Zen teacher herself at both the Diamond Sangha (USA) and, under Willigis Jaeger Roshi, at the Sanbo-Kyodan School (Germany) (Marsha Linehan Biography, 2019).

DBT proved to be effective for chronically suicidal patients and people with borderline personality disorder. It was also found to be effective for people with depression, drug and alcohol problems, post-traumatic stress disorder (PTSD) and various mood disorders (Hayes, 2011).

The RCTs for third-wave treatments generally used research methodology that was significantly less stringent than most CBT studies.

They found, however, that the mean effect size was moderate for both ACT and DBT, and that none of the third-wave therapies met the criteria to be labelled empirically supported treatments (Öst, 2008).

The ACT and DBT studies' limitations may be the reason why they were not included in the meta-analyses of mindfulness interventions. They have, however, been added to the list of different psychotherapies used in the UK IAPT programme.

We should now take a final, holistic look at the aspects of mindfulness, Buddhist meditation and psychotherapy that have been explored in the previous chapters. This book has explored mindfulness, Buddhist meditation and psychotherapy by considering the work of the leading scholars and pioneers of these fields. It has also referred to the best books and scientific articles on these subjects. In some cases, direct quotes have been included from these sources, so readers can make up their own minds about them.

If we try to answer to the question "what is mindfulness today?", we still have to face the conceptual problem of the transition from "Buddhist meditation" to "meditation without Buddhism".

Buddhism is the main religion of several Asian countries, each with their own traditional school. This ancient religion only arrived in the West relatively recently. In the East, however, it is deeply ingrained in the culture and history of several countries, where its deep roots transcend religion and should more properly be considered in an anthropological light. When devoted and enlightened pioneers brought Buddhism to the West around a century ago, it had to set down new roots in a modern culture that was steeped in a very different, Christian history. In fact, the first adherents of Buddhism in the West should probably be seen not as traditional Buddhists, but converts from Christianity. It will probably take several generations before we see exactly how Buddhist traditions take on a new life in the West.

In the West, one of the aspects of Buddhism people were most interested in was meditation, and it continues to be the main focus of occidental Buddhism to this day. There is interest in all the different forms of meditation and traditions, such as Soto, Rinzai, Mahayana, Theravada, Hinayana, Tibetan, Vajrayana, as well as other minor or recent forms. In the West, the first people to transmit Buddhist teachings from the traditional lineage were teachers trained in Asia, who passed them on to new, local pupils. It would now be useful to trace the progress of these new teachers and discover how exactly Buddhist disciplines and meditative practices are changing and developing in the West. It would be prudent, however, not to expect Buddhism or the practices related to it to spread especially quickly or widely, given the fact it has historically avoided overt proselytising.

The Western phenomenon of mindfulness, however, continues to spread rapidly, moving further and further away from its origins in Buddhist meditation and increasingly taking on local characteristics. There is, though, also enthusiasm for meditation and Buddhism outside mindfulness. A prominent example is Robert Wright's recent book, *Why Buddhism Is True: The Science and Philosophy of Meditation and Enlightenment* (Wright, 2017).

There are now many expressing concern about the direction of mindfulness. Robert Scharf has noted that there were other ideas similar to Kabat-Zinn's mindfulness: in particular among the Burmese Buddhist reform movements of the first half of the twentieth century. There were also earlier precedents in Buddhist history, such as the innovations of medieval Chinese Zen (Chan) and Tibetan Dzogchen. These were attempts to make Buddhist practices accessible to laypeople who did not want to adopt the reclusive, ascetic lifestyle of the monasteries. They promised astonishingly quick results, but were met with suspicion and criticism by traditional Buddhists. Scharf also points out that people who are interested in the therapeutic effects of mindfulness are often not aware of the controversies that have shrouded the history of mindfulness and meditation (Sharf, 2014).

In his book *Mindlessness: The Corruption of Mindfulness in a Culture of Narcissism*, Thomas Joiner has raised his concern that the original idea behind mindfulness may have been undermined by the narcissistic, egoistic and solipsistic turn that contemporary culture has taken (Joiner, 2017). Miguel Farias and Catherine Wikholm, following their experiences with yoga and meditation with prisoners, use their book *The Buddha Pill: Can Meditation Change You?* to critically examine the benefits and limitations of mindfulness, arguing that in some cases it can have unexpected negative consequences (Farias & Wikholm, 2015).

In *What's Wrong with Mindfulness (And What Isn't): Zen Perspectives*, a group of experts explain how removing mindfulness from Buddhism may set a dangerous precedent. In particular, they focus on the unintended side effects of exposing a spiritual tradition to the demands of capitalism, and offer hints to a deeper understanding of where mindfulness comes from and where it might be headed (Rosenbaum & Magid, 2016). David Forbes, a professor of contemplative education at Brooklyn College, also addresses the financial implications and possible impact of capitalism on mindfulness in his new book *Mindfulness and Its Discontents*, which is due to be published in 2019. Forbes was also one of the editors of a recent collection of contributions on the developments of mindfulness (Purser, Forbes, & Burke, 2016). His upcoming book is expected to cover many of the concerns we have seen here. When announcing the publication of the book, Sean Illing warned that in the USA, mindfulness and meditation have a capitalism problem. He also wondered whether the mindfulness movement would be able to resist the pressure to become a tool of self-absorption, or whether it would be the latest victim of the self-industry (Illing, 2017).

Others have expressed their concerns even more openly. In his article "Beyond McMindfulness", which appeared in the *Huffington Post* in July 2013, Ronald E. Purser coined the term "McMindfulness" ("Beyond McMindfulness", 2013). The article went viral on social media, and gained widespread attention. In it, Purser expressed his concerns about "self-care" being incorporated into Western corporate capitalism and neoliberalism (Purser & Milillo, 2014). There was also a recent article in *The Guardian* expressing alarm at how capitalism had captured the mindfulness industry. Many have connected the astonishing amount of business mindfulness generates with the simultaneous loss of the ethics behind meditation—even in its new secular context (Purser, 2018; Purser & Milillo, 2014). Purser's new book on these themes, *McMindfulness: How Mindfulness Became the New Capitalist Spirituality*, is expected to published in mid-2019 (Purser, 2019).

In the UK, mindfulness has been adopted and developed in different ways, and it has managed to avoid many of the problems with commercial competition, individualism and perceptions of narcissism and solipsism. Several initiatives were launched there, but the most relevant one is certainly the combination of mindfulness and CBT to form MBCT. This came about as an evolution of CBT, which was delivered by the National Health Service through its IAPT programme. The programme developed a stepped care protocol for treating of depression, delivered outside traditional psychiatric circuits. Its aim was to avoid the need for antidepressant drugs as much as possible. First the programme offered psychological support and psychotherapy (CBT), then MBCT was also offered—particularly in cases of recurrent depressive episodes. MBCT and other interventions were introduced after trials, following the best evidence-based procedures, showed their effectiveness. The principles for trialling interventions are set out in the government agency NICE's guidelines.

Over the course of its 2500 years of history, something completely unforeseeable happened to Buddhist meditation: it became a medical tool. When mindfulness was combined with cognitive behavioural psychotherapy to form MBCT, like any medical drug, device or intervention, it was assessed and proved to be not only clinically effective, but also cost-effective, for treating patients suffering from mood disorders.

Some problems appear, however, when this process is examined in detail. Buddhism and Buddhist meditation are to do with existential suffering, *dukkha*: the individual mental reaction to unavoidable events such as old age, disease and death. The IAPT programme and MBCT, however, focus on treating subjects with clinical depression, a mental disorder that is medically diagnosed using the APA's DSM, as well as psychometric scales. The procedure is essentially ticking boxes in a questionnaire for deciding whether a patient is sick or not. There is a similar problem with evaluating the outcome of interventions. Patients are evaluated against a psychometric scale and assessors decide whether a patient has improved, been cured or showed no response based on how much their questionnaire score has changed.

How mindfulness instructors are trained is evidently crucial. In the USA, one of the most respected MBSR training providers is Kabat-Zinn's original institution. In its approach, the practice of meditation is still quite recognisable, although it has been adapted for the programme.

In the UK, meditation is less easily recognisable in MBCT. In fact, in studies of the practice there, it is only referred to indirectly, through a reference to the book by Segal et al. on MBCT for depression. It does not even play a central role in the book either (Segal, Williams et al., 2013). Similarly, when the IAPT set out an MBCT training curriculum, it clearly defined how therapists should be qualified and certified. It did not, however, make any mention of the term "meditation" (IAPT, 2017). This absence is surprising given the evidence showing the effectiveness of meditative practices. Essentially, therapists using MBCT are qualified for cognitive therapy, but given no certification for meditation.

If we forget for the moment the many commercial applications of mindfulness, we can see that it is now playing a significant role in mental health, medicine and psychiatry. The gap between the spiritual origins of meditation and evidence-based medicine is clear. As psychotherapies developed, they abandoned their humanist, existential and interpersonal aspects and transformed themselves based on advances in neuroscience and cognitivism. Meditation and mindfulness became part of this process. MBCT became one of the tools available to biological psychiatry for treating "mental disorders". It was a cost-effective alternative to antidepressant drugs, with similar outcomes. Many see the prescription of antidepressant drugs as simplistic and affected by a form of mechanistic reductionism. Some even apply this criticism to the criteria used by regulatory agencies for authorising antidepressant drugs (Giraldi, 2017).

In recent years there have been extraordinary scientific advances in medicine—particularly the rapidly evolving field of neuroscience. As a result, the powerful tools of neuroscience have been applied to meditation and mindfulness—for example, by Goleman and Davidson (Goleman & Davidson, 2017a, 2017b). Their efforts are laudable, and have certainly made significant contributions to our understanding of the brain and how meditation affects it. It is difficult to see, however, how these studies and all the technological advances like meditation smartphone apps, as well as gadgets such as Neurosky, will help people struggling to cope with difficult life events.

This has been brilliantly explored by John Horgan in his 2010 book *The Undiscovered Mind: How the Brain Defies Explanation*

(Horgan, 1999). Even more relevant to meditation and mindfulness is the book *Rational Mysticism: Dispatches from the Border Between Science and Spirituality*, written by the same author in 2003 (Horgan, 2003). Both are carefully researched and enriched by stimulating interviews with pioneers of these fields. He concludes, essentially, that science is still struggling to grapple with vital questions like the nature of the mind, the mind-body relationship and the nature of consciousness.

There have also been criticisms of the exaggerated conclusions drawn from various neuroscience studies, which try to draw public interest by both simplifying and amplifying results beyond their limited meaning and often flawed technical grounding (Legrenzi & Umiltà, 2011). Hilary and Steven Rose raise similar and even broader concerns about what they term "Neurotechnosciences" in their book *Genes, Cells and Brains: The Promethean Promises of the New Biology*. The book extends these worries to areas of modern biology such as genomic sciences (Rose & Rose, 2012).

Overall, meditation is still preserved and practised in Buddhist groups in Western countries. It has also, however, been integrated into mindfulness, where various practitioners have tried to pull it away from its roots in Buddhism. As a result, it has been popularised in a wide range of different fields. There have even been efforts to use it as an investigative tool in neuroscience. Mindfulness-based interventions (in which it is increasingly difficult to trace the remnants of meditation) have also been integrated into cognitive psychotherapies.

Cognitive and cognitive behavioural psychotherapies developed when "talking cures" were brought into the world of science and medicine. In a recent development of cognitive psychotherapy, mindfulness was combined with it to form MBCT (in which meditation is even less traceable). MBCT is a mental health intervention, and was thus adopted by psychiatry. This was in no small part because of American psychiatry, which had already been transformed by the rise of biological psychiatry and efforts to adopt the principles of evidence-based medicine. Now, therefore, when MBCT is applied outside psychiatric institutions, practitioners also go to great lengths to use the principles of evidence-based medicine. This leads to similar problems to those already seen when they are applied to mindfulness and meditation. It is particularly concerning when the DSM criteria and psychometric scales are used outside psychiatry—as happens with traditional cognitive and third-wave cognitive therapies—and even in the UK's IAPT and mindfulness programmes.

There have been serious doubts raised—on empirical and theoretical grounds—about psychiatric interventions for serious mental diseases. It is easy to see how these concerns could be even more marked for milder conditions and mood variations that may simply be based on normal emotions. The numerous contradictory facets of psychiatry have been collected, updated and critically analysed by Nikolas Rose in his book *Our Psychiatric Future*. The chapters cover issues that should be publicly debated. They cover, for example, what psychiatry is, whether there really is an epidemic of mental disorders, if it could be caused by social factors, the problems with diagnosis, the question of whether mental disorders are "brain disorders", whether there is a future for psychiatry and psychopharmacology, and the question of whether another form of psychiatry is possible. In the end, Rose says that there are seven "hard questions", and that the answers to these should shape the future of psychiatry. Rose's book opens the door to a psychiatry that is still evidence-based and rigorous, but is also more attuned to the realities of mental health, social medicine and psychiatry (Rose, 2019).

Innovative developments in psychiatry are possible: one major example is Community Mental Health Care in Trieste. Since Franco Basaglia's appointment in 1971 as director of the former San Giovanni mental hospital, Trieste has played a major international role in community mental health care. When it was deinstitutionalised, the Department of Mental Health (DMH) became a laboratory for social psychiatry innovation, developing a "whole system, whole community" approach. The DMH provides care through a network of community services, but also places great emphasis on working with the wider community to promote mental health and a strong society. The DMH is a World Health Organization Collaborating Centre, which played a major role in internationally disseminating best practice for community mental health (Bennett, 1985; Mezzina, 2014; WHO Collaborating Centre for Research and Training in Mental Health, 2019).

At DMH, modern, evidence-based psychiatric interventions are integrated into a network of socio-sanitary services that are provided through community care. Each available intervention is put in a sort of virtual "toolbox", and is used flexibly in the most appropriate individualised way. The main focus is on respect for the health, personality and rights of subjects, with the aim of supporting the best possible recovery (Mezzina, 2014). It is through a similarly open approach that meditation and mindfulness could be integrated into their interventions. A new tool to be approached with an open, but critically watchful mind. It may be possible to make meditation and mindfulness one of the options for those who are willing to use it, while at the same avoiding the constraints and rigidity that so often accompany psychiatric procedures in institutions.

Buddhism has only recently become available to the West. It has given a very large number of people access to an extraordinary message, set of values and path to leading a full life where sufferings can be addressed, attenuated and overcome. Buddhism is being integrated into this new world in a relatively short time—not long, in the grand scheme of things—after it was first introduced to the West by early pioneers. While traditional practices are still followed and gaining more and more ground, there are also attempts to develop a new "secular", "agnostic" form in the West that is less anchored to Eastern religious practices. There is a similar process at work with meditation, which has become increasingly popular in the West. It has developed along new lines in the form of mindfulness, which is also being integrated into psychotherapy using the principles of neuroscience and biological psychiatry. It is impossible to foresee how Buddhism and meditation will develop in Western culture. Only with time will we be able to see these extraordinarily interesting changes take shape—changes that affect not only the science of the mind, human culture and spiritualism, but also our most deeply rooted individual values.

## References

Batchelor, S. (2011). *Confession of a Buddhist atheist*. New York: Spiegel & Grau.

Baucher, H., Fontanarosa, P. B., & Golug, R. M. (2016). JAMA welcomes the US preventive services task force. *JAMA, 315*(4), 351–354.

Bennett, D. (1985). The changing pattern of mental health care in Trieste. *International Journal of Mental Health, 14*(1–2), 70–92. https://doi.org/10.1080/00207411.1985.11448989.

Benson, H., Dusek, J., Sherwood, J., Lam, P., Bethea, C., Carpenter, W., et al. (2006). Study of the therapeutic effects of intercessory prayer (STEP) in cardiac bypass patients: A multicenter randomized trial of uncertainty and certainty of receiving intercessory prayer. *American Heart Journal, 151*(4), 934–942. https://doi.org/10.1016/j.ahj.2005.05.028.

Beyond McMindfulness. (2013). Retrieved from https://www.huffpost.com/entry/beyond-mcmindfulness_b_3519289. Accessed 20 April 2019.

Butler, A., Chapman, J., Forman, E., & Beck, A. (2006). The empirical status of cognitive-behavioral therapy: A review of meta-analyses. *Clinical Psychology Review, 26*(1), 17–31. https://doi.org/10.1016/j.cpr.2005.07.003.

Caplan, P. (1996). *They say you're crazy.* Reading, MA: Addison-Wesley.

Christodoulou, G. N. (2012, October 10). *Depression as a consequence of the economic crisis.* WHO. Depression: A Global Crisis World Mental Health Day, pp. 14–18. Retrieved from https://www.who.int/mental_health/management/depression/wfmh_paper_depression_wmhd_2012.pdf. Accessed 4 April 2019.

Crane, R. S., Eames, C., Kuyken, W., et al. (2013). Development and validation of the mindfulness-based interventions—Teaching assessment criteria (MBI:TAC). *Assessment, 20,* 681–688.

Dawkins, R. (2006). *The god delusion.* London: Bantam Press.

Farias, M., & Wikholm, C. (2015). *The Buddha Pill: Can meditation change you?* London: Watkins Publishing.

Fisher, D. (2010). *Mindfulness and the cessation of suffering: An exclusive new interview with mindfulness pioneer Jon Kabat-Zinn.* Retrieved from https://www.lionsroar.com/mindfulness-and-the-cessation-of-suffering-an-exclusive-new-interview-with-mindfulness-pioneer-jon-kabat-zinn/. Accessed 4 April 2019.

Frances, A. (2014). *Saving normal.* New York: William Morrow.

Frances, A. (2016, January 26). Screen everyone for depression? Good intention, very bad idea. *New Scientist.* Retrieved from https://www.newscientist.com/article/2075249-screen-everyone-for-depression-good-intention-very-bad-idea/. Accessed 4 April 2019.

Gilbody, S., Littlewood, E., Hewitt, C., Brierley, G., Tharmanathan, P., Araya, R., et al. (2015). Computerised cognitive behaviour therapy (cCBT) as treatment for depression in primary care (REEACT trial): Large scale pragmatic randomised controlled trial. *BMJ,* h5627. https://doi.org/10.1136/bmj.h5627.

Giraldi, T. (2017). *Unhappiness, sadness and 'depression'.* Cham: Springer.

Goleman, D., & Davidson, R. (2017a). *The science of meditation: How to change your brain, mind and body.* London: Penguin Life.

Goleman, D., & Davidson, R. (2017b). *Altered traits.* New York: Penguin Random House.

Greenberg, G. (2013). *The book of woe.* Melbourne: Scribe.

Harvey, P. (2013). *An introduction to Buddhist ethics.* Cambridge, UK: Cambridge University Press.

Hayes, S. (2011). *Mindfulness and acceptance.* New York [u.a.]: Guilford.

Heine, S., & Wright, D. (2008). *Zen ritual.* Oxford: Oxford University Press.

Herbert, J., & Gaudiano, B. (2005). Introduction to the special issue on the placebo concept in psychotherapy. *Journal of Clinical Psychology, 61*(7), 787–790. https://doi.org/10.1002/jclp.20125.

Hofmann, S., Sawyer, A., Witt, A., & Oh, D. (2010). The effect of mindfulness-based therapy on anxiety and depression: A meta-analytic review. *Journal of Consulting and Clinical Psychology, 78*(2), 169–183. https://doi.org/10.1037/a0018555.

Horgan, J. (1999). *The undiscovered mind.* New York: Simon & Schuster.

Horgan, J. (2003). *Rational mysticism.* Boston: Houghton Mifflin.

Hunot, V., Moore, T., Caldwell, D., Furukawa, T., Davies, P., Jones, H., et al. (2013). 'Third wave' cognitive and behavioural therapies versus other psychological therapies for depression. *Cochrane Database of Systematic Reviews.* https://doi.org/10.1002/14651858.cd008704.pub2.

Hunsley, J., & Di Giulio, G. (2002, Spring/Summer). Dodo bird, Phoenix, or urban legend? The question of psychotherapy equivalence. *The Scientific Review of Mental Health Practice, 1*(1), 11–22.

IAPT. (2015). *Psychological therapies: Annual report on the use of IAPT services England, 2014/15.* Retrieved from https://files.digital.nhs.uk/publication-import/pub19xxx/pub19098/psyc-ther-ann-rep-2014-15.pdf. Accessed 4 April 2019.

IAPT. (2017). *Improving access to psychological therapies: Mindfulness-based cognitive therapy national MBCT training curriculum version 1.0.* Retrieved from https://www.hee.nhs.uk/sites/default/files/documents/MBCT%20in%20IAPT%20curriculum.pdf. Accessed 4 April 2019.

Illing, S. (2017). *Mindfulness meditation in America has a capitalism problem*. Retrieved from https://www.vox.com/science-and-health/2019/3/29/18264703/mindfulness-meditation-buddhism-david-forbes. Accessed 4 April 2019.

Insel, T. (2013). *Director's blog: Transforming diagnosis*. National Institute of Mental Health. http://www.nimh.nih.gov/about/director/2013/transforming-diagnosis.shtml. Accessed 9 April 2015.

Joiner, T. (2017). *Mindlessness*. Oxford: Oxford University Press.

Kabat-Zinn, J. (1982). An outpatient program in behavioral medicine for chronic pain patients based on the practice of mindfulness meditation—Theoretical considerations and preliminary-results. *General Hospital Psychiatry, 4*, 33–47.

Kahl, K., Winter, L., & Schweiger, U. (2012). The third wave of cognitive behavioural therapies. *Current Opinion in Psychiatry, 25*(6), 522–528. https://doi.org/10.1097/yco.0b013e328358e531.

Kaltenthaler, E., Parry, G., & Beverley, C. (2004). Computerized cognitive behaviour therapy: A systematic review. *Behavioural and Cognitive Psychotherapy, 32*(1), 31–55. https://doi.org/10.1017/s135246580400102x.

Kirsch, I., Deacon, B. J., Huedo-Medina, T. B., Scoboria, A., Moore, T. J., & Johnson, B. T. (2008). Initial severity and antidepressant benefits: A metaanalysis of data submitted to the Food and Drug Administration. *PLoS Medicine, 5*(2), e45. https://doi.org/10.1371/journal.pmed.0050045.

Kirsch, I., & Sapirstein, G. (1998). Listening to prozac but hearing placebo: A meta-analysis of antidepressant medication. *Prevention & Treatment, 1*(0002a). http://dx.doi.org/10.1037/1522-3736.1.1.12a.

Kocovski, N., & MacKenzie, M. (2016). Mindfulness-based cognitive therapy for depression: Trends and developments. *Psychology Research and Behavior Management*, 125. https://doi.org/10.2147/prbm.s63949.

Kutchins, H., & Kirk, S. (1999). *Making us crazy*. London: Constable.

Kuyken, W., Hayes, R., Barrett, B., Byng, R., Dalgleish, T., Kessler, D., et al. (2015). Effectiveness and cost-effectiveness of mindfulness-based cognitive therapy compared with maintenance antidepressant treatment in the prevention of depressive relapse or recurrence (PREVENT): A randomised controlled trial. *The Lancet, 386*(9988), 63–73. https://doi.org/10.1016/s0140-6736(14)62222-4.

Legrenzi, P., & Umiltà, C. (2011). *Neuromania*. Oxford: Oxford University Press.

Lilienfeld, S., & Arkowitz, H. (2012). Are all psychotherapies created equal? *Scientific American Mind, 23*(4), 68–69. https://doi.org/10.1038/scientificamericanmind0912-68.

Maj, M. (2011). *Clinical depression vs understandable sadness. Is the difference clear and is it relevant to treatment decisions*? Festschrift volume for Prof. George Christodoulou (pp. 174–178). Athens: Beta Publishers. www.paeeb.com—editions.

Marsha Linehan Biography. (2019). University of Washington. Retrieved from https://blogs.uw.edu/linehan/biography/. Accessed 4 April 2019.

Mezzina, R. (2014). Community mental health care in Trieste and beyond. *The Journal of Nervous and Mental Disease, 202*(6), 440–445. https://doi.org/10.1097/nmd.0000000000000142.

Mindful Nation UK. (2015). *Report by the mindfulness all-party parliamentary group (MAPPG).* https://www.themindfulnessinitiative.org.uk/images/reports/Mindfulness-APPG-Report_Mindful-Nation-UK_Oct2015.pdf. Accessed 4 April 2019.

NIMH. (2006). *Sequenced treatment alternatives to relieve depression (STAR*D).* ClinicalTrials.gov, http://www.clinicaltrials.gov/ct/show/NCT00021528?order=1. Accessed 20 March 2019.

Oasis Institute for Mindfulness-Based Professional Education & Teacher Training. (2019). Retrieved from https://www.umassmed.edu/cfm/training/. Accessed 4 April 2019.

Öst, L. (2008). Efficacy of the third wave of behavioral therapies: A systematic review and meta-analysis. *Behaviour Research and Therapy, 46*(3), 296–321. https://doi.org/10.1016/j.brat.2007.12.005.

Purser, R. (2018). Critical perspectives on corporate mindfulness. *Journal of Management, Spirituality & Religion, 15*(2), 105–108. https://doi.org/10.1080/14766086.2018.1438038.

Purser, R. (2019). *McMindfulness.* London: Repeater.

Purser, R., Forbes, D., & Burke, A. (2016). *Handbook of mindfulness.* [S.l.]: Springer, Switzerland.

Purser, R., & Milillo, J. (2014). Mindfulness revisited. *Journal of Management Inquiry, 24*(1), 3–24. https://doi.org/10.1177/1056492614532315.

Rāhula, W. (1974). *What the Buddha taught* (revised ed.). New York: Grove Press.

Richards, D., Ekers, D., McMillan, D., Taylor, R., Byford, S., Warren, F., et al. (2016). Cost and outcome of behavioural activation versus cognitive behavioural therapy for depression (COBRA): A randomised, controlled, non-inferiority trial. *The Lancet, 388*(10047), 871–880. https://doi.org/10.1016/s0140-6736(16)31140-0.

Rose, N. (2019). *Our psychiatric future.* Cambridge, UK: Polity Press.

Rose, H., & Rose, S. (2012). *Genes, cells, and brains*. London: Verso.
Rosenbaum, R., & Magid, B. (2016). *What's wrong with mindfulness (and what isn't)*. Somerville, MA: Wisdom Publications.
Rush, A. J., Warden, D., Wisniewski, S. R., et al. (2009). STAR*D. Revising conventional wisdom. *CNS Drugs, 23*(8), 627–647.
Segal, Z. V., Teasdale, J. D., Williams, J. M., & Gemar, M. C. (2002). The mindfulness-based cognitive therapy adherence scale: Inter-rater reliability, adherence to protocol and treatment distinctiveness. *Clinical Psychology and Psychotherapy, 9,* 131–138.
Segal, Z., Williams, J., Teasdale, J., & Kabat-Zinn, J. (2013). *Mindfulness-based cognitive therapy for depression*. New York: Guilford Press.
Shapiro, A., & Shapiro, E. (2000). *The powerful placebo*. Baltimore: Johns Hopkins University Press.
Sharf, R. (1995). Buddhist modernism and the rhetoric of meditative experience. *Numen, 42*(3), 228–283. https://doi.org/10.1163/1568527952598549.
Sharf, R. (2014). Is mindfulness Buddhist? (and why it matters). *Transcultural Psychiatry, 52*(4), 470–484. https://doi.org/10.1177/1363461514557561.
Shedler, J. (2010). The efficacy of psychodynamic psychotherapy. *American Psychologist, 65*(2), 98–109. https://doi.org/10.1037/a0018378.
Sinyor, M., Schaffee, A., & Levitt, A. (2010). The sequenced treatment alternatives to relieve depression (STAR*D) trial: A review. *La Revue Canadienne de Psychiatrie, 55*(3), 126–137.
Siu, A., Bibbins-Domingo, K., Grossman, D., Baumann, L., Davidson, K., Ebell, M., et al. (2016). Screening for depression in adults. *JAMA, 315*(4), 380. https://doi.org/10.1001/jama.2015.18392.
Snelling, J. (1998). *The Buddhist handbook*. London: Rider.
Stierhoff, C. (2019). *The deception of Buddhist-based mindfulness in our schools and the dangers it poses*. American Center for Law and Justice. Retrieved from https://aclj.org/religious-liberty/the-deception-of-buddhist-based-mindfulness-in-our-schools-and-the-dangers-it-poses. Accessed 4 April 2019.
Thase, M. E. (2016). Recommendations for screening for depression in adults. *JAMA, 315*(4), 349–352.
The Mindful Initiative. (2018). https://www.themindfulnessinitiative.org.uk/mindful-nation-uk. Accessed 4 April 2019.
Thoma, N., Pilecki, B., & McKay, D. (2015). Contemporary cognitive behavior therapy: A review of theory, history, and evidence. *Psychodynamic Psychiatry, 43*(3), 423–461. https://doi.org/10.1521/pdps.2015.43.3.423.

Tovote, K., Schroevers, M., Snippe, E., Emmelkamp, P., Links, T., Sanderman, R., et al. (2017). What works best for whom? Cognitive behavior therapy and mindfulness-based cognitive therapy for depressive symptoms in patients with diabetes. *PLoS One, 12*(6), e0179941. https://doi.org/10.1371/journal.pone.0179941.

Vallury, K., Jones, M., & Oosterbroek, C. (2015). Computerized cognitive behavior therapy for anxiety and depression in rural areas: A systematic review. *Journal of Medical Internet Research, 17*(6), e139. https://doi.org/10.2196/jmir.4145.

Van Dam, N., van Vugt, M., Vago, D., Schmalzl, L., Saron, C., Olendzki, A., et al. (2017). Mind the hype: A critical evaluation and prescriptive agenda for research on mindfulness and meditation. *Perspectives on Psychological Science, 13*(1), 36–61. https://doi.org/10.1177/1745691617709589.

Wampold, B., & Imel, Z. (2015). *The great psychotherapy debate*. New York: Routledge.

Warden, D., Rush, A. J., Trivedi, M. H., et al. (2007). The STAR*D project results: A comprehensive review of findings. *Current Psychiatry Reports, 9*(6), 449–459.

WHO Collaborating Centre for Research and Training in Mental Health. (2019). Retrieved from http://www.euro.who.int/en/health-topics/noncommunicable-diseases/mental-health/partners/who-collaborating-centres-working-in-mental-health/who-collaborating-centre-for-research-and-training-in-mental-health. Accessed 4 April 2019.

World Federation for Mental Health. (2012). *Depression*. A Global Crisis World Mental Health Day. https://www.who.int/mental_health/management/depression/wfmh_paper_depression_wmhd_2012.pdf. Accessed 28 April 2019.

Wright, R. (2017). *Why Buddhism is true*. New York: Simon & Shuster.

Ziliak, S. (2008). *The cult of statistical significance*. Ann Arbor, MI: University of Michigan Press.

# Index




T. Giraldi, *Psychotherapy, Mindfulness and Buddhist Meditation*, https://doi.org/10.1007/978-3-030-29003-0

The manufacturer's authorised representative in the EU is Springer Nature Customer Service Centre GmbH, Europaplatz 3, 69115 Heidelberg, Germany. If you have any concerns regarding our products, please contact ProductSafety@springernature.com

Printed and bound by CPI Group (UK) Ltd, Croydon, CR0 4YY
05/10/2026
02228125-0005